My Correct Views on Everything

Titles by Leszek Kolakowski
The Two Eyes of Spinoza and Other Esssays on Philosophers (St. Augustine's Press)
Religion: If There Is No God . . . On God, the Devil, Sin, and Other Worries of the So-Called Philosophy of Religion (St. Augustine's Press)
Husserl and the Search for Certitude (St. Augustine's Press)
Bergson (St. Augustine's Press)
Main Currents of Marxism, 3 vol. (Oxford University Press)
The Presence of Myth (The University of Chicago Press)
Modernity on Endless Trial (The University of Chicago Press)
On Freedom, Fame, Lying and Betrayal (Westview Press)

Other Titles of Interest from St. Augustine's Press
Zbigniew Janowski, *Augustinian-Cartesian Index*
Rémi Brague, *Eccentric Culture: A Theory of Western Civilization*
Francisco Suarez, *On Creation, Conservation, & Concurrence: Metaphysical Disputations 20–22*
Francisco Suarez, *Metaphysical Demonstration to the Existence of God*
John of St. Thomas, *Introduction to the Summa Theologiae of Thomas Aquinas*
William of Ockham, *Ockham's Theory of Terms: Part I of the Summa Logicae*
William of Ockham, *Ockham's Theory of Propositions: Part II of the Summa Logicae*
Roger Bacon, Roger *Bacon's Philosophy of Nature. Translation of De multiplicatione specierum and De speculis comburentibus*
Thomas Aquinas, *Disputed Questions on Virtue*
Roger Scruton, *An Intelligent Person's Guide to Modern Culture*
Roger Scruton, *On Hunting*
Roger Scruton, *Art and Imagination: A Study in the Philosophy of Mind*
Roger Scruton, *Aesthetic Understanding*
Josef Pieper, *Leisure, the Basis of Culture*
Josef Pieper, *Scholasticism: Personalities and Problems*
Josef Pieper, *The Silence of St. Thomas*
Mario Enrique Sacchi, *The Apocalypse of Being: The Esoteric Gnosis of Martin Heidegger*
Friedrich Nietzsche, *On the Future of Our Educational Institutions*
Friedrich Nietzsche, *Prefaces to Unwritten Works*
René Girard, *A Theater of Envy: William Shakespeare*
Stanley Rosen, *The Question of Being: A Reversal of Heidegger*
Stanley Rosen, *Nihilism: A Philosophical Essay*

My Correct Views on Everything

Leszek Kolakowski

Edited by Zbigniew Janowski

St. Augustine's Press
South Bend, Indiana
2005

Copyright © 2005 by Leszek Kolakowski

All rights reserved. No part of this book may be reproduced, stored in a retrieval system, or transmitted, in any form or by any means, electronic, mechanical, photocopying, recording, or otherwise, without the prior permission of St. Augustine's Press.

Manufactured in the United States of America.

1 2 3 4 5 6   10 09 08 07 06 05

Library of Congress Cataloging in Publication Data
Kolakowski, Leszek.
    [Selections. English. 2004]
    My correct views on everything / Leszek Kolakowski; edited by Zbigniew Janowski.
       p. cm.
    Includes bibliographical references and index.
    ISBN 1-58731-525-4 (alk. paper)
    1. Philosophy. 2. Kolakowski, Leszek - Bibliography. I. Janowski, Zbigniew. II. Title.
B4691.K5862E5 2004b
199'.438 - dc22   2004011719

∞ *The paper used in this publication meets the minimum requirements of the American National Standard for Information Sciences – Permanence of Paper for Printed Materials, ANSI Z39.48-1984.*

ST. AUGUSTINE'S PRESS
www.staugustine.net

Contents

A Very Short Introduction	vii
Amid Moving Ruins	1
1. My Correct Views on Everything	3
2. The Marxist Roots of Stalinism	27
3. The Myth of Human Self-Identity	45
4. What Is Socialism?	62
5. Totalitarianism and the Virtue of the Lie	66
6. Communism as a Cultural Force	77
7. What Is Left of Socialism?	91
8. The Heritage of the Left	99
9. Genocide and Ideology	106
10. The Devil in History: Leszek Kolakowski in an Interview with George Urban	121
What Is Wrong with God?	139
11. A Layman Pronounces upon the Catechism	141
12. Jesus Christ – Prophet and Reformer	150
13. Leibniz and Job: The Metaphysics of Evil and the Experience of Evil	164

14. Concern with God in an Apparently Godless Era	173
15. Crime and Punishment	184
16. On Natural Law	194

Who Are We? — 203

17. On Collective Identity	205
18. The Demise of the Historical Man	216
19. On Our Relative Relativism	227
20. What Are Universities For?	236
21. Neutrality and Academic Values	244
22. Where Are Children in Liberal Philosophy?	257
23. Man Does Not Live by Reason Alone: Leszek Kolakowski in an Interview with Nathan Gardels	269

Bibliography of Leszek Kolakowski's Major Writings	279
Leszek Kolakowski	283

A Very Short Introduction

Like my previous volume, *The Two Eyes of Spinoza and Other Essays on Philosophers*, with which mankind was blessed by Mr. Bruce Fingerhut of St. Augustine's Press, this collection has been prepared by two persons: my friend Zbigniew Janowski, who found all the texts, selected, and edited them, and my daughter Agnieszka, who translated a number of them from the French, the Polish, or my notoriously lame English.

The first part of this collection deals with questions and burdens imposed on us by communism and its historical vicissitudes. After all that has happened since 1989, the topic might seem obsolete, or of interest only as a historical study. I wish it were obsolete, but I am not sure it is. Communism was not the crazy fantasy of a few fanatics, nor the result of human stupidity and baseness; it was a real, very real part of the history of the twentieth century, and we cannot understand this history of ours without understanding communism. We cannot get rid of this specter by saying it was just "human stupidity," or "human corruptibility." The specter is stronger than the spells we cast on it. It might come back to life.

The second part consists of a few remarks concerning, mainly, the Catholic Church of today and some parts of its historical background.

The third part of the collection deals with various unpleasant dilemmas of our civilization: liberal ideologies, relativist illusions, the moral foundation of law, our attitudes toward history, the place of universities in our world. None of these dilemmas is properly solved; everything is left ambiguous. I want to believe that this is not just a result of my ineptitude, but perhaps also of the incurable ambiguity of reality itself.

There are in this collection two texts which are perhaps in need of an explanation; both were written in Polish, a long time ago. The text "What Is Socialism?" was, unsurprisingly, confiscated by censors from a weekly journal in Poland; copies of it, however, circulated "illegally," and it was even displayed (not by myself) on a billboard at Warsaw University. This was in 1956; even for me it is not easy to believe that such a remote past really existed. Short as it was, this satirical piece was long enough to provoke the fury of the Communist Party leaders - something to boast of. The essay on Jesus Christ was published in 1956. I do not find anything original in it. Nonetheless it became a text of some renown in Poland, perhaps because it appeared in an atheist weekly.

Enough of explanations.

Oxford, November 3, 2002

AMID MOVING RUINS

My Correct Views on Everything

"An Open Letter to Leszek Kolakowski"[1]

Dear Leszek Kolakowski,

First, I must introduce myself, since this is an unusual kind of letter. You don't know me, but I know you well.

This must be familiar enough to a man with an international reputation. He must often be beset with the importunities of strangers.

But my claim is more insistent and vulgar than that. I am the stranger who walks into the house, slaps you on the back, sits down at your table, and jests about your youthful escapades, on the pretext of a claim to distant relationship of which you know nothing. I am, in political terms, your mother's brother's stepson. I am an impossible and presumptuous guest, and an uninvited one – you may even suspect that I am an impostor – but the courtesies of kinship disallow you from throwing me from your house.

We were both voices of the Communist revisionism of 1956. . . . But there was a closer and more continuing identity in our preoccupations. We both passed from a frontal critique of Stalinism to a stance of Marxist revisionism; we both sought to rehabilitate the utopian energies within the socialist tradition; we both stood in an ambiguous position, critical and affirmative, to the Marxist tradition. We both were centrally concerned with the radiating problems of historical determinism on the one hand, and of agency, moral choice, and individual responsibility on the other.

[1] This first section consists of a fragment of a letter from E.P. Thompson, published as "An Open Letter to Leszek Kolakowski," *The Socialist Register* (1973), pp. 1–100. Kolakowski's full answer appears below (see footnote 3).

When I say that "we both" initiated similar enquiries, I don't, of course, suggest that we both did so with equal success. The inadequacy of my own writings is testified to by the silence into which they have fallen. Your own writing, on the other hand, still seems to me to be among the few constructive and enduring consequences of that experience. Your sustained polemic, "Responsibility and History,"[2] first published in *Nowa Kultura* in 1957, remains without equal.

In 1956 we lived through a common experience, but we experienced it in different ways.... You Poles were the worst old Adamists of All! Your poets – Tuwim and Wazyk – your film-makers and sociologists, and, worst of all, your Leszek Kolakowski.... Your voice was the clearest voice out of Eastern Europe in those years, although you didn't offer the easiest answers.... But I was explaining a point of history, why I feel that I have some petty claim of relationship to you (I owe also, of course, for your writings and for your courage, in 1956 and again in 1966, a much greater debt). My claim is a trivial and abstract one. At a certain moment, partly out of a sense of solidarity with you and your comrades, I and others like me took up certain intellectual and political positions. We refused to disavow "Communism" because Communism was a complex noun which included Leszek Kolakowski. I am sure that the solidarity expressed in little, academically un-reputable journals in England did you no good whatsoever. We brought you neither thanks nor tank-traps; not even an audience among a "reputable" British public.... I feel, when I turn over your pages in *Encounter*, a sense of injury and betrayal. My feelings are no affair of yours; you must do what you think is right. But they explain why I write, not an article or polemic, but this open letter.

And yet – I return to the first lines of this letter – I have some right to speak frankly, for I am (or was) some kinsman of yours. There was a time when you, and the causes for which you stood, were present in our innermost thoughts. And in those days (only fifteen years distant!) whose meanings are now forgotten or falsified, when a "new left" was first projected, we shared another kinsman in our friend, C. Wright Mills. It was Mills who defined this relationship, in words better than any of mine:

> I can no longer write seriously without feeling contempt for the indifferent professors and smug editors who so fearlessly fight the cold war, and for the cultural bureaucrats and hacks, the intellectual thugs of the official line who so readily have

---

2 See L. Kolakowski, *Toward a Marxist Humanism. Essays on the Left Today* (New York: Grove Press Inc., 1968). The English edition of this book appeared under the title *Marxism and Beyond: On Historical Understanding and Individual Responsibility* (London: Pall Mall Press, 1969). Editor's note.

abdicated the intellect in the Soviet Bloc. I can no longer write with moral surety unless I know that Leszek Kolakowski will understand where I stand. . . .

I do not think the time has gone by for such a struggle. I think it is with us, every day. In any case, can we meet one day and have a drink? I owe you more than one. And can we still drink to the fulfilment of that moment of common aspiration: "1956"?

Yours fraternally,

E.P. Thompson

"My Correct Views on Everything: A Rejoinder to E.P. Thompson."[3]

Dear Edward Thompson,

Why I am not very happy about this public correspondence is because your letter deals as much (at least) with personal attitudes as with ideas. However, I have no personal accounts to settle either with Communist ideology or with the year 1956; this was settled long ago. But if you insist,

> Let us begin and carry up this corpse
> Singing together. . . .[4]

In a review of the last issue of *Socialist Register* by Raymond Williams, I read that your letter is one of the best pieces of Leftist writing in the last decade, which implies directly that all or nearly all the rest was worse. He knows better and I take his word. I should be proud to have occasioned, to a certain degree, this text, even if I happen to be its target. And so, my first reaction is one of gratitude.

My second reaction is of *embarras de richesses*. You will excuse me if I make a fair choice of topics in my reply to your 100 pages of Open Letter (not well segmented, as you will admit). I will try to take up the most controversial ones. I do not think I should comment on the autobiographical pages, interesting though they are. When you say, for example,

---

3 Reprinted from *The Socialist Register*, 1974.
4 From Robert Browning's poem, "A Grammarian's Funeral Shortly after the Revival of Learning in Europe." Editor's note.

that you do not go to Spain for holidays, that you never attend a conference of Socialists without paying a part of the costs out of your own pocket, that you do not participate in meetings funded by the Ford Foundation, that you are like Quakers of old who refused to take off their hats before authorities, etc., I do not think it advisable to reply with a virtue-list of my own; this list would probably be less impressive. Neither am I going to exchange the story of your dismissal from the *New Left Review* for all the stories of my expulsions from different editorial committees of different journals[5]; these stories would be rather trivial.

My third reaction is of sadness, and I mean it. Incompetent though I am in your field of studies, I know your reputation as a scholar and historian. I found it regrettable to see in your Letter so many Leftist clichés which survive in speech and print owing to three devices. First, the refusal to analyze words and the use of verbal hybrids purposely designed to confound the issues. Second, the use of moral or sentimental standards in some cases and of political and historical standards in other similar cases. Third, the refusal to accept historical facts as they are. I will try to say more precisely what I mean.

Your letter contains some personal grievances and some arguments on general questions. I will start with a minor personal grievance. Oddly enough, you seem to feel offended by not having been invited to the Reading[6] conference and you state that if you had been invited you

5   In 1956, after the Hungarian Revolution, Khrushchev insisted that the communist leaders in satellite communist countries organize trials of the revisionists, among them Kolakowski. Fortunately, Wladyslaw Gomulka, the First Secretary of the Communist party of Poland, did not consent to this, but instead viciously attacked Kolakowski in 1957. In 1958 Kolakowski, along with other "revisionists," was expelled from the influential weekly *Nowa Kultura*; in 1959, after the publication of "Karl Marx and the Classical Definition of Truth" (included in *The Two Eyes of Spinoza and Other Essays on Philosophers* [South Bend, Indiana: St. Augustine's Press, 2004]), upon the request of the Soviets, he was expelled from *Studia Filozoficzne*, of which he was editor-in-chief. After delivering his famous speech on the tenth anniversary of the Polish October, Kolakowski found it difficult to publish anything. His translation of Spinoza's works was published, however, without his name. He was also expelled from the editorial board of two prestigious collections in the Wydawnictwo Naukowe publishing house: Biblioteka Klasykow Filozofii (The Library of Classics of Philosophy) and Biblioteka Pisarzy Reformacyjnych (The Library of Reformation Writers).

6   The Reading conference – whose topic was "Is There Anything Wrong with the Socialist Idea?" (originally conceived as "What Is Wrong with the Socialist Idea?") – was organized by Robert Cecil, Stuart Hampshire, Leszek Kolakowski, and George Weidenfeld, and sponsored by the publishing house Weidenfeld and Nicholson and the Graduate School of Contemporary European Studies, Reading University. The papers delivered at this confer-

would have refused to attend anyway on serious moral grounds. I presume, consequently, that if you had been invited, you would have felt offended as well and so no way out of hurting you was open to the organizers. Now, the moral ground you cite is the fact that in the organizing committee you found the name of Robert Cecil. And what is sinister about Robert Cecil is that he once worked in the British diplomatic service. And so, your integrity does not allow you to sit at the same table with someone who used to work in British diplomacy. O blessed Innocence! You and I, we were both active in our respective Communist Parties in the '40s and '50s, which means that, whatever our noble intentions and our charming ignorance (or refusal to get rid of ignorance) were, we supported, within our modest means, a regime based on mass slave labor and police terror of the worst kind in human history. Do you think that there are many people who could refuse to sit at the same table with us on these grounds? No, you are innocent, while I do not feel, as you put it, the "sense of the politics of those years" when so many Western intellectuals were converted to Stalinism.

From your casual comments on Stalinism, I gather that your "sense of politics of those years" is obviously subtler and more differentiated than mine. First, you say that a part (a part, I do not omit that) of the responsibility for Stalinism lies with the Western powers. You say, second, that "to a historian, fifty years is too short a time in which to judge a new social system, if such a system is arising." Third, we know, as you say, "times when communism has shown a most human face, between 1917 and the early 1920s and again from the battle of Stalingrad to 1946."

Everything is right on some additional assumptions. Obviously, in the world in which we live, important events in one country are usually to be credited in part to what happened in other countries. You will certainly not deny that a part of the responsibility for German Nazism lay upon the Soviet Union. I wonder how this affects your judgment on German Nazism?

Your second comment is revealing, indeed. What is fifty years "to a historian"? The same day as I am writing this, I happen to have read a book by Anatol Marchenko relating his experiences in Soviet prisons and concentration camps in the early 1960s (not 1930s). The book was published in Russian in Frankfurt in 1973. The author, a Russian worker, was caught when he tried to cross the Soviet border to Iran. He was lucky to have done this in Khrushchev's time when the regrettable errors of J.V.

ence were subsequently published as *The Socialist Idea: A Reappraisal*, L. Kolakowski and S. Hampshire eds., preface by L. Kolakowski, (New York: Basic Books, 1974). Kolakowski's paper, "The Myth of Human Self-Identity: The Unity of Civil and Political Society in Socialist Thought," is included in this volume. Editor's note.

Stalin were over (yes, regrettable, let us face it, even if in part accounted for by the Western powers). And so he got only six years of hard labor in a concentration camp. One of his stories is about three Lithuanian prisoners who tried to escape from a convoy in a forest. Two of them were quickly caught, shot many times in the legs, ordered to get up (which they could not do), then kicked and trampled by guards. Finally, they were bitten and torn up by police dogs (such an amusement, survival of capitalism), and only then stabbed to death with bayonets. All this with witty remarks by the officer, of the kind "Now, free Lithuania, crawl, you'll get your independence straight off!" The third prisoner was shot and, reputed to be dead, was thrown under corpses in the cart. Discovered later to be alive, he was not killed (de-stalinization!) but left for several days in a dark cell with his festering wounds. He survived only because his arm was cut off.

This is one of thousands of stories you can read in many now available books. Such books are rather reluctantly read by the enlightened Leftist elite. First, because they are largely irrelevant, second, they supply us only with small details (after all, we agree that some errors were committed) and because many of them have not been translated. (Did you notice that if you meet a Westerner who has learnt Russian you have at least 90% chance of meeting a bloody reactionary? Progressive people do not enjoy the painful effort of learning Russian. They know better anyway.)

And so, what is fifty years to a historian? Fifty years covering the life of an obscure Russian worker Marchenko or of a still more obscure Lithuanian student who has not even written a book? Let us not hurry to judge a "new social system." Certainly I could ask you how many years you needed to assess the merits of the new military regime in Chile or in Greece, but I know your answer: there is no analogy – Chile and Greece remain within capitalism (factories are privately owned) while Russia started a new "alternative society" (factories are state owned, as is land, as are all its inhabitants). As genuine historians we can wait for another century and keep our slightly melancholic but cautiously optimistic historical wisdom.

Not so, of course, with "that beast," "that old bitch, consumer capitalism" (your words). Wherever we look, our blood boils. Here we may afford to be ardent moralists again and we can prove – as you do – that the capitalist system has a "logic" of its own that all reforms are unable to cancel. The national health service, you say, is impoverished by the existence of private practice, and equality in education is spoilt because people are trained for private industry etc. You do not say that reforms are doomed to failure; you only explain that as long as reforms do not destroy capitalism, capitalism is not destroyed, which is certainly true.

My Correct Views on Everything

And you propose "a peaceful revolutionary transition to an alternative socialist logic." You think apparently that this makes perfectly clear what you mean. I think, on the contrary, that it is perfectly obscure unless, again, you imagine that once the total state ownership of factories is granted, there remain only minor technical problems on the road to your utopia. But this is precisely what remains to be proved, and the *onus probandi* lies on those who maintain that these (insignificant "to a historian") fifty years of experience may be discarded by the authors of the new blueprint for the socialist society. (In Russia there were "exceptional circumstances," weren't there? But there is nothing exceptional about Western Europe.)

Your way of interpreting these modest fifty years (fifty-seven now) of the new alternative society is also revealed in your occasional remarks about the "most human face of communism" between 1917 and the early '20s and between Stalingrad and 1946. What do you mean by "human face" in the first case? The attempt to rule the entire economy by the police and army, resulting in mass hunger with uncountable victims, in several hundred peasants' revolts, all drowned in blood (a total economic disaster, as Lenin would admit later, after having killed and imprisoned an indefinite number of Mensheviks and SRs for predicting precisely that)? Or do you mean the armed invasion of seven non-Russian countries which had formed their independent governments, some socialist, some not (Georgia, Armenia, Azerbaijan, Ukraine, Lithuania, Latvia, Estonia; God knows where are all these curious tribes live)? Or do you mean the dispersion by soldiers of the only democratically elected Parliament in Russian history, before it could utter one single word? The suppression by violence of all political parties, including socialist ones, the abolition of the non-Bolshevik press and, above all, the replacement of law with the absolute power of the party and its police in killing, torturing and imprisoning anybody they wanted? The mass repression of the Church? The Kronstadt uprising? And what is the most human face in 1942–46? Do you mean the deportation of eight entire nationalities of the Soviet Union with hundreds of thousands of victims (let us say seven, not eight; one was deported shortly before Stalingrad)? Do you mean sending to concentration camps hundreds of thousands of Soviet prisoners of war handed over by the Allies? Do you mean the so-called "collectivization" of the Baltic countries, if you have an idea about reality of this word?

I have three possible explanations for your statement. First, that you are simply ignorant of these facts. This I find incredible, considering your profession as a historian. Second, that you use the word "human face" in a very Thompsonian sense which I do not grasp. Third, that you, like most communists, both orthodox and critical, believe that everything is all right in the communist system as long as the leaders of the party are not murdered. This is, in fact, the standard way communists become "critical" – when they realize that the new alternative socialist logic does not spare the communists themselves and in particular party leaders. Did you notice that the only victims Khrushchev mentioned by name in his speech of 1956 (whose importance I am far from underestimating) were *pur sang* Stalinists like himself, most of them (like Postychev) hangmen of merit with uncountable crimes committed before they became victims themselves? Did you notice in memoirs or critical analyses written by many ex-communists (I will not quote names, excuse me) that their horror only suddenly emerged when they saw communists being slaughtered? They always are pleading the innocence of the victims by saying "but these people were communists"! (Which, incidentally, is a self-defeating defense, for it suggests that there is nothing wrong in slaughtering non-communists. This implies that there is an authority to decide who is and who is not a communist, and this authority can be only the same rulers who keep the gun. Consequently, the slaughtered are by definition non-communists and everything is all right.).

Well, Thompson, I really do not attribute to you this way of thinking. Still I cannot help noticing your use of double standards of evaluation. And when I say "double standards" I do not mean indulgence for the justifiable inexperience of the "new society" in coping with new problems. I mean the use, alternately, of political or moral standards to similar situations. This I find unjustifiable. We must not be fervent moralists in some cases and *Real-politikers* or philosophers of world history in others, depending on political circumstances.

This is a point I would like to make clear to you if we are to understand each other. I will quote to you (from memory) a talk with a Latin-American revolutionary who told me about torture in Brazil. I asked: "What is wrong with torture?" and he said: "What do you mean? Do you suggest it is all right? Are you justifying torture?" And I said: "On the contrary, I simply ask you if you think that torture is a morally inadmissible monstrosity." "Of course," he replied. "And so is torture in Cuba?" I asked. "Well," he answered, "this is another thing. Cuba is a small country under the constant threat of American imperialists. They have to use all means of self-defense, however regrettable." Then I said: "Now, you cannot have it both ways. If you believe, as I do, that torture is abominable and inadmissible on moral grounds, it is such, by definition, in all circumstances. If however there are circumstances where it can be tolerated, you can condemn no regime for applying torture, since you assume that there is nothing essentially wrong with torture itself. Either you condemn torture in Cuba in exactly the same way you do for Brazil, or you refrain from condemning the Brazilian police for torturing people. In fact, you cannot condemn torture on political grounds, because in most cases it is perfectly efficient and the torturers get what they want. You can condemn it only on moral grounds and then, necessarily, everywhere in the same way, in Batista's Cuba, in Castro's Cuba, in North Vietnam and in South Vietnam."

This is a banal but important point which I hope is clear to you. I simply refuse to join people whose hearts are bleeding to death when they hear about any, major or minor (and rightly condemnable), injustice in the US and suddenly become wise historiosophists or cool rationalists when told about worse horrors of the new alternative Society.

This is one, but not the only, reason for the spontaneous and almost universal mistrust people from Eastern Europe nourish towards the Western New Left. By a strange coincidence the majority of these ungrateful people, once they come to settle in Western Europe or in the US, pass for reactionaries. These narrow empiricists and egoists extrapolate a poor few decades of their petty personal experience (logically inadmissible, as you rightly observe) and find in it pretexts to cast doubt on the radiant socialist future, elaborated on the best Marxist-Leninist grounds by ideologists of the New Left for the Western countries.

This is a topic I will pursue somewhat further. I assume that we do not differ in accepting facts as they are and that we do not get knowledge of existing societies by deducing from a general theory. Again, I will quote my talk with a Maoist from India. He said: "The cultural revolution in China was a class struggle of poor peasants against kulaks." I asked: "How do you know that?" and he replied: "From Marxist-Leninist theory." I commented: "Yes, that is what I guessed." (He did not understand, but you do.) This is not enough, however, for, as you know, any properly vague ideology is always able to absorb (meaning: to discard) all facts without giving up any of its ingredients. And the trouble is that most people are not dedicated ideologists. Their shallow minds work in such a way as if they believed that nobody has ever seen capitalism or socialism but only sets of small facts they are incapable of interpreting theoretically. They simply notice that people in some countries are better off than in others, that in some of them production, distribution, and services are much more efficient than in others, that here people enjoy civil and human rights and freedom and there they do not. (I should rather say "freedom" in quotation marks, as you do, to use the word "freedom" in quotation marks when applied to Western Europe. I do realize that this is a part of the absolutely obligatory Leftist spelling: what a "freedom," indeed, enough to burst one's sides with laughter. And we, people without a sense of humor, do not laugh.)

AMID MOVING RUINS

I am not trying to make you believe that you live in paradise and we in hell. In my country, Poland, we do not suffer hunger, people are not being tortured in prisons, we have no concentration camps (in contrast to Russia), in the last couple of years we have had only a few political prisoners (in contrast to Russia), and many people go abroad relatively easily (again, in contrast to Russia). Still, we are a country deprived of sovereignty, and this not in the sense Mr. Foot and Mr. Powell fear that Britain could lose her sovereignty because of joining the Common Market, but in a sadly direct and palpable sense: in that all key sectors of our life, including the army, foreign policy, foreign trade, important industries, and ideology, are under the tight control of a foreign empire which exerts its power with considerable meticulousness (e.g., preventing specific books from being published or specific information from being divulged, not to speak of more serious matters). Still, we appreciate immensely our margins of freedom when we compare our position with that of entirely liberated countries like the Ukraine or Lithuania which, as far as the right to self-government is concerned, are in a much worse situation than the old colonies of the British empire were. And the point is that these margins, important though they are (we can still say and publish significantly more than people elsewhere in the "ruble zone," except for Hungary), are not supported by any legal guarantees at all and can be (as they used to be) canceled every night by a decision taken by party rulers in Warsaw or in Moscow. And this is simply because we got rid of this fraudulent bourgeois device of division of powers and we achieved the socialist dream of unity, which means that the same apparatus has legislative, executive, and judicial power in addition to its power of controlling all means of production; the same people make law, interpret it, and enforce it: king, Parliament, army chief, judge, prosecutor, policeman, and (new socialist invention) owner of all national wealth and the only employer at one and the same desk – what better social unity can you imagine?

You are proud of not going to Spain for political reasons. Unprincipled that I am, I was there twice. It is unpleasant to say that this regime, oppressive and undemocratic though it is, gives its citizens more freedom than any socialist country (except, perhaps, for Yugoslavia). I am not saying this with *Schadenfreude*, but with shame, keeping in mind the pathos of the civil war. The Spanish frontiers are open (never mind the reason, which is, in this case, thirty million tourists each year), and no totalitarian system can work with open frontiers. They have censorship after, and not before, publication (my own book was published in Spain and then confiscated, but only after one thousand copies had been sold[7];

---

7 *El hombre sin alternativa* (Madrid: Alianza Editorial, 1970), the translation of

we all should like to have the same conditions in Poland). You find in Spanish bookshops Mani, Trotsky, Freud, Marcuse, etc. Like us, they have no elections and no legal political parties, but, unlike us, they have many forms of organization which are independent of the state and the ruling party. They are sovereign as a state.

You will probably say that I am talking in vain because you clearly stated that you are far from seeing your ideal in the existing socialist states and that you were thinking in terms of a democratic socialism. You did, indeed, and I am not accusing you of being an admirer of the socialist secret police. Still, what I am trying to say is very relevant to your article for two reasons. First, you consider the existing socialist states as (imperfect, to be sure) beginnings of a new and better social order, as transitional forms which went beyond capitalism and are heading towards utopia. I do not deny that this form is new, but I do deny that it is in any respect superior to the democratic countries of Europe. I defy you to prove the opposite, i.e., to show a point in which the existing socialism may claim its superiority, except for the notorious advantages all despotic systems have over democratic ones (less trouble with people). The second, and equally important, point is that you pretend to know what democratic socialism means to you, yet you do not know. You write: "My own utopia, two hundred years ahead, would not be like Morris's 'epoch of rest.' It would be a world (as D. H. Lawrence would have it) where the 'money values' give way before the 'life values,' or (as Blake would have it) 'corporeal' will give way to 'mental' war. With sources of power easily available, some men and women might choose to live in unified communities, sited, like Cistercian monasteries, in centres of great natural beauty, where agricultural, industrial and intellectual pursuits might be combined. Others might prefer the variety and pace of an urban life which rediscovers *some* of the qualities of the city-state. Others will prefer a life of seclusion, and many will pass between all three. Scholars would follow the disputes of different schools, in Paris, Jakarta or Bogota."

This is a very good sample of socialist writing. It amounts to saying that the world should be good, and not bad. I am entirely on your side on this issue. I share without restrictions your (and Marx's, and Shakespeare's, and many others') analysis to the effect that it is very deplorable that people's minds are occupied with the endless pursuit of money, that needs have a magic power of infinite growth, and that the profit motive, not use value, rules production. Your superiority consists in that you know exactly how to get rid of all this and I do not.

> the German collection of essays *Der Mensch ohne Alternative: Von der Möglichkeit und Unmöglichkeit, Marxist zu sein.*

Amid Moving Ruins

Why the problems of the only existing communism, which Leftist ideologists put aside so easily ("all right, this was done in exceptional circumstances, we won't imitate these patterns, we will do better," etc.), are crucial for socialist thought is because the experiences of the "new alternative society" have shown very convincingly that the only universal medicine these people have for social evils (state ownership of the means of production) is not only perfectly compatible with all disasters of the capitalist world, with exploitation, imperialism, pollution, misery, economic waste, national hatred, and national oppression, but that it adds to them a series of disasters of its own: inefficiency, lack of economic incentives and, above all, the unrestricted role of the omnipotent bureaucracy, a concentration of power never known before in human history. Just a stroke of bad luck? No, you do not say exactly so, you simply prefer to ignore the problem, and rightly so. All attempts to examine this experience lead us back not only to contingent historical circumstances but to the very idea of socialism and the discovery of incompatible demands hidden in this idea (or at least demands whose compatibility remains to be proved). We want a society of small communities with a large autonomy, do we not? And we want central planning in the economy. Let us try to think now how both work together. We want technical progress and we want perfect security for people; let us look closer how both could be combined. We want industrial democracy and we want efficient management: do they work well together? Of course they do, in the leftist heaven everything is compatible and everything settled, lamb and lion sleep in the same bed. Look at the horrors of the world and see how easily we can get rid of them once we make a peaceful revolution toward the new socialist logic. The Middle East war and Palestinian grievances? Of course, this is the result of capitalism; let us make the revolution and the question is settled. Pollution? Of course, no problem at all, just let the new proletarian state take over the factories and there will be no pollution. Traffic jams? This is because capitalists do not care a damn about human comfort, just give us power (in fact, this is a rather good point, in socialism we have far fewer cars and correspondingly fewer traffic jams). People die from hunger in India? Of course, American imperialists eat their food, but once we make the revolution, etc. Northern Ireland? Demographic problems in Mexico? Racial hatred? Tribal wars? Inflation? Criminality? Corruption? Degradation of educational systems? There is such a simple answer to everything and, moreover, the same answer to everything!

This is not a caricature, not in the slightest. This is standard pattern of thought of those who have overcome the miserable illusions of reformism and invented a beneficial device for solving all problems of mankind, and this device consists in a few words which, when repeated often enough, start looking as if they had content: revolution, alternative society, etc. And we have in addition a number of negative words to provoke horror, for instance "anti-communism" or "liberal." You use these words as well, Edward, without explanation, aware though you must be that the purpose of these words is to mingle many different things and to produce vague negative associations. What is, in fact, the anti-communism you do not profess? Certainly, we know people who believe that there are no serious social problems in the Western world except for the communist danger, that all social conflicts here are to be explained by a communist plot, that the world would be a paradise if only sinister communist forces did not interfere, and that the most hideous military dictatorships deserve support if only they suppress communist movements. You are not anti-communist in that sense? Neither am I. But you will be called anti-communist if you do not strongly believe that the actual Soviet (or Chinese) system is the most perfect society the human mind has invented so far, or if you wrote a piece of purely scholarly work on the history of communism without lies. And there is a great number of other possibilities in between. The convenience of the word "anti-communism," the bogey-man of leftist jargon, is precisely to put all of them in the same sack and never to explain the meaning of the word. The same with the word "liberal." Who is a "liberal"? Perhaps a nineteenth-century free-trader who proclaimed that the state should forbear from interfering in the "free contract" between workers and employers and that workers' unions were contrary to the free contract principle? Do you suggest that you are not "liberal" in this sense? This is very much to your credit. But according to the unwritten revolutionary OED, you are "liberal" if you imagine in general that freedom is better than slavery (I do not mean the genuine, profound freedom people enjoy in socialist countries, but the miserable formal freedom invented by the bourgeoisie to deceive the toiling masses). And the word "liberal" has the easy task of amalgamating these and other things. And so, let us proclaim loudly that we spurn liberal illusions, but let us never explain exactly what we mean.

Should I go on with this progressive vocabulary? Just one more word which, I emphasize, you do not use in this sound sense: "fascist" or "fascism." This is an ingenious discovery, with a fair range of applications. Sometimes a fascist is a person I disagree with but, because of my ignorance, I am unable to debate with, so I would do better to kick him. When I collect my experiences, I notice that a fascist is a person who holds one of the following beliefs (by way of example): 1) that people should wash themselves, rather than go dirty; 2) that freedom of the press in America is preferable to the ownership of the whole press by one ruling party; 3) that people should not be jailed for their opinions, both communist and anti-communist; 4) that racial criteria, in favor of either whites or blacks, are inadvisable in admission to Universities; 5) that torture is condemnable, no matter who applies it. (Roughly speaking, "fascist" was the same as "liberal.") A fascist is, by definition, a person who happened to have been in jail in a communist country. The refugees from Czechoslovakia in 1968 were sometimes met in Germany by very progressive and absolutely revolutionary leftists with placards saying, "fascism will not pass."

And you blame me for making a caricature of the New Left. I wonder what such a caricature would be. Still, your irritation (this is one of the few points where your pen flares up) is understandable. You quote from an interview I gave to the German Radio (and later translated from German into English and published in *Encounter*) two or three general sentences where I expressed my disgust with New Leftist movements, as I knew them in America and Germany, but – this is the point – I did not specify which movements I meant. I said instead vaguely "some people" etc. This means that I did not specifically exclude the *New Left Review* in 1960–63 when you were associated with it or I even tacitly included you in my statement. Here you got me. I did not specifically exclude the *New Left Review* in 1960–63 and, I admit, I did not even keep it in mind when I was talking to the German journalist. I thought that to say "some new leftists," etc. is rather like saying, e.g., "some British academics are drunkards." Do you think that many academics would be offended by such a (admittedly not very ingenious) statement, and if so, which ones? My comfort is that if I happen to say publicly such things on the New Left, my socialist friends somehow never feel that they could be included even if they are not specifically excluded.

But I cannot delay any longer. I hereby solemnly declare that in an interview to the German Radio in 1971, when I was talking about leftist obscurantism, I was not thinking of the *New Left Review* in 1960–63, with which Edward Thompson was involved. Will that be all right?

You are right, Edward, that we, people from Eastern Europe, have a tendency to underestimate the gravity of the social issues democratic societies face and we may be blamed for that. But we cannot be blamed for not taking seriously people who, unable though they are to remember correctly any single fact from our history or to say which barbaric dialect we speak, are perfectly able instead to teach us how liberated we are in the East. Neither can we take seriously those who have a rigorously scientific solution for humanity's illnesses, and this solution consists in repeating a few phrases we heard for thirty years on each celebration on the 1st of May and read in any party propaganda brochure. (I am talking about the attitude of progressive radicals; the conservative attitude to the problem of the East is different and can be summarized briefly: "This would be awful in our country, but for these tribes it is good enough.")

When I was leaving Poland at the end of 1968 (I had not been in any Western country for at least six years), I had a somewhat vague idea of what the radical student movement and different Leftist groups or parties might be. What I saw and read I found pathetic and disgusting in nearly all (still, not all) cases. I do not shed tears for a few windows smashed in demonstrations. That old bitch, consumer capitalism, will survive it. Neither do I find scandalous the rather natural ignorance of young people. What impressed me was mental degradation of a kind I had never seen before in any Leftist movement. I saw young people trying to "reconstitute" universities and to liberate them from horrifying, savage, monstrous, fascist oppression. The list of demands, with variations, was very similar on campuses all over the world. These fascist pigs of the Establishment want us to pass examinations while we are making the revolution; let them give all of us A grades without examinations. Curiously enough, the anti-fascist warriors wanted to get their degrees and diplomas in such fields as mathematics, sociology or law, and not in such as carrying posters, distributing leaflets or destroying offices. And sometimes they got what they wanted. The fascist pigs of the Establishment gave them grades without examinations. Very often there were demands for abolishing altogether some subjects of teaching as irrelevant, e.g., foreign languages (these fascists want us, internationalist revolutionaries, to waste time in learning languages. Why? To prevent us from making world revolution). In one place revolutionary philosophers went on strike because they got a reading list including Plato, Descartes, and other bourgeois idiots, instead of relevant great philosophers like Ché Guevara and Mao. In another, revolutionary mathematicians passed a motion that the department should organize courses on the social tasks of mathematics and (this is the point) each student should be able to attend this course as many times as he wanted and each time get credit for it, which meant that he could get the diploma in mathematics exactly for nothing. In still another place, the noble martyrs of the world revolution demanded to be examined only by other students they would choose themselves, and not by these old reactionary pseudo-scholars. Professors should be appointed (by students, of course) according to their political views, students admitted on the same grounds. In several cases in the US, the vanguard of the oppressed toiling masses set fire to university libraries (irrelevant pseudo-knowledge of the Establishment). Needless to say, you could hear that there is no difference, no difference at all, between life on a California campus and a Nazi concentration camp. And all were Marxists, of course, which meant they knew three or four sentences written by Marx or Lenin, in particular the sentence "the philosophers have only interpreted the world, in various ways; the point, however, is to change it" (what Marx wanted to say in this sentence, it is obvious to them, was that it made no sense to learn).

I could carry on this list for pages but this may suffice. The patterns are always the same: the great socialist revolution consists, first of all, in giving us privileges, titles, and power for our political opinions and in destroying the old reactionary academic values like knowledge and logical abilities (but these fascist pigs should give us money, money, money).

And what about the workers? There are two rival views. One (pseudo-Marcusian) says that these bastards were bribed by the bourgeoisie and one cannot expect anything more from them. Now the students are the most oppressed and the most revolutionary class of society. Another (Leninist) says that workers have a false consciousness and do not understand their alienation because the capitalists give them wrong papers to read, but we, revolutionaries, store in our heads the correct consciousness of the proletariat. We know what the workers should think and, in fact, do think without knowing it; consequently we deserve to take power (but not in this stupid electoral game which, as has been scientifically proved, is just for deceiving the people).

You say complacently "revolutionary farce." All right, it is. But to say this is not enough. This is not a farce capable of turning society upside down, but it is capable of destroying the university. This is a performance worth worrying about (some German universities already look like party schools).

Let us go back to the more general question we discussed earlier in private letters. You defend the movement I just described by saying ". . . but there was a Vietnam war." Very much so, indeed, to put it elegantly. And many other things, no doubt. Traditional German universities had some intolerable features. Italian and French universities had others of their own. There are many things in any society and in any university to justify protest. And this is my point: you will find no political movement in the world which has no good and well justified claims. If you look at mutual accusations of parties vying for power you always find some well-chosen and well-grounded points in their claims and attacks, and you do not take it as a reason to support all of them. Nobody is altogether wrong, and you are right, of course, in saying that those who joined the communist parties were not altogether wrong. When you look at Nazi propaganda again in the Weimar Republic, you will find a great number of well-justified points. They said that the Versailles Treaty was a shame, and it was; that the democracy was corrupted, and it was; they attacked aristocracy, plutocracy, the power of bankers and, incidentally, the pseudo-freedom, irrelevant to the real needs of the people and serving dirty Jewish newspapers. But this was not a good reason to say "all right, they do not behave very decently and some points in their ideas are rather silly, but they are not wrong in many questions, so let us give them a qualified support." At least, many people refused to say so. In fact, had the Nazis not had many good points in attacking the existing regime, they would not have won, and there would not have been such a phenomenon as the ranks of *Rotfront* passing with unfolded colors over to the SA. This is the reason why, when I saw movements imitating the same patterns of behavior and imitating a part of the same ideology (viz. in all points concerning "formal" freedom and all democratic institutions, tolerance, and academic values), I could not be strongly impressed by the observation: "but there was a Vietnam war."

You say that we should help the blind to recover their sight. I accept this advice with a slight restriction: it is difficult to apply when you have to do with people who are omniscient and all-seeing anyway. I do not remember having ever refused a discussion with people who were ready to have one. The trouble is that some were not ready, and this precisely because of their omniscience, which I lacked. True, I was almost omniscient (yet not entirely) when I was twenty years old, but, as you know, people grow stupid when they grow older. I was much less omniscient when I was twenty-eight and still less now. Nor am I capable of satisfying those who look for perfect certainty and for immediate global solutions to all the world's calamities and misery. Still, I believe that in approaching other people we should, as far as we are able to do so, follow the Jesuit, rather than the Calvinist, method. This means, we ought to presuppose that nobody is totally and hopelessly corrupted, that everybody, no matter how perverted and limited, has some good points and some good intentions. This is admittedly easier to say than to practice and I do not think that either of us is a perfect master in this maieutic art.

* * *

Your proposal to define yourself (and myself) by the allegiance to the "Marxist tradition" (as opposed to the system, the method, the heritage) seems to me elusive and vague. I am not sure of the meaning you confer on this attachment unless you simply find it important to be called "Marxist," but you say you do not. Neither do I. I am not interested at all in being "a Marxist" or in being so called. There are certainly only a few people working in the human sciences who would not acknowledge their debt to Marx. I am not one of them. I readily admit that without Marx our thinking about history would be different and in many respects worse than it is. To say this is rather trivial. Still, I think that many important tenets of Marx's doctrine are either false or meaningless, or else true only in a very restricted sense. I think that the labor theory of value is a normative device without any explanatory power whatsoever; that none of the well-known general formulae of historical materialism to be found in Marx's writings is admissible and that this doctrine is valid only in a strongly qualified sense; that his theory of class consciousness is false and that most of his predictions proved to be erroneous (this is admittedly a general description of what I feel, I am not trying to justify my conclusions here). If I admit nevertheless to still thinking, in historical (not in philosophical) matters, in terms inherited in part from the Marxist legacy, do I accept an allegiance to the Marxist tradition? Only in such a loose sense that the same statement would be equally true if I substituted for "Marxist" – "Christian," "skeptical," "empiricist." Without belonging to any political party or sect, to any Church, to any philosophical school, I do not deny my debt to Marxism, to Christianity, to skeptical philosophy, to empiricist thought and to a few other traditions (more specifically Eastern-European and less interesting to you). Neither do I share the horror of "eclecticism" if the opposite of eclecticism is philosophical or political bigotry (as it usually is in the minds of those who terrify us with the label of eclecticism). In this poor sense, I admit to belonging to the Marxist tradition, among others. But you seem to imply more. You seem to imply the existence of a "Marxist family" defined by spiritual descendence from Marx and to invite me to join it. Do you mean that all people who in one way or another call themselves Marxist form a family (never mind that they have been killing each other for half a century and still are) opposed as such to the rest of the world? And that this family is for you (and ought to be for me), a place of identification? If this is what you mean, I cannot even say that I refuse to join this family; it simply does not exist in a world where the great Apocalypse can most likely be triggered by a war between two empires both claiming to be perfect embodiments of Marxism.

* * *

In your letter there are several points which I should broach not because of their importance but because of the unpleasantly demagogic way you discuss them. I will take up two of them. You quote an article of mine containing a remark which I thought was a platitude: that exploited classes have not been allowed to participate in the development of spiritual culture. You appear as a spokesman of the excluded working class and you explain to me, with indignation, that the working class developed a sense of solidarity, loyalty, etc. In other words, I said

My Correct Views on Everything

this rather to deplore than to exalt the fact that the exploited were denied access to education and you show disgust at my alleged view that the working class has no morals. This is not a misreading but a sort of absurd *Hineinlesen*, which makes any discussion impossible. And then, when I stigmatized as obscurantist the idea of a new, socialist logic or science (again, a truism, as I saw it), you explain that the point is not to change logic but that Marx wanted to change property relations. Did he, really? Well, what can I say except that you opened my eyes? And if you think that the question of a "new logic" or "new science" as opposed to "bourgeois logic" and "bourgeois science" was not at issue, you are entirely wrong. This was not an extravagance but a standard pattern of thinking and talking among Marxist-Leninist-Stalinists. These patterns were inherited intact by the dozens of Lenins, Trotskys, and Robespierres you could find on any American or German campus.

The second point is your comment on one sentence I uttered in the same interview you quoted. It said that "men have no fuller means of self-identification than through religious symbols" and that "religious consciousness . . . is an irreplaceable part of human culture."[8] Here, you explode: "By what right (you say), what study of its tradition and sensitivity, may you assume this as a universal in the heart of an ancient Protestant Island, doggedly resistant to the magic of religious symbolism. . . ." I apologize for many reasons. First, that I gave my interview to a German journalist in the heart of the ancient Protestant Island instead of doing this on German soil. Second, that I failed to explain – which I assumed, wrongly, to be known – that a "religious symbol" is not necessarily, contrary to what you obviously believe, a picture, a sculpture, a rosary etc., but everything people believe that gives them a way of communicating with the Supernatural or conveys its energy. (Jesus Christ himself is a symbol, not only a crucifix.) I did not invent this use of the word but, since I did not explain it in my interview, I offended your iconoclastic English tradition. Does this lexical explanation appease somewhat your Protestant conscience hurt by a superstitious Ultramontanist? And you accuse me – that beats everything – of not justifying, in this interview, my belief in the permanence of the religious phenomenon. It was indeed thoughtless not to quote entirely, in this interview, all the books and articles I have written on the subject to support this view. You had no reason whatsoever to read these books (one of them, over eight hundred dense pages, and dealing mostly with sectarian movements of the seventeenth century, is so boring that it would be inhuman to ask you to wade through it[9]) – at least you had no such reason as long as you

8 *Encounter* (October, 1971), pp. 44–45. Editor's note.
9 *Swiadomosc Religijna i wiez koscielna. Studia nad chrzescijanstwem bezwyznaniowym*

were not trying to criticize my views on the subject. Therefore your indignant "By what right . . ." seems to be more appropriate when retorted to you.

Unfortunately, your article teems with instances when you shift the subject and try to make yourself believe that I said something you think I should have said, on the basis of some general beliefs you attribute to me. I am sure you do this unconsciously, according to a peculiar logic of beliefs which has always been very characteristic of dogmatic communist thinking, where the difference between those reasonings which are truth-functional and those which are not entirely disappears; however, even if it were true that A entails B, it would not follow that if someone believes A, he believes B. The willful rejection of this rather unsophisticated distinction has always allowed the communist press to give its readers information constructed approximately in this way: "The American President said that, in defiance of the protest of the whole of peace-loving mankind, he would carry on with the genocidal war in Vietnam" or "Chinese leaders declare that their jingoist, anti-Leninist policy aims at the destruction of the socialist camp in order to help imperialists." There is a consistency in this grotesque Wonderland logic and I rather dislike its echoes in your reasoning. But there is more than that. Since you think about society in categories or global "systems" – capitalism or socialism – you believe that: 1) socialism, imperfect though it is, is essentially a higher stage of mankind's development, and this superiority of the "system" is valid irrespective of whether or not it can be shown in any particular facts related to human life; 2) all negative facts to be found in the non-socialist world – apartheid in South Africa, torture in Brazil, hunger in Nigeria, or inadequate health service in Britain are to be imputed to the "system," while similar facts occurring within the socialist war have to be accounted for by the "system" as well, yet not socialist, but the same capitalist system (survival of the old society; impact of encirclement etc.); 3) whoever does not believe in the superiority or the socialist "system" so conceived is bound to believe that "capitalism" is in principle admirable and to justify or to conceal its monstrosities, i.e., to justify apartheid in South Africa, hunger in Nigeria etc. Hence your desperate attempts to force me to say something I have not.

XVII wieku (Warsaw: PWN, 1965). (The French translation appeared in 1969 as *Chrétiens sans église: La conscience religieuse et le lien conféssionnel au XVIIème siècle* [Paris: Gallimard, 1969]; The Spanish edition was published in 1984.) A chapter from this book appeared in English, as "Dutch Seventeenth-Century Non-Denominationalism and *Religio Rationalis* in L. Kolakowski, *The Two Eyes of Spinoza and Other Essays on Philosophers* [South Bend, Indiana: St. Augustine's Press, 2004], pp. 27–83. Editor's note).

My Correct Views on Everything

(True, since you consider my case not entirely lost, you try to wake up my conscience and explain, for example, that there are spies and bugging devices in Western countries. Really? Are you not joking?) Needless to say, this peculiar way of reasoning is absolutely irrefutable because it is able to neglect all empirical facts as irrelevant (anything bad that happens within the "capitalist system" is by definition the product of capitalism; anything bad that happens in "the socialist system" is by the same definition the product of the same capitalism). Socialism is defined within this "system-thinking" as total or nearly total state ownership of the means of production. You obviously cannot define socialism in terms of the abolition of hired labor, since you know that if empirical socialism differs in this respect from capitalism, this is only in restoring direct slave labor for prisoners, half-slave labor for workers (abolition of the freedom to change one's place of work) and the mediæval *glebae adscriptio* for peasants. So, within this construction it is consistent to believe that with the abolition of private ownership the roots of evil, if not all actual evil, on earth are eradicated. But these three statements I mentioned are nothing else but the expression of an ideological commitment, incapable of being either validated or disproved empirically. You say that to think in terms of a "system" yields excellent results. I am quite sure it does, not only excellent, but miraculous; it simply solves all the problems of mankind in one stroke. This is why people who have not reached this level of scientific consciousness (like myself) do not know this simple device for the salvation of the world, that is known to any sophomore in Berlin or Nebraska, viz. the socialist world revolution.

* * *

I have obviously not exhausted the topics of your text, which restores the dignity of the vanishing art of epistolography. But I believe I have touched on the most controversial ones. The gulf dividing us at the moment is unlikely to be bridged. You still seem to consider yourself a dissident communist or a sort of revisionist. I do not see myself this

10 L. Kolakowski's final split with official communist ideology can be traced back to 1966, when, on October 21, he delivered the speech "The Development of Polish Culture in the Last Decade" on the tenth anniversary of the Polish October at Warsaw University. (The transcript of this speech, recorded at the meeting by agents of the security police and recently discovered in the Archives of the Communist Security Police, was published in *Dzieje Najnowsze*, No. 4 [1994]). A few months later Kolakowski was viciously attacked by Wladyslaw Gomulka, the First Secretary of the Polish Communist Party, as the "main ideologue of the so-called revisionism," and was removed from its ranks. On March 25, 1968, after the delivery of anoth-

way, and have not for a very long time.[10] You seem to define your position in terms of discussions from 1956, and I do not. This was an important year and its illusions were important, too. But they were crushed just after they appeared. You probably realize that what was labeled "revisionism" in the people's democracies is virtually dead (possibly with the exception of Yugoslavia), which means that both young and old people in these countries stopped thinking about their situation in terms of "genuine socialism," "genuine Marxism," etc. They want (more often than not in a passive way) more national independence, more political and social freedom, better living conditions, but not because there is anything specifically socialist in these claims. The official state ideology is in a paradoxical position. It is absolutely indispensable, for it is the only way in which the ruling apparatus can legitimize its power; and it is believed by nobody – neither the rulers nor the ruled (both well aware of the unbelief of the others and of their own). In Western countries, virtually every intellectual who considers himself socialist (and even communist) will admit in private talk that the socialist idea is in deep crisis; few will admit this in print. Here buoyant jauntiness is obligatory and we must not sow doubt and confusion "among the masses" or supply our foes with arguments. I am not sure if you agree that this is a self-defeating policy. I rather think you do not.

In the meantime some traditionally socialist institutions seem to have crept into capitalist societies in a rather unexpected way. Even the most short-sighted politicians realize now that not everything can be bought for money; that a moment might come when no money will buy us clean air, clean water, more land or wasted natural resources. And so, "use value" comes back, slowly, into the economy. A paradoxical "socialism" resulting from the fact that mankind does not know what to do with garbage. The result is growing bureaucracy and the growing role of power centers. The only medicine communism has invented – centralized, uncontrolled, state ownership of national assets and one-party rule – is worse than the illnesses it is supposed to cure; it is less efficient economically and it makes the bureaucratic character of social relations an absolute principle. I appreciate your ideal of the decentralized society

---

er speech at the Writers Union (February 29, 1968; the text of this speech was published in *Obecnosc* [London: Aneks, 1987]), Kolakowski was expelled from Warsaw University and stripped of all his scholarly titles, as the official document stated, for "forming the opinions of young people in a direction glaringly contradictory to the dominant tendency of the development of the country." At the same time he was subjected to constant police surveillance. Between 1968 and 1981, Kolakowski was on the Index of authors whose publications could not be published, cited, or even referred to. Editor's note.

with a large autonomy for small communities and I share your attachment to this tradition. But it is silly to deny powerful forces resulting from technological development itself, and not from the existence of private property, leading toward greater and more powerful central bureaucracy. If you pretend to know a simple means to cope with this situation, if you imagine you have found the solution in saying, "we will make a peaceful revolution and socialism will reverse this trend," you delude yourself and fall victim to verbal magic. The more society depends on the complex technological network it created, the more problems have to be regulated by central powers, the more powerful state bureaucracy becomes, the more political democracy and more "formal" "bourgeois" freedom is needed to restrain the ruling apparatus and to secure for individuals their shrinking rights to remain individuals. There will never be, and there cannot be any economical or industrial democracy without political ("bourgeois") democracy with everything it entails. We do not know how to harmonize the contradictory tasks contemporary society imposes upon us. We can only try to reach an uncertain balance between these tasks because we have no blueprint for a conflictless and secure society. I will repeat what I wrote once elsewhere: "In private life there is the attitude of those who think about how to gain at one blow the capital that would allow them to spend the rest of their life without worries, in peace and security; and there is the attitude of those who must worry about how to survive until tomorrow. I think that human society as a whole will never be in the happy position of a pensioner, living on dividends and having the guarantee of secure life to the end, thanks to capital once acquired. Its position will be rather similar to that of a journeyman who must worry about how to survive until tomorrow. Utopians are people who dream about ensuring for mankind the position of pensioner and who are convinced that this position is so splendid that no sacrifices (in particular no moral sacrifices) are too great to achieve it."

This does not mean that socialism is a dead option. I do not think it is. But I do think that this option was destroyed not only by the experience of socialist states, but because of the self-confidence of its adherents, by their inability to face both the limits of our efforts to change society and the incompatibility of the demands and values which made up their creed. In short, that the meaning of this option has to be revised entirely, from the very roots.

And when I say "socialism" I do not mean a state of perfection but rather a movement trying to satisfy demands of equality, freedom, and efficiency, a movement that is worth the trouble only as far as it is aware not only of the complexity of problems hidden in each of these values separately but also of the fact that they limit each other and can be implemented only through compromises. We make fools of ourselves and of others if we think (or pretend to think) otherwise. All institutional changes have to be treated entirely as a means at the service of these values and not as ends in themselves. They must be judged correspondingly, taking into account the price we pay in one value when we reinforce another. Attempts to consider any of these values as absolute and to implement them at all costs, not only are bound to destroy the other two, but must lead to the destruction of the other one as well. Nota bene, this is a discovery of venerable antiquity. Absolute equality can be established only within a despotic system of rule which implies privileges, i.e., destroys equality; total freedom means anarchy and anarchy results in the domination of the physically strongest, i.e., total freedom turns into its opposite; efficiency as a supreme value calls again for despotism and despotism is economically inefficient above a certain level of technology. If I repeat these old truisms it is because they still seem to go unnoticed in utopian thinking; and this is why nothing in the world is easier than writing utopias. I wish we could agree on this point. If we do, we can agree on many others, even after exchanging a few caustic remarks, which, I hope, we will be generous enough to forgive each other. Such agreement will be much less likely if you keep believing that communism was in principle an excellent contrivance, somewhat spoilt in less than excellent application. I hope to have explained to you why, for many years, I have not expected anything from attempts to mend, to renovate, to clean up or to correct the communist idea. Alas, poor idea. I knew it, Edward. This skull will never smile again.

Yours in friendship,

Leszek Kolakowski

The Marxist Roots of Stalinism[1]

The Questions We Ask and the Questions We Don't

When we ask about the relation between Marxism and the Stalinist ideology and system of power, the main difficulty is in how to formulate the question. This can be done, and in fact has been done, in a number of ways. Some of the resulting questions are unanswerable or pointless; others are rhetorical, since the answers are obvious.

An example of a question that is both unanswerable and pointless: "What would Marx have said had he lived to see his ideas embodied in the Soviet system?" If he had lived, he would inevitably have changed. If by some miracle he were resurrected now, his opinion about which practical interpretation of his philosophy is the best one would be just one opinion among others, and could easily be dismissed by saying that a philosopher is not necessarily infallible in recognizing the implications of his own ideas.

Examples of questions to which the answers are obvious and indisputable: "Was the Stalinist system causally generated by Marxist theory? Do Marx's writings contain any implicit or explicit value judgments that conflict with the value system established in Stalinist societies?" The answer to the first question is obviously "no": there has never been a society entirely begotten by an ideology or entirely explicable by the ideas of those who contributed to its origin. Anyone is Marxist enough to admit that. All societies reflect in their institutions their members' and makers' (mutually conflicting) ideas about how society ought to be, but no society has ever been produced from such ideas alone – from conceptions of it before its existence. To imagine that a society could ever spring up entirely from a utopia (or indeed from a *kakotopia*) would

---

1 Reprinted from *Stalinism: Essays in Historical Interpretation*, ed. by Robert C. Tucker (New York: Norton, 1977).

amount to believing that human communities are capable of doing away with their history. This is common sense – a platitude, and a purely negative one at that. Societies have always been molded by what they thought about themselves, but this dependence has never been more than partial.

The answer to the second question is obviously "yes," and is irrelevant to our problem. It is easily established that Marx never wrote anything to the effect that the socialist kingdom of freedom would consist in one-party despotic rule; that he did not reject democratic forms of social life; that he expected socialism to lead to the abolition of economic coercion *in addition to*, and not *as opposed to*, political coercion; and so on. Nevertheless, his theory may logically imply consequences that are incompatible with his ostensible value judgments; or it may be that empirical circumstances prevented its being implemented in any other way. There is nothing odd in the fact that political and social programs, utopias and prophecies lead to outcomes not only very different from but significantly in conflict with the intentions of their authors; empirical connections previously unnoticed or neglected may make it impossible to implement one part of the utopia without abandoning some other ingredient. This, again, is common sense, and trivial. Most of what we learn in life is about which values are compatible and which mutually exclusive; and most utopians are simply incapable of learning that there *are* incompatible values. More often than not, this incompatibility is empirical, not logical, and this is why their utopias are not necessarily self-contradictory in logical terms, only impracticable, because of the way the world is.

Thus in discussing the relationship between Stalinism and Marxism I dismiss as irrelevant pronouncements like "This would make Marx turn in his grave" or "Marx was against censorship and in favor of free elections," whether or not their truth could be decided with certainty (which is somewhat doubtful in the case of the former).

My own curiosity would be better expressed in another way: was (or is) the characteristically Stalinist ideology that was designed to justify the Stalinist system of societal organization a legitimate (even if not the only possible) interpretation of Marxist philosophy of history? This is the milder version of my question. The stronger version is: was every attempt to implement all the basic values of Marxist socialism likely to generate a political organization that would bear the unmistakable marks of Stalinism? I shall argue for an affirmative answer to both questions, while realizing that saying "yes" to the first does not logically entail "yes" to the second: it is logically consistent to maintain that Stalinism was one of several admissible variants of Marxism and to deny that the very content of Marxist philosophy favored this particular version more strongly than any other.

How Can "Stalinism" be Identified?

It makes little difference whether we use the word "Stalinism" to refer to a well-defined period of one-man despotism in the Soviet Union (i.e., roughly from 1930 to 1953) or to any system that clearly manifests similar features. Nevertheless, the question of the degree to which post-Stalinist Soviet and Soviet-style states are essentially extensions of that system is obviously not a terminological one. For a number of reasons, however, the second, less historical and more abstract definition, which stresses the continuity of the system, is more convenient.

"Stalinism" may be characterized as an (almost perfect) totalitarian society based on state ownership of the means of production. I use the word "totalitarian" in its common sense of a political system where social ties have been entirely replaced by state-imposed organization and where, consequently, all groups and all individuals should be guided in their actions only by goals which are goals of the state, and which the state has defined as such. In other words, an ideal totalitarian system would entail the utter destruction of civil society: it would be a system in which the state and its organizational instruments were the only forms of social life, and where all forms of human activity – economic, intellectual, political, and cultural – were allowed and imposed (the distinction between what is allowed and what is imposed tending to disappear) only if they were at the service of state goals (again, as defined by the state). In such a system, every individual (including the rulers themselves) is considered the property of the state.

The concept so defined – and in so defining it I believe I do not differ from most authors who have dealt with the subject – calls for a few explanatory remarks.

First, it is clear that in order to achieve the perfect shape, a totalitarian principle of organization requires state control of the means of production. In other words, a state which leaves significant parts of productive activity and economic initiative in the hands of individuals, and in consequence permits segments of society to be economically independent of the state, cannot attain the ideal form. Therefore totalitarianism has the best chances of fulfilling this ideal within a socialist economy.

Second, it should be stressed that no absolutely perfect totalitarian system has ever existed. However, we do know some societies with a very strong, built-in, and constantly operative tendency to "nationalize" all forms of individual and community life. Both Soviet and Chinese society are, or have been, in certain periods, very close to this ideal; so was Nazi Germany, even if it did not last long enough to develop itself fully, and even though it was satisfied with subordinating economic activity to state goals through coercion, without nationalizing everything. Other fascist states were (or are) far behind Germany on this path; nor have European socialist states ever achieved the Soviet level of totalitarianism, despite a permanent and undiminished determination to do so.

It is unlikely that the *entelechia* of totalitarianism could ever be realized in an ideal form. There are forms of life – among them familal, emotional, and sexual relationships – which stubbornly resist the pressure of the system; they have been subjected to all sorts of strong state pressure, but apparently never with complete success (at least not in the Soviet state; perhaps more was achieved in China). Similarly with individual and collective memory, which the totalitarian system constantly tries to annihilate by reshaping, rewriting, and falsifying history according to current political needs. Factories and labor are obviously easier to nationalize than feelings; and hopes easier than memories. Resistance to state ownership of the past is an important part of anti-totalitarian movements.

Third, the above definition implies that not every despotic system or reign of terror is necessarily totalitarian. Some, even the bloodiest, may have limited goals, and may not need to absorb all forms of human activity within them. The worst forms of colonial rule, in their worst periods, were usually not totalitarian; the goal was to exploit the subjugated countries economically, and many spheres of life which were neutral from this point of view could be left more or less untouched. Conversely, a totalitarian system does not need to use terror permanently as a means of oppression.

In its perfect form, totalitarianism is an extraordinary form of slavery: slavery without masters. It converts all people into slaves; because of this it bears certain marks of egalitarianism.

I realize that the concept of totalitarianism, applied in this way, has of late increasingly been dismissed as "outdated" or "discredited"; its validity has been questioned. Yet I know of no analysis, either conceptual or historical, that does discredit it, although I am acquainted with many earlier analyses which justify it. Indeed, the prediction that communism would mean state-ownership of persons appears in Proudhon; and so many well-known authors have pointed out (whether or not they used the word "totalitarianism" in doing so) that this was what did in fact happen in Soviet society, and gone on to describe it, that it would be pointless pedantry to quote them here.

The Main Stages of Stalinist Totalitarianism

The Soviet variety of totalitarianism spent many years ripening before reaching its apogee. The main stages of its growth are well known, and need only to be briefly mentioned.

In the first stage, the basic forms of representative democracy – parliament, elections, political parties, a free press – were done away with.

The second stage (which overlapped with the first) is known by the misleading name of "war communism." The name suggests that the policies of this period were conceived of as temporary and exceptional measures to cope with the monstrous difficulties imposed by civil war and intervention. In fact, it is clear from the relevant writings of the leaders – in particular Lenin, Trotsky, and Bukharin – that they all envisaged this economic policy (the abolition of free trade, coercive requisitioning of "surplus" – i.e., whatever the local leadership considered to be surplus – from the peasants, universal rationing, forced labor) as a permanent achievement of the new society, and that it was eventually abandoned not because the war conditions which had made it necessary no longer existed, but as a result of the economic disaster it had caused. Both Trotsky and Bukharin were emphatic in their assurances that forced labor was an organic part of the new society.

Important elements of the totalitarian order that was set up in this period persisted and became permanent components of Soviet society. One such lasting achievement was the destruction of the working class as a political force: the abolition of the soviets as an independent expression of popular initiative and the end of independent trade unions and political parties. Another was the suppression – not yet definitive – of democracy within the party itself: the ban on factional activity. Throughout the NEP era the totalitarian traits of the system were extremely strong, despite the fact that free trade was accepted and that a large section of society – the peasants – enjoyed economic independence from the state. Both politically and culturally, the NEP meant mounting pressure of the party-owned state on all centers of initiative that were not yet, or not entirely, state-owned, although it was only in subsequent stages of development that full success was achieved in this respect.

The third stage was forced collectivization, which amounted to destroying the last social class not yet nationalized and gave the state full control over economic life. Which did not mean, of course, that it enabled the state to engage in real economic planning: it did not.

The fourth stage was to destroy the party itself, through purges; for it was still a potential, though no longer actual, non-nationalized force. Although no effective forces of rebellion survived within it, many of its members, especially the older ones, remained loyal to the traditional party ideology. Thus even if they were perfectly obedient, they were (rightly) suspected of dividing their loyalties between the actual leader and the inherited ideological value system – in other words, of being potentially disloyal to the leader. It had to be made clear to them that ideology was whatever the leader at any given moment said it was. The massacres successfully accomplished this task; they were the work of an ideological *Führer*, not a madman.

The Mature Face of Stalinism

Each stage of this process was deliberately decided and organized, although not all were planned in advance. The result was a fully stateowned society that came very close to the ideal of perfect unity, cemented by party and police. It was both perfectly integrated and perfectly fragmented, and for the same reason: integrated in that all forms of collective life were entirely subordinated to, and imposed by, one ruling center, and fragmented in that civil society had been to all intents and purposes destroyed, and each citizen, in all his relations with the state, faced the omnipotent apparatus alone, an isolated and powerless individual. Society was reduced to a thing like a "sack of potatoes," as Marx said of French peasants in the *Eighteenth Brumaire*.

This situation – a unified state organism facing atom-like individuals – defined the all-important features of the Stalinist system. They are well known and have been much-described, but it is worth briefly mentioning a few of the ones most relevant to our topic.

First, the abolition of law. Law persisted, to be sure, as a set of procedural rules governing public life. But as a set of rules which could infringe upon the state's omnipotence in its dealings with individuals it was entirely abolished. In other words, it could contain no rules which might restrict the principle that citizens are the property of the state. In its crucial points totalitarian law had to be vague, so that its application might hinge on the arbitrary and changing decisions of the executive authorities, and so that each citizen could be considered a criminal whenever these authorities chose so to consider him. The notable examples have always been political crimes as defined in penal codes; these are constructed in such a way that it is well-nigh impossible for a citizen not to commit crimes almost daily. Which of these crimes are actually prosecuted and how much terror is used depends on the political decisions of the rulers. In this respect nothing has changed in the post-Stalinist period: the law remains characteristically totalitarian, and neither the transition from mass to selective terror nor the better observance of procedural rules is relevant – as long as they do not limit the effective power of the state over individual lives – to its persistence. People may or may not be jailed for telling political jokes; their children may or may not be forcibly taken away from them if they fail in their legal duty to raise them in the communist spirit (whatever this means). Totalitarian lawlessness consists not in the actual application of extreme measures always and everywhere but in the fact that the law gives individuals no protection against whatever forms of repression the state wants to use at any given moment. The law as a mediator between the state and the people disappears, and is converted into an endlessly malleable instrument of the state. In this respect the Stalinist principle persists unchanged.

Second, one-person autocracy. This seems to have been a natural and "logical" outcome of the perfect-unity principle which was the driving force in the development of the totalitarian state. In order to achieve its full shape, the state required one and only one leader, endowed with limitless power. This was implicit in the very foundations of the Leninist party (in accordance with Trotsky's often quoted prophesy of 1903, soon forgotten by the prophet himself). The whole progress of the Soviet system in the 1920s consisted in a step-by-step narrowing of the forum where conflicting interests, ideas, and political tendencies could be expressed. For a short period they continued to be articulated publicly in society, but their expression was gradually confined, in a narrowing upward movement: first to the party; then to the party apparatus; then to the Central Committee; and finally to the Politburo. But here, too, expressions of social conflict could be prevented, although the sources of conflict had not been eradicated. It was Stalin's well-grounded contention that even here, in this narrowest caucus, conflicting expressions of opinion, if allowed to continue, would convey the pressure of those conflicting interests which still survived within society. This is why the destruction of the civil society could not be fully accomplished so long as different tendencies or factions had room to express themselves, even in the supreme party organ.

The changes which occurred in the Soviet system after Stalin – the transition from personal tyranny to oligarchy – seem most salient here. They resulted from an incurable contradiction inherent in the system: perfect unity of leadership, required by the system and embodied in personal despotism, was incompatible with other leaders' need for a minimum of security. Under Stalin's rule they were demoted to the same precarious status as other people – the status of slaves. All their enormous privileges could not protect them against a sudden fall from grace, imprisonment and death. The oligarchical rule after Stalin was a sort of mutual security pact among the party apparatus. But such a contract, insofar as it is in fact applied, runs counter to the principle of unity. In this sense the decades after Stalin's death may properly be described as an ailing form of Stalinism.

Nevertheless, Soviet society, even in its worst periods, has never been ruled by the police. Stalin governed the country and the party with the aid of the police machine, but he governed as party leader, not as chief of police. The party, which for a quarter of a century was identical with Stalin, never lost its all-embracing sway.

Third, universal spying as the principle of government. People were encouraged – and compelled – to spy upon one another, but this was obviously not how the state defended itself against real dangers; rather, it was a way of pushing the principle of totalitarianism to its extreme. As citizens, people were supposed to live in a perfect unity of goals, desires, and thoughts – all expressed through the mouth of the leader. As individuals, however, they were expected to hate one another and to live in constant mutual hostility. Only thus could the isolation of individuals from one another achieve perfection. In fact, the unattainable ideal of the system seems to have been one where everyone is at the same time an inmate of a concentration camp and a secret police agent.

Fourth, the apparent omnipotence of ideology. This is a point on which, in all discussions of Stalinism, there is more confusion and disagreement than on any other. This is evident if we look at the exchange of views on the subject between Solzhenitsyn and Sakharov. The former says, roughly, that the whole Soviet state, in both its home and its foreign policy, in both economic and political matters, is subjugated to the overwhelming rule of Marxist ideology, and that it is this (false) ideology which is responsible for all the disasters that have struck both the state and the society. The latter replies that the official state ideology is dead and that no one any longer takes it seriously, so it is silly to imagine that it could be a real force in guiding and shaping practical policies.

It seems that both these observations are valid, within certain limits. The point is that the Soviet state has an ideology built into its very foundations, from the very beginning, as the only principle of its legitimacy. Certainly, the ideological banners under which the Bolshevik party seized power in Russia (peace and land for the peasants) had no specifically socialist, let alone Marxist, content. But it could only establish its monopoly rule on the Leninist ideological principle: as a party which by definition was the only legitimate mouthpiece of the working class and of all the "toiling masses," of their interests, goals, and desires (even if these were unknown to the masses themselves), and which owed its ability to "express" the will of the masses to its "correct" Marxist ideology. A party that wields despotic power cannot abandon the ideology which justifies this power and which remains, in the absence of free elections or an inherited royal charisma, the only basis of its legitimacy. In such a system of rule ideology is indispensable, no matter how few or many people believe it, who they are and how seriously they take it; and it remains indispensable even if – as is now the case in European socialist countries – there are virtually no more believers left, either among the rulers or among the ruled. The leaders clearly cannot afford to reveal the real and notorious principles of their policy without risking the utter collapse of the system of power. A state ideology believed by no one must be binding on all if the entire fabric of the state is not to crumble.

This does not mean that the ideological considerations appealed to in order to justify each step in practical policy are real, independent forces before which Stalin or other leaders bowed. But to a certain extent they do limit this policy. The Soviet system, both under and after Stalin, has always pursued the *Realpolitik* of a great empire, and its ideology had to be vague enough to sanctify any given policy: NEP and collectivization, friendship with the Nazis and war with the Nazis, friendship with China and the condemnation of China, support for Israel or support for Israel's foes, Cold War and detente, the tightening of the internal regime and its relaxation, the oriental cult of the satrap and the denunciation of that cult. And still this ideology preserves the Soviet state and holds it together.

It has often been pointed out that the Soviet totalitarian system is not intelligible unless we take into account the historical background of Russia, with its strongly pronounced totalitarian traits. The autonomy of the state and its overwhelming powers over civil society was stressed by Russian historians of the nineteenth century, and this view was endorsed, with some qualifications, by a number of Russian Marxists (such as Plekhanov, in his *History of Russian Social Thought*, and Trotsky in his *History of the Russian Revolution*). After the revolution this background was repeatedly referred to as the genuine source of Russian communism (Berdyaev). Many authors (Kucharzewski was one of the first) saw in Soviet Russia a direct extension of the czarist regime; they saw it in, among other things, her expansionist policy and her insatiable hunger for new territories, and also in the "nationalization" of all citizens and the subordination of all forms of human activity to the state's goals. Several historians have published very convincing studies on the subject (most recently R. Pipes and T. Szamuely), and I do not question their conclusions. But this historical background does not explain the peculiar function of Marxist ideology in the Soviet order. Even if we go so far as to admit (with Amalrik) that the whole meaning of Marxism in Russia ultimately consisted in injecting a shaky ideological empire with flesh and blood that would allow it to survive for a time before definitively falling apart, the question of how Marxism fitted into this task still remains unanswered. How could the Marxist philosophy of history, with its ostensible hopes, aims, and values, supply the totalitarian, imperialist, and chauvinist state with an ideological weapon?

It could and it did; and it did not even need to be essentially distorted, merely interpreted in the appropriate way.

Stalinism as Marxism

In discussing this question I am assuming that Marx's thought from 1843 onwards was propelled by that same value-laden idea for which he was continually seeking a better form of expression. Thus I agree with those who emphasize the strong continuity of Marx's intellectual development; I do not believe that there was any significant, much less violent, break in the growth of his main ideas. But I will not argue here in favor of this controversial – although by no means original – view.

In Marx's eyes the original sin of man, his *felix culpa*, responsible both for great human achievements and for human misery, was the division of labor – and its inevitable result, the alienation of labor. The extreme form of alienated labor is exchange value, which dominates the entire process of production in industrial societies. It is not human needs but the endless accumulation of exchange value in the form of money that is the main driving force behind all human productive efforts. This has transformed human individuals, with their personal qualities and abilities, into commodities which are sold and bought according to the anonymous laws of the market, within a system of hired labor. It has generated the alienated institutional framework of modern political societies; and it has produced an inevitable split between people's personal, selfish, self-centered lives as members of civil society on the one hand and, on the other, the artificial and obscure community which they form as members of a political society. As a result, human consciousness was bound to suffer an ideological distortion: instead of affirming human life and its own function as an "expression" of that life, it built a separate, illusory kingdom of its own, designed to perpetuate this split. With private property, the alienation of labor divided society into hostile classes struggling for the distribution of the surplus product; finally, it gave rise to the class in which all society's dehumanization was concentrated, and which was consequently destined both to demystify consciousness and to restore the lost unity of human existence. This revolutionary process starts with smashing the institutional mechanisms which protect existing labor conditions and ends with a society where, with all the basic sources of social conflict removed, the social process is subordinated to the collective will of the individuals associated in it. These latter will then be able to unfold all their individual potentialities not against society but for its enrichment; their labor will have been gradually reduced to the necessary minimum, and free time will be enjoyed in the pursuit of cultural creativity and high-quality entertainment. The full meaning of both history and present struggles is revealed only in the romantic vision of the perfectly united mankind of the future. Such unity implies no more need for the mediating mechanisms which separate individuals from the species as a whole. The revolutionary act that will close the "pre-history" of mankind is both inevitable and directed by free will; the distinction between freedom and necessity will have disappeared in the consciousness of the proletariat as it becomes aware of its own historical destiny through the destruction of the old order.

I suspect it was both Marx's anticipation of man's perfect unity and his myth of the historically privileged proletarian consciousness that led to his theory's being turned into the ideology of the totalitarian movement; not because he conceived of it in such terms, but because its basic values could not be realized in any other way. It was not that Marx's theory lacked a vision of future society; it did not. But even his powerful imagination could not stretch so far as to envisage the transition from "pre-history" to "genuine history" and come up with the proper social technology for converting the former into the latter; this step had to be carried out by practical leaders. And that necessarily implied adding to the inherited body of doctrine and filling in the details.

In his dream of a perfectly unified humanity Marx was not, strictly speaking, a Rousseauist; Rousseau did not believe that the lost spontaneous identity of each individual with the community would ever be restored and the poison of civilization effaced from human memory. But this was precisely what Marx did believe: not because he believed that jettisoning civilization and returning to the primitive happiness of a savage state was possible or desirable, but because he believed that the irresistible progress of technology would ultimately overcome (dialectically) its own destructiveness and offer humanity a new unity – a unity based not on the suppression of needs but on freedom from wants. In this respect he shared the hopes of the St. Simonists.

Marx's liberated mankind needs none of the machinery with which bourgeois society settles conflicts among individuals or between them and society: law, state, representative democracy, and negative freedom, as conceived and proclaimed in the Declaration of Human Rights. Such machinery is characteristic of societies ruled economically by the market and composed of isolated individuals with their conflicting interests; it is what they must rely on to maintain their stability. The state and its legal skeleton protect bourgeois property by coercion and impose rules on conflicts; their very existence presupposes a society where human activities and desires naturally clash with each other. The liberal concept of freedom implies that my freedom inevitably limits the freedom of my fellow men, and this is indeed the case if the scope of freedom coincides with the scale of ownership. Once the bourgeois order is replaced by a system of communal property, this machinery no longer has any purpose. Individual interests converge with universal ones, and there is no more need to shore up society's unstable equilibrium with regulations that define the limits of individual freedom. And it is not only the "rational" instruments of liberal society that are then done away with: inherited tribal and national ties will also disappear. In this respect the capitalist order paves the way for communism: under the cosmopolitan power of capital and as a result of the internationalist consciousness of the proletariat, the old, irrational loyalties crumble away. The end of this process is a community where nothing is left except the individual and the human species as a whole, and where individuals will directly identify their own lives, abilities, and activities as social forces: they will have no need of political institutions or traditional national ties to mediate this experience of their identity.

How can this be achieved? Is there a technique for effecting such social transsubstantiation? Marx did not answer this question, and from his point of view it seems wrongly put: the point was not to find a technique of social engineering after drawing an arbitrary picture of a desirable society, but to identify and "express" theoretically the social forces which are already at work to bring such a society about. And expressing them meant practically reinforcing their energy and providing them with the self-knowledge necessary for their conscious self-identification.

There were a number of possible practical interpretations of Marx's message, depending on which values one considered fundamental to the doctrine and which formulations one interpreted as basic clues to the whole. There seems nothing wrong with the interpretation which became the Leninist-Stalinist version of Marxism. It went as follows:

Marxism is a ready-made doctrinal body, identical with the class-consciousness of the proletariat in its mature and theoretically elaborated form. Marxism is true both because it has "scientific" value and because it articulates the aspirations of the "most progressive" social class. The distinction between "truth" in the genetic and the ordinary sense of the word has always been obscure in the doctrine; it was taken for granted that the "proletariat," by virtue of its historical mission, has a privileged cognitive position, and therefore that its vision of the social "totality" has to be right. Thus the "progressive" automatically becomes the "true," whether or not this truth could be confirmed by universally accepted scientific procedures.

This is a simplified version of the Marxist concept of class consciousness. Certainly, the party's claim to have a monopoly on truth did not automatically follow from it; the equation also required the specifically Leninist notion of the party. But there was nothing anti-Marxist in this notion. If Marx did not have a theory of the party, he did have a concept of a vanguard group which was supposed to articulate the latent consciousness of the working class, and he saw his own theory as an expression of that consciousness. The idea that a "proper" working class revolutionary consciousness had to be instilled into the spontaneous workers' movement from without was one that Lenin took from Kautsky and supplemented with an important addition: that since only two basic ideologies can exist in a society torn by class struggle between the bourgeoisie and the proletariat, it follows that an ideology which is not proletarian – i.e., not identical with the ideology of the vanguard party – is necessarily bourgeois. Thus, since the workers are incapable of producing their own class ideology unaided, the ideology they will produce by their own efforts must be a bourgeois one. In other words, the empirical, "spontaneous" consciousness of the workers can only generate what is essentially a bourgeois *Weltanschauung*. Consequently, the Marxist party, while being the only vehicle for truth, is also entirely independent of the empirical (and by definition bourgeois) consciousness of the workers (except that it sometimes has to make tactical concessions in order not to run too far ahead of the proletariat if it is canvassing for its support).

This remains true after the seizure of power. As the sole possessor of truth, the party may completely discard (except in a tactical sense) the (inevitably immature) empirical consciousness of the masses. Indeed it must do so: it cannot do otherwise without betraying its historical mission. It knows both the "laws of historical development" and the proper connections between the "base" and the "superstructure," and is therefore perfectly able to discern which elements of the real, empirical consciousness of the people deserve destruction as surviving remnants from a past historical epoch. Religious ideas clearly fall into this category, but so does everything that makes the minds of the people different in content from the minds of their leaders.

Within this conception of the proletarian consciousness, the dictatorship over minds is entirely justified: the party really does know better than society what society's genuine (as opposed to empirical) desires, interests, and thoughts are. And once the spirit of the party is incarnated in one leader (as the highest expression of society's unity), we have the ultimate equation: truth = proletarian consciousness = Marxism = the party's ideology = the party leaders' ideas = the chief's decisions. The theory which endows the proletariat with a sort of cognitive privilege culminates in the statement that Comrade Stalin is never wrong. And there is nothing un-Marxist in this equation.

The concept of the party as the sole possessor of truth was of course strongly reinforced by the expression "the dictatorship of the proletariat," which Marx used casually two or three times without explanation. Kautsky, Martov, and other Social Democrats could argue that what Marx meant by "dictatorship" was the class content of government rather than its form, and that the term was not to be understood in opposition to a democratic state; but Marx did not specifically say anything of the sort in this context. And there was nothing obviously wrong in taking the word "dictatorship" at its face value, to mean precisely what Lenin meant and expressly said: a reign based entirely on violence and not limited by law.

Beside the question of the party's "historical right" to impose its despotism on all domains of life, there was the question of the content of this despotism. This was solved in a way that was basically in keeping with Marx's predictions. Liberated mankind was supposed to abolish the distinction between state and civil society, to eliminate all the mediating devices that had prevented individuals from achieving a perfect identity with the "whole," to destroy the bourgeois freedom that entailed conflicts of private interests, and to demolish the system of hired labor which compelled workers to sell themselves like commodities. Marx did not spell out exactly how this unity was to be achieved, except for one indisputable point: the expropriation of the expropriators – i.e., the elimination of the private ownership of the means of production. One could, and ought, to argue that once this historical act of expropriation has been performed, all remaining social conflicts are merely the expression of a backward (bourgeois) mentality left over from the old society. But the party knows what the content of the correct mentality corresponding to the new relations of productions should be, and it is naturally entitled to suppress all phenomena which are out of keeping with it.

What would, in fact, be the appropriate technique to reach this desirable unity? The economic foundations have been laid. One could argue that Marx did not mean for civil society to be suppressed or replaced by the state, but rather expected the state to wither away, leaving only the "administration of things," with political government becoming superfluous. But if the state is by definition an instrument of the working class on its road to communism, it cannot, by definition, use its power against the "toiling masses," only against the relics of capitalist society. And how could the "administration of things," or economic management, not involve the use and distribution of labor, i.e., of all working people? Hired labor – the free market of the labor force – was to be eliminated. This duly happened. But what if communist enthusiasm alone proves an insufficient incentive for people to work? Clearly, this means that they are imprisoned in bourgeois consciousness, which it is the task of the state to destroy. Consequently, the way to eliminate hired labor is to replace it by coercion. And how is the unity of civil and political society to be implemented if only the political society expresses the "correct" will of the people? Here again, whatever opposes and resists that will is by definition a survival of the capitalist order; so once more the only way toward unity is through the destruction of civil society by the state.

Whoever argues that people should be educated to cooperate freely and without compulsion must answer the question: at what stage and by what means can such education be successful? It is certainly counter to Marx's theory to expect it to be possible in capitalist society, where the working people are weighed down by the overwhelming influence of bourgeois ideology. (Did not Marx say that the ideas of the ruling class are ruling ideas? Is it not pure utopia to hope for a moral transformation of society in a capitalist order?) And after the seizure of power, education is the task of the most enlightened vanguard of society; compulsion is used only against the "survivals of capitalism." So there is no need to distinguish between the production of the "new man" of socialism and sheer coercion; in consequence, the distinction between liberation and slavery is inevitably blurred.

The question of freedom (in the "bourgeois" sense) becomes irrelevant in the new society. Did not Engels say that genuine freedom should be defined as the extent to which people were capable of both subjugating their natural environment and consciously regulating social processes? On this definition, the more society is technologically advanced, the freer it is; and the more social life is submitted to a unified directing force, the freer it is. Engels did not mention that this regulation of society would necessarily involve free elections or any other bourgeois contrivances of the sort; and there is no reason to maintain that a society entirely regulated by one center of despotic power is not perfectly free in this sense.

One can find many quotations in Marx and Engels to the effect that throughout human history the "superstructure" has been at the service of the corresponding relations of property in a given society, that the state is nothing but a tool for keeping intact the existing relations of production, and that the law cannot but be a weapon of class power. It is valid to conclude that the same situation continues in the new society, at least as long as communism in its absolute form has not entirely dominated the earth. In other words, the law is an instrument of the political power of the "proletariat," and since it is just a technique for wielding power (its main task being, more often than not, to cover up violence and deceive the people), it makes no difference whether the victorious class rules with the help of the law or without it. What matters is the class content of power, not its "form." Moreover, it also seems valid to conclude that the new "superstructure" must serve the new "base"; this means, among other things, that cultural life as a whole must be entirely subordinated to political "tasks" as defined by the "ruling class," speaking through the mouth of its most conscious element. It is therefore arguable that universal servility as the guiding principle of cultural life in the Stalinist system was a proper deduction from the "base-superstructure" theory. The same applies to the sciences: again, did not Engels say that the sciences should not be left to themselves, without theoretical philosophical guidance, lest they fall into all sorts of empiricist absurdities? And indeed this was how many Soviet philosophers and party leaders from the start justified the control of all the sciences (in their content as well as their scope of interest) by philosophy – i.e., by party ideology. In the 1920s Karl Korsch had already pointed out the obvious connection between philosophy's claim to supremacy and the Soviet system of ideological tyranny over the sciences.

Many critical Marxists considered this to be a caricature of Marxism. I would not deny this. I would add, however, that one can talk meaningfully of "caricature" only if the caricature resembles the original – as in this case it does. Nor would I deny the obvious fact that Marx's thought was much richer, subtler, and more differentiated than it might seem from the few quotations which are endlessly repeated in Leninist-Stalinist ideology to justify the Soviet system of power. Still, I would argue that these quotations are not necessarily distortions: that the dry skeleton of Marxism adopted by Soviet ideology was a greatly simplified but not a falsified guide to building a new society.

The idea that the whole theory of communism may be summed up by the single phrase "abolition of private property" was not invented by Stalin. Nor did he come up with the idea that wage labor cannot exist without capital, or that the state must have centralized control over the means of production, or that national hostilities will disappear together with class antagonisms. All these ideas are, as we know, clearly stated in the *Communist Manifesto*. Taken together, they do not merely suggest but logically imply that once the factories and the land are state-owned, as was to happen in Russia, society is basically liberated. This was precisely the claim made by Lenin, Trotsky, and Stalin.

The point is that Marx really did consistently believe that human society would not be "liberated" without achieving unity. And there is no known technique apart from despotism whereby the unity of society can be achieved: no way of suppressing the tension between civil and political society except by the suppression of civil society; no means of eliminating the conflicts between the individual and the "whole" except by the destruction of the individual; no way toward a "higher," "positive" freedom – as opposed to "negative," "bourgeois" freedom – except through the suppression of the latter. And if the whole of human history is to be conceived in class terms – if all values, all political and legal institutions, ideas and moral norms, religious and philosophical beliefs, all forms of artistic creativity, etc., are nothing but instruments of "real" class interests (and there are many passages to this effect in Marx's writings) – then it does follow that the new society must start by a violent break in cultural continuity from the old one. (In fact the continuity cannot be entirely broken, and in Soviet society a selective continuity was accepted from the beginning; the radical quest for "proletarian culture" was only a short-lived extravagance sponsored by the leadership. The emphasis on selective continuity grew stronger with the development of the Soviet state, mostly as a result of its increasingly nationalist character.)

I suspect that utopias – visions of a perfectly unified society – are not simply impracticable but become counter-productive as soon as we try to create them by institutional means. This is because institutionalized unity and freedom are opposing notions. A society that is deprived of freedom can be unified only in the sense that the expression of conflicts is stifled: the conflicts themselves do not go away. Consequently, it is not unified at all.

I do not deny the importance of the changes that took place in the socialist countries after Stalin's death, although I maintain that the political constitution of these countries has remained intact. But the main point about them is that, however reluctantly it is done, allowing the market some limited impact on production and abandoning or even just loosening rigid ideological control in certain areas of life amounts to renouncing the Marxist vision of unity. What these changes reveal is the impracticability of that vision; they cannot be interpreted as symptoms of a return to "genuine" Marxism – no matter what Marx "would have said."

An additional – although certainly not conclusive – argument in favor of the above interpretation lies in the history of the problem. It would be utterly false to say that "no one could have predicted" such an outcome of Marxist humanist socialism. Anarchist writers actually did predict it, long before the socialist revolution: they thought that a society based on Marx's ideological principles would produce slavery and despotism. Here, at least, mankind cannot complain that it was deceived by History and surprised by the unpredictable connections of things.

The question discussed here is one of "genetic vs environmental" factors in social development. Even in genetic enquiry, when the properties under investigation are not precisely definable, or when they are mental rather than physical (like "intelligence," for example), it is very difficult to distinguish the respective roles of these factors; how much more difficult, then, to distinguish between the "genetic" and the "environmental" in our social inheritance – between an inherited ideology and the contingent conditions in which people try to implement it. It is common sense that both factors are at work in any particular case, and that we have no way of calculating their relative importance and expressing it in quantitative terms. To say that "genes" (the inherited ideology) are entirely responsible for how the child turns out is just as silly as saying that the "environment" (contingent historical events) can entirely account for it. (In the case of Stalinism, these two unacceptably extreme positions are expressed respectively as the view that Stalinism was in fact "no more than" Marxism realized and as the view that it was "no more than" a continuation of the czarist empire.) But although we cannot perform a calculation and assign each set of factors its "fair share" of responsibility, we can still reasonably ask whether or not the mature form was anticipated by the "genetic" conditions.

The continuity I have tried to trace back from Stalinism to Marxism appears in still sharper outline when we look at the transition from Leninism to Stalinism. The non-Bolshevik factions (the Mensheviks, not to mention the liberals) were aware of the general direction Bolshevism was taking, and predicted its outcome fairly accurately, just after 1917; moreover, the despotic character of the new system was soon attacked within the party itself (by the "Workers' Opposition" and then the Left Opposition – e.g., Rakovsky) long before Stalinism was securely established. The Mensheviks saw all their predictions borne out in the 1930s, and Trotsky's belated rejoinder to their "we told you so" is pathetically unconvincing. They may have predicted what would happen, he argued, but still they were quite wrong, for they believed that despotism would come as a result of Bolshevik rule; it has indeed come, he said, but as a result of a bureaucratic coup. *Qui vult decipi, decipiatur*.

The Myth of Human Self-Identity
The Unity of Civil and Political Society in Socialist Thought[1]

These remarks are not historical. Their aim is to point out a soteriological myth hidden in the traditional Marxist anticipation of socialism as based on the identity of civil and political society. I will try to show a continuity (though not an identity) between this soteriology and contemporary totalitarian variants of socialism and to say why the Marxian ideal of unity is in my opinion impracticable. Some brief historical remarks may nevertheless be useful to bring into relief the background against which Marxian thought seems to have developed.

Marx's ideas on the relationship of civil society to the state took shape in his criticism of four doctrines which differed widely in the negative influence they exerted on his thought. They are: (1) Hegel's and then Lassalle's theory of the state; (2) the classical liberal concept of the state; (3) anarchist (mostly Bakuninist) criticism of the state; (4) totalitarian communism.

The first two of these may be called liberal in the sense that they both involved the separation of political from civil society as a permanent feature of human life, and both rejected the idea that the state could ever replace civil society or, at the other extreme, become superfluous; in other words, they were neither totalitarian nor anarchist. Both Hegel and Lassalle, however, departed from classical liberal tenets in that they went beyond a purely utilitarian concept of the state and attributed an autonomous value to it as the highest form of human community. The classical liberal doctrine envisaged the state in strictly utilitarian terms, as a necessary device for setting well-defined legal limits to the conflicts

1 Originally a lecture delivered at the Reading Conference, 1973. Published in *The Socialist Idea: A Reappraisal*, edited by L. Kolakowski and S. Hampshire (New York: Basic Books, 1974).

of particular interests that inevitably arise in any society and thus preventing society from turning into an unrestricted war of all against all, i.e., from eventually falling prey to the tyranny of the strongest.

When confronted with Marx's strictures on Bakunin, we may sometimes feel it difficult to square them with his criticism of Lassalle; the former is attacked for denouncing the state as the main source of all social evil, the latter for worshiping it as the most splendid achievement of the human spirit. We may say, however, that Marx's basic conception of the relationship between political and civil society, as expounded in 1843 in the unfinished *Critique of the Hegelian Philosophy of Right* and in *The Jewish Question*, persisted intact throughout his intellectual development, and there are no grounds for maintaining that it was ever denied in later writings.

To be sure, Marx started in Feuerbachian fashion by blaming Hegel for his "inversion" of the relation of "subject" to "predicate" in dealing with the question. For Hegel, he says, real human subjects become predicates of the universal substance embodied in the state. The real priorities are thus reversed, since "the universal" can be only a property of an individual being, and the genuine subject is always finite. It is not the state that creates "real individuals"; the state, on the contrary, is "objectified man." The stated aim of democracy is to restore the state to its real human creators. When stating that "the universal" needs human subjectivity to reach its own perfection, Hegel not only makes the separation of the state from human beings permanent but sanctions the illusion of the state as the embodiment of the universal interest. Indeed, Hegel believed that the spirit of the state, its superiority over all particular interests, is incorporated in the consciousness of state functionaries, since only they can identify their particular interest with the universal interest and make possible the synthesis of the general good with the aspirations of particular layers of society. Consequently, Hegelian philosophy supports the ideological illusion of the Prussian bureaucracy that considers itself the incarnation of the universal interest. Marx stresses, however, that when bureaucracy becomes an autonomous principle and when the interest of the state gains independence as the interest of the bureaucracy – and is thus a "real" interest – bureaucracy must fight against the aspirations of the other particular orders which gave birth to it.

Marx thus took over the Hegelian distinction between civil society and the state, while denying their permanence and the necessity of their separation. Civil society is a mass of conflicting individual and group aspirations; everyday life, with all its conflicts and struggles, is the realm of private desires and private endeavors. To Hegel, its conflicts are rationally moderated, kept in check and synthesized in the superior will of the state, this will being independent of any particular interest. To

Marx the state, at least in its present form, far from being a neutral mediator, is the tool of particular interests disguised as the illusory universal will. Man as citizen and as private person is two different, separate beings, but only the latter, the member of the civil society, is the "real" concrete being; as a citizen he participates in the abstract community that owes its reality to ideological mystification. This mystification was unknown in medieval society, where class divisions were directly expressed in the political order, i.e., the segmentation of civil society was reflected in the political organism. Modern societies, where class stratification has no direct political validity, split social life into two realms, and this division is carried over into each individual existence, so that it has become a contradiction within every human being, torn between his status as a private person and his role as a citizen. Consequently, political emancipation – in defiance of Bruno Bauer's philosophy – must not be confused with human emancipation. The former may politically eliminate – i.e., render politically insignificant – the differences between people in matters of ownership or religion, and thus liberate the state from religious or class distinctions (by, for example, the abolition of ownership qualifications in political activities or of legal privileges for certain denominations). But this change, important though it may be, does not abrogate either religious or class divisions in society; and it leaves untouched the separation of civil from political society. The former is still a realm of real life, egoistic and isolated for every individual; the latter lends life its collective character, but only in an abstract, illusory form. The aim of human – as opposed to political – emancipation is to restore to collective life its real character, or to restore the collective character to civil society. At the end of the *Jewish Question* we find an important sentence which expresses – still in philosophical and embryonic form, not yet in class terms – the great Marxist hope for universal human emancipation; a hope that was to continue determining all Marx's further efforts to outline his vision of a society that will have abolished for ever the dichotomy between man's personal and his collective existence:

> Only when real, individual man reabsorbs into himself the abstract citizen and becomes a species-being, in his everyday life, in his individual work, and in his individual relationships; only when man recognizes and organizes his "forces propres," his own powers, as social powers, and, consequently, no longer separates from himself social force in the shape of political force – only then will human emancipation be accomplished.

No one would claim that this sentence contains everything Marx would say later about the meaning of the future kingdom of freedom.

But everything he said grew out of this initial hope. In the quoted sentence the concept of "human emancipation" is not accompanied by any mention of class struggle or the mission of the proletariat. And yet the same vision of man returning to perfect unity, experiencing his personal life directly as a social force, makes up the philosophical background of Marxian socialism. In all later writings which were to define his position in contrast to liberal, anarchist, and communist totalitarian doctrines, the same eschatological concept of unified man remains.

What is wrong with this hope? Is there any historical connection between the Marxian vision of unified man and the fact that real communism appears only in totalitarian form, i.e., as the tendency to *replace* all crystallizations of civil society by coercive organs of the state? How can this connection be grasped?

While we cannot examine in detail the intricacies of the problems in the chronicles of Marxist doctrine here, I must summarize, however crudely, the most important points of the Marxist criticism of the four approaches just mentioned.

Anarchism, i.e., Stirner and Bakunin. Bakunin's concept was based on three premises. First, that state institutions are the main sources of all social evil. Second, that people left to themselves and free of the burden of political machinery will develop their natural ability for friendly cooperation within loosely-organized small communities. Third, that any attempt to rebuild the state, once the existing state has been crushed, will end in another, still worse version of the same tyranny: a new apparatus composed of the former workers of the old cannot but reinforce continuing slavery; the upstarts who run it will be instantly converted into traitors of their class and will protect their freshly acquired privileges from that class. To Marx the first two arguments were obviously wrong and based on ignorance of well-established historical facts. Since the origin of the state must be sought in civil society, and not conversely, Bakunin's demand for the demolition of the state amounts to putting the cart before the horse. Existing political bodies do not produce exploitation but express it; briefly, the alienation of labor precedes political alienation. To dissolve the political framework of the capitalist order while retaining the relations of production unaltered would be to preserve conditions that would be bound to recreate the same framework within a short time. As to the third point, Marx never dealt with it. The issue remained open for his followers. His comment on the Paris Commune, in particular his statement that the working class cannot take over the existing state machinery but must smash it, was certainly welcomed by Bakunin's acolyte Guillaume as a shift towards the anarchist standpoint. But wrongly so, as later writings (especially the *Critique of the Gotha Program*) would reveal.

The Myth of Human Self-Identity

The classical liberal concept corresponded to the idealized model of capitalist society as analyzed in *Capital*. Marx was aware, of course, that the real patterns of capitalist economy do not coincide perfectly with this model, which presupposes that the state is utterly inactive in economic life and allows the laws of free competition to work unbridled. Still, this was the model he was dealing with in his major work. The liberal concept – the state limited to the role of watchman, not interfering in the "free contract" relations between entrepreneurs and wage earners (not to speak of other aspects of industrial activity) – was not, strictly speaking, "wrong" in Marx's eyes, insofar as it matched the genuine tendency of capital. What was wrong was the ideological delusion that this kind of separation met the inalterable requirements of human nature or that, once laid down, it would last indefinitely. According to this concept, the maximum productive efficiency and consequently the optimum general good is secured within a political framework based on minimum interference in economic relations. The state has to care about security; welfare and wealth will look after themselves. Marx's anticipated organization of society was exactly the opposite: political government would become superfluous while economic management, "the administration of things," would exhaust the functions of the public organs. The expression "withering away of the state" comes from Engels but it fits into Marxist predictions. The question arises: what premises do we have to admit in order to believe that a social organization free from any mediating and coercive power and from any political bodies is practicable? What conditions would make conceivable a society which can administer "things" without "governing people"?

Hegel's and Lassalle's cult of the state was attacked by Marx from another point of view. Lassalle did not, of course, share the ideal of the economic neutrality of the state. On the contrary, he believed that workers, through the parliamentary system, could influence the state and compel it to help in organizing independent productive co-operatives which would eventually dominate economic life. For Marx, Lassalle utterly neglected the class character of the existing state and cherished a utopian fancy that the state, which is in fact a self-defensive device of the privileged classes, may be employed as an organ of socialist transformation. By considering the state as a value in itself and overlooking its class function Lassalle reveals his historical ignorance.

Marx did not deny that the state apparatus may play an independent role in the class struggle. This happens, he thought, in exceptional circumstances, which he analyzed in the case of "Bonapartism." Moments of temporary autonomy for the state occur as a result of stalemate in a violent class war. Marx did not try to synthesize his general view of the state as an organ of class domination and his remarks on

49

these exceptional conditions. Nor did he set down any theoretical view about how the socially indispensable functions of the state can coexist with its role as the oppressive instrument of the propertied classes. No wonder that what the Marxist movement took over from its founder was the crude idea that the state is "nothing more" than an organ of class rule, the fist of the owners held over the head of the exploited, and that, since the basic class antagonisms are irreconcilable, the "capitalist state" can never be at the service of workers' welfare.

Marx's criticism of totalitarian utopias takes up much less space in his writings. It does appear in the 1844 Manuscripts as criticism of primitive egalitarian communism, willing to destroy anything that cannot become the private property of all (i.e., everything that distinguishes individuals from each other), and to abolish all the talents and personal qualities which make cultural creativity possible. Far from promising the assimilation of the alienated world, this communism pushes alienation to the extreme when it tries to debase society as a whole to the present condition of workers. To this Marx opposes what he calls "the positive abolition of private property," an expression he did not explain and does not seem to have used subsequently. Its meaning may be guessed from the context, which deals with religious alienation and the anticipated abolition of atheism: the latter loses all meaning once human self-affirmation no longer depends on the negation of God to become positive self-affirmation. This may suggest, by analogy, a meaning for the "positive" abolition of private property: a society which no longer depends on the negation of private property is probably a society in which the very question of private property has disappeared from people's consciousness and no longer troubles them. Nor does this explanation give us any plain clue to the meaning of communism, except that Marxian criticism bears out what we can easily gather from elsewhere: that in Marx's imagination "communist man" was modeled (in contrast to many utopias of the Enlightenment) on images of the universal giants of the Hellenic and Renaissance worlds, rather than on the pattern of barracks and monasteries. This last point cannot be disputed. What remains obscure is the relation of this buoyant perspective and the structure of the imaginary communist world to the gloomy realities of the actual one.

The pattern of Marxian thought on the question may be expressed as follows:

1. The alienation of labor can be accounted for by the division of labor resulting from technical development.

2. The alienation of labor induced class divisions and gave birth to a special apparatus intended chiefly to protect, by coercive measures, the vested interests of the privileged strata.

The Myth of Human Self-Identity

3. In medieval European societies the fabric of this apparatus directly reflected class structure and its function was obvious.

4. In industrial societies the political superstructure and civil society became separated, not in the sense that the former stopped serving the latter, but in the sense that the true nature of political society has been concealed behind legal equality and personal freedom. Consequently, the image of the relations between the two was bound to become blurred in the minds of those involved.

5. At the same time, traditional social ties and loyalties have been utterly shattered in a society where the profit motive rules economic activity unchallenged. As a result, political society – distorted though its image may be in the social perception – is the only form of (apparent) community, the only place where individuals recognize (in the abstract) the social character of their existence.

6. This results in the almost perfect split of every individual into his real but self-centered life in civil society, on the one hand, and his communal but abstract existence as state member on the other. Social functions (especially work) are perceived as private matters and particular interests (in political functions) wear the mask of social service.

7. The state may emerge as an autonomous social force only in the exceptional circumstances of a temporary equilibrium in the class war. Nor is the state likely to take over important economic functions within the capitalist order.

8. The task of communism is to reunite the two aspects of human life which have become sundered, the personal and the collective. Not by destroying the former (as primitive communism would have it) nor by simply removing the latter while leaving civil society to look after itself (as anarchist dreams would have it), but by organizing a society organically incapable of producing separate political organisms.

9. This restoration of human unity will be brought about by the violent smashing of the protective shell of the existing state, expropriating the exploiting classes and handing over the means of production to the producers. Once the latter are in a position to command all the accumulated forces of production, they will naturally abolish the profit motive in their economic activity and subordinate it exclusively to social needs.

10. Given these conditions, class antagonisms will no longer emerge and, consequently, no organs of political rule will be needed. The public organs will be entirely devoted to the "administration of things," the education and the welfare of the people.

11. As a result, the rift between the social and personal functions of individuals, but also between subject and object of the historical process (transparency of social relations, control of associated individuals over

the processes of their lives, etc.), between man and his natural setting, between desires and duties, and between essence and existence, will be healed.

What became of this scheme and, in particular, of its prospects? Among socialists hardly anyone before the October Revolution seriously doubted its validity. Lenin's *State and Revolution,* written a couple of months before October, may seem like a day-dream today, but it must have looked the same on the very first day after the seizure of power. The totalitarian development of post-revolutionary Russian society is often accounted for not only by the exceptional conditions (non-exceptional ones, alas, are not found) at the moment of revolution (an overwhelmingly agrarian society, isolation and the collapse of hopes of revolution in the West, economic devastation, political exhaustion), but also by the peculiar tradition of this country in the relation between civil society and the state. According to some Russian historians of the nineteenth century, the predominance of the state over civil society went so far that, far from being a product of class division, the state itself produced social classes by a series of measures imposed from above; the very size of the underpopulated territory and the need for constant military protection from invasions compelled the state to build up a larger and larger apparatus of administration and war and to harness the entire economic activity of the country to the service of the state. All important economic changes were due to the initiative of the state. As a result, the main features of what we today call a totalitarian system were virtually non-existent in the pre-revolutionary tradition: the overriding principle that all citizens' activities (including economic ones) must have aims which coincide with those of the state; that no spontaneous crystallizations of social life may be permitted unless they conform to the aims of the state; that each citizen is the property of the state. The unusual autonomy of the Russian state in relation to civil society was not denied by Russian Marxists (Plekhanov, Trotsky), even if they did not go as far as those who devolved on the former the entire responsibility for the construction of the latter, including the very formation of social classes. But this is not the question with which we are dealing here. The question is whether, apart from peculiar circumstances and the peculiar tradition of the country where the first attempt was made to found a social organization on Marxist premises, there are grounds for any suppositions about the connection between these premises and the real results of this attempt. To ask this does not amount to posing the frivolous and unanswerable question: "What would Marx say if he saw the work of his followers?" since it is obvious that he could not see it without surviving for many decades longer than he did, and therefore without changing in ways that we cannot possibly guess. Nor is the question about whether the patterns of contemporary communism were, so to speak, fully preordained by, or prefigured in, the Marxist scheme. Obviously, an ideology is always weaker than the social forces which happen to be its vehicle and try to carry its values. Consequently, since none of the real interests involved in social struggles are reducible to the simplicity of an ideological value system, we may be certain in advance that no political organism will be the perfect embodiment of its ideology. We can assert this of Marxism, as of any other ideology, without historical knowledge. For those concerned about the prospects of socialist development the real question is: does inquiry into the Marxist idea of the unity of civil and political society suggest that any attempt to set up such a unity is likely to produce an order with strongly pronounced totalitarian traits?

It should be stressed that I am not, in 1973, the first to broach this topic (otherwise I could be suspected of seeking a pre-established harmony between an idea and its subsequent embodiment in order to resolve intellectual anomalies and arrange the contingency of history into a semblance of order). The same question was repeatedly raised – mostly by anarchists and syndicalists, but also by some Marxists – long before an answer could be found in the empirical realities of the socialist state. The main reason advanced for asking it was that Marx was deluding himself in predicting a socialist organization with centralized economic management but without political power and social oppression. Such a system, according to Bakunin's criticism, was bound to engender a new class of rulers either from working-class renegades or from the intelligentsia. Waclaw Machajski even maintained that Marxist socialism was an ideological tool devised by the intelligentsia in its attempt to replace the then-privileged classes and seize power in order to profit from their socially inherited cultural and intellectual superiority. Sorel insisted that all leaders who expected the socialist revolution to be carried through by political parties were just the new would-be revolutionary despots and that, no matter how democratic the phraseology they used, people like Jaurès or Turati announced only another form of oppression over the working class. Similar utterances can be quoted from French syndicalists and Proudhonists. Sorel expected a new oppressive society to emerge from any program of political (i.e., party-sponsored) revolution, as opposed to a movement of real workers. The latter could win only if they succeeded in abolishing the supremacy of intellectuals and becoming masters of production directly, not through political functionaries or managers.

Socialists did not, of course, accept this line of reasoning. Some of them, however, pointed out the dangers of a new despotism that could emerge if the revolution occurred in "immature" conditions or if the leaders failed to interpret the meaning of Marxist socialism properly.

Jaurès wrote that if socialism resulted in a group of rulers who not only wielded political power but also controlled all economic decisions, this would mean endowing a handful of people with an omnipotence such that the might of Asiatic despots would pale in comparison. Plekhanov, in his polemics against revolutionary populism, noted that if by chance a conspiratorial movement succeeded in seizing power in economically backward conditions, it would only establish a kind of oriental satrapy, or renew czarist despotism on a communist basis. He repeated similar warnings against the Bolsheviks, who were, in his opinion, the heirs of the *narodnik* conspiracy, rather than Marxists.

There were others who emphasized the moral rather than economic preconditions of socialist society, if this society were not to degenerate into a new oppressive class system. I quote Edward Abramowski, a theorist of anarcho-syndicalism, who is less known in the West, being a Pole. He wrote in 1897:

> May we venture an opinion that a socialist system could be founded without a previous stage of moral revolution? That communist institutions could be established without the requirement of first finding the corresponding needs in human souls, without foundations in the consciousness of people? [...] Let us suppose for a moment that a revolutionary Providence, a conspiratorial group professing socialist ideals, happily succeeds in mastering the state machinery and establishes communist institutions with the help of the police disguised in new colors. Let us suppose that the consciousness of the people takes no part in this process and that everything is carried out by the force of sheer bureaucratism. Then what happens? [...] The new institutions have removed the fact of legal ownership, but ownership as a moral need on the part of the people has remained; they have banned official exploitation in production, but have preserved all the external factors from which injustice arises – factors that would always have a large enough field in which to operate, if not in the economic sphere, then in all other fields of human relations. To stifle aspirations to ownership the organization of communism would have to enforce extensive state powers; the police would replace those natural needs from which social institutions grew and by virtue of which they freely develop. Moreover, the defense of new institutions would only be possible for a state founded on principles of absolutism, since any effective democracy in a society beset by violence under the new system would threaten that system

with rapid decay, and would bring back all the old social laws – laws that would have survived in human souls, untouched by revolution. Thus communism would not only be extremely superficial, and impotent, but would turn into a state power oppressing individual freedom; instead of the former classes two new classes would emerge – citizens and state functionaries – and their antagonism would necessarily appear in all domains of social life. Consequently, if communism in such an artificial form, without a moral transformation of the people, could even survive, it would contradict itself; and it would be a social monster such as no oppressed class has ever dreamt of, least of all the proletariat that is fighting for human rights and is called upon by History itself to achieve the liberation of man.[2]

Thus the concept of the rise of a socialist "new class" did not wait for Burnham. It was anticipated long before it could be found in experience (after the October Revolution, Kautsky seems to have been the first to apply this concept to the new society, in 1919). We must, however, make a distinction between critics who warned against the new communist class society that would result if the revolution failed to find appropriate economic or moral conditions, and those who claimed to have found the germ of a totalitarian order in the very concept of socialism as elaborated by Marx. The two kinds of arguments are logically independent.

Let us turn to the latter kind, as we know it from anarchist writers. I think there is considerable justification for this criticism; and one does not need to share anarchist ideals, or even to consider them either feasible or consistent, in order to think so. I will try to repeat in modified form those critiques which are noteworthy, and to adduce some other remarks on the subject, not necessarily taken from the same sources.

1. The crucial point in the Marxist ideal of unity is his distinction – inherited from the "utopian" socialists – between the administration of things and the governing of people. This distinction is vague, since we cannot imagine how things can be administered without people being used, controlled, and organized for this purpose. Management of the economy involves control over people, and it is not *prima facie* clear what is meant by saying that this would be not "political" but purely "economic" control. It is self-evident that economic planning involves the planning of the labor force and labor organization. In effective planning and management three kinds of instruments can be employed: material

2 Edward Abramowski, "Etyka a rewolucja," in *Filozofia spoleczna. Wybor pism* (Warsaw, 1965), pp. 179–80.

incentives, moral motivations, and physical coercion. The first presupposes a free labor market (economic activity depending on private motives, on striving after personal profit, and on competition between working individuals) and is hardly compatible with the Marxian image of the unity of social and personal life. The second presupposes a formidable moral revolution in men's minds; what reason is there to believe that such a revolution is likely or possible? The experience of socialist countries speaks clearly against any hope of using moral incentives as a lasting and efficient basis for production; most of the slogans intended to arouse "enthusiasm for work" were used rather to cover various kinds of pressure and coercion. It seems hardly necessary to stress the incompatibility of the third kind of instrument with the Marxist program. If, however, we read the notorious attacks of Trotsky on Kautsky from 1920, we notice that to him the system of compulsory labor was not a transitory necessity of the civil war period but a permanent feature of socialist society.

> The principle itself of *compulsory labor* service has just as radically and permanently *replaced* the principle of free hiring as the socialization of the means of production has replaced capitalist property. . . . The only solution of economic difficulties that is correct from the point of view *both of principle and practice is to treat the population of the whole country as the reservoir of the necessary labor power.* . . . The foundation of the militarization of labor are those forms of state compulsion without which the replacement of capitalist economy by socialist will forever remain an empty sound. No social organization except the army has ever considered itself justified in subordinating citizens to itself in such a measure, and controlling them by its will on all sides to such a degree, as the state of the proletarian dictatorship considers itself justified in doing, and does. . . . For we have no way to socialism except by the authoritative regulation of the economic forces and resources of the country, and the centralized distribution of labor-power in harmony with the general state plan. The labor state considers itself empowered to send every worker to the place where his work is necessary [*emphasis added*].[3]

Trotsky does, to be sure, mention the "enthusiasm for work" of the working class, but he is aware that the planned economy cannot rely upon this factor. His idea, roughly speaking, is: Let the workers work –

3 Leon Trotsky, *The Defense of Terrorism: A Reply to Karl Kautsky* (London: Labour Publishing Co., 1921), pp. 126, 125, 130, 131.

for almost nothing – and go where we want them to go, from revolutionary enthusiasm. If they will not, they shall be persuaded to do so by the policeman's gun." In other words, Trotsky promised us socialism conceived as a permanent concentration camp. He did not seem worried about the possible incompatibility of this program with Marxist doctrine. Two circumstances may nonetheless be adduced in his favor. First, a free market for the labor force does indeed seem to run counter to the Marxist concept of socialism. Second, he offered a practical solution to a question that Marx left unanswered. Indeed, if we set aside the free market, then only moral motivation and coercion are left as possible stimuli for work; and the second has proved utterly unreliable. In fact, all three factors have been employed, in differing proportions, in the history of socialist states. Material incentives now seem to be on the way to becoming the prevailing factor in economic organization.

2. Following on the question of stimuli for work, the question arises of stimuli for production itself. Marx recognized that civil society is ruled by private interest and that, left to themselves, people will produce and trade anyway; but they cannot master the global results of their joint productive activity, which turns against them in the form of quasi-natural catastrophic laws. If the motive of private profit in production is eliminated, however, the organizational body of production – i.e., the state – becomes the only possible subject of economic activity and the only remaining source of economic initiative. This must lead, not by bureaucratic ambition but by necessity, to a tremendous growth in the tasks of the state and its bureaucracy. And this is indeed what happened. The civil society – as opposed to the state apparatus – is left economically passive and deprived of any reason for economic initiative, and any possibility of it. Without impulses from the state apparatus no economic activity arises in society, except on the fringes, in the form of small private producers who are considered insignificant and may be dismissed as relics of the past. Whatever is not planned by state organs is simply not produced, regardless of social needs. Some changes, slowly and reluctantly initiated in socialist countries to restore the influence of the market on production, prove economically efficient to a certain degree, but in the same degree run counter to the Marxian version of unity.

These two circumstances may justify the suspicion that, far from leading to the promised fusion of civil with political society, the Marxian vision of unified man is likely to entail the cancerous growth of a quasi-omnipotent bureaucracy that will attempt to shatter and paralyze civil society and carry the (rightly denounced) anonymity of public life to its extreme consequences.

3. This tendency becomes still more likely if we consider the third point: the question of the autonomy of political bodies as distinct from

social classes. It is in fact difficult to imagine what reasons could be advanced in favor of the belief that, once social classes (in Marx's sense, i.e., based on the criteria of the ownership of the means of production and the appropriation of surplus value) have been abolished, the conflict of private interests will stop. The class struggle in capitalist society is a historical form of the struggle for the distribution of surplus product. Why should we presume that the same struggle for surplus product would not continue within an economy based on public ownership (whether this is an authoritarian or a democratic system)? And since public ownership must inevitably beget social layers endowed with privileges in controlling the means of production, the labor force, and the instruments of coercion, what reasons could we possibly have for denying that all possible means would be employed to safeguard the position of these layers and increase their privileges? (Unless, of course, we predict a sudden restoration of angelic nature to the human race.)

It is arguable that, in dealing with these questions and in predicting man's return to the lost unity of his social and personal existence, Marx admitted, among others, two very common false premises: that all human evil is rooted in social (as distinct from biological) circumstances, and that all important human conflicts are ultimately reducible to class antagonisms. Thus he entirely overlooked the possibility that some sources of conflict and aggression may be inherent in the permanent characteristics of the species and are unlikely to be eradicated by institutional changes. In this sense he really remained a Rousseauist. He also overlooked the formidable force of human aspirations for power for its own sake and the extreme antagonisms arising from relations of power as such, that is, irrespective of the social origin of given ruling bodies. Of all the famous sentences that have had a dizzying career in history, this is one of the most striking in its falsity: that the history of all hitherto existing societies is the history of class struggles. The belief that political bodies are nothing more than instruments of classes; that their interests may always be identified with the interests of the classes they are supposed to represent; that they do not produce interests of their own of any significance; and that people delude themselves if they imagine they are striving for other values (for freedom or for power, for equality or for national goals) as values in themselves, since these values are only vehicles for class interests – all these beliefs are the consequences of this one sentence. They gave Marxism its stupendous efficiency and its catechismal simplicity. Needless to say, Marx's detailed analyses show that his thought was much subtler and more differentiated than this sentence would suggest. But without espousing this belief he would not have been able to nourish his hope for a unified man.

Let us conclude.

The Myth of Human Self-Identity

1. There is no reason to believe that the restoration of the perfect unity of the personal and communal life of every individual (i.e., the perfect, internalized identity of each person with the social whole, with no tension between his personal aspirations and his various social loyalties) is possible, and least of all that it could be secured by institutional means. Marx believed such identity had been achieved in stagnant primitive communities; but even if this romantic image is well-founded, nothing substantiates the hope that it can be resuscitated in the predictable future: this would presuppose an unprecedented moral revolution running counter to the whole course of history. To believe that the initial basis for such unity may be coercive (i.e., by the violent destruction of civil society and its replacement by the omnipotence of an oppressive state), and that from this an internalized, voluntary unity will subsequently grow, amounts to believing that people who have been compelled to do something by fear will later do the same thing willingly and cheerfully. From everything we know about human behavior the opposite is much more likely.

2. The social equivalent of this unity of person was envisaged as the unity of civil and political society. This in its turn was conceived of as a community in which political power had become unnecessary. But such a community is inconceivable unless one of two conditions is fulfilled. The first: that no conflicts of interest arise between groups or individuals, so that economic management need not be associated with political power, and public instruments of mediation or moderation are unnecessary. Only if all conflicts of human interests were rooted in class divisions (in the Marxist sense of the word) – which is obviously not the case – could this condition ever be satisfied. The second: that all decisions in public matters, however insignificant, are taken directly by the community as a whole in a democratic manner. Such a system, if practicable, would not eliminate conflicts of interest (and thus would not comply with the requirements of perfect unity), but could moderate them without creating separate political bodies for the purpose. This ideal was patterned, in anarchist thought, on the model of medieval Swiss villages, and of course cannot be attributed to Marx. If not for historical, then for technical reasons it is obviously impracticable in any community larger than a medieval Swiss village. Societies based on the (universal, and still spreading) interdependence of all the elements of their technological and economic structures are bound to produce separate bodies for economic management and for mediating the conflicting aspirations of their different segments, and these bodies will in turn always produce their own particular interests and loyalties.

3. The growth of the economic responsibilities of central power is an undeniable tendency in many different political systems. The trend

towards nationalizing larger and larger segments of the production, trade, and exchange systems is inevitably accompanied by the rise of bureaucracy, and the same is true of all the areas which by widespread consent are acknowledged to be the responsibility of central power: the welfare, health, and education systems, the control of wages, prices, investment and banking, the protection of the natural environment, and the exploitation of natural resources and land. It is difficult (although not impossible) to be consistent when fulminating at the same time against the growth of bureaucracy and against the uncontrolled wastefulness involved in the operation of private industry; more often than not, increasing control over private business means increasing bureaucracy. The urgent question is how society can restrain its expanding bureaucracy, not how it could dispense with it. Representative democracy presupposes separate bodies with separate privileges in deciding on public matters; thus it cannot secure the ideal of the perfect unity of civil and political society. One can say, in general, that representative democracy entails a great number of vices and only one virtue. Its vices and dangers are easily found in Marxist literature. Its one virtue is that as yet no one has come up with anything better.

* * *

I believe that socialist thought in its traditional areas of concern (how to ensure for working society more equality, more security, more welfare, more justice, more freedom, more participation in economic decisions) cannot at the same time entertain prospects of the perfect unity of social life. The two kinds of preoccupation run against each other. The dream of perfect unity could be realized only as a caricature that would deny its original intention: as an artificial unity imposed by force from above, with the political body preventing real conflicts and real segmentation of the civil society from expressing themselves. This body is almost automatically compelled to crush all spontaneous forms of economic, political, and cultural life. Thus the rift between civil and political society, instead of being healed, is deepened.

To the question of whether this outcome was somehow inscribed in original Marxian thought, the answer is certainly "no" if "inscribed" means "intended." All the evidence indicates that the initial intention was the opposite of what grew out of it. But this initial intention is not, as it were, innocent. It could scarcely be realized in any very different form, not because of contingent historical circumstances but because of its very content.

The dream of a perfectly unified human community is probably as old as human thought about society; romantic nostalgia was only a later

The Myth of Human Self-Identity

incarnation. It is a dream that was philosophically reinforced by that element in European culture which arose from Neoplatonism. There is no reason to expect that this dream will ever disappear, for it has strong roots in our awareness of the split which humanity suffered at the very beginning of its existence, when it emerged from its animal innocence. Nor is there any reason to expect that it can ever come true, except in the cruel form of despotism; and despotism is a desperate simulation of paradise.

What Is Socialism?[1]

We intend to tell you what socialism is. But first we must tell you what it is not – and our views on this matter were once very different from what they are at present.

Here, then, is what socialism is not:
- a society in which someone who has committed no crime sits at home waiting for the police;
- a society in which it is a crime to be the brother, sister, son, or wife of a criminal;
- a society in which some people are unhappy because they say what they think and others are unhappy because they do not;
- a society in which some people are better off because they do not think at all;
- a society in which some people are unhappy because they are Jews and others are happier because they are not;
- a state whose soldiers are the first to set foot in the territory of another country;
- a state where people are better off because they praise their leaders;
- a state where one can be condemned without trial;
- a society whose leaders appoint themselves;
- a society in which ten people live in one room;
- a society that has illiterates and plague epidemics;

1 Written in Polish ("Co To Jest Socjalizm?") in 1956 for the student journal *Po Prostu*. The entire article was censored. Thereafter the journal was proscribed. The text was affixed by students to the notice board of Warsaw University, but was soon removed by the authorities. It has since circulated widely in manuscript form. The English translation appeared in *The New Leader*, vol. 40 (February 18, 1957), pp. 9–10; reprinted in E. Stillman, ed., *Bitter Harvest: The Intellectual Revolt behind the Iron Curtain* (New York: Praeger, 1959), and in Paul Oestreicher, ed., *The Christian-Marxist Dialogue* (New York: Macmillan, 1969).

What Is Socialism?

- a state that does not permit travel abroad;
- a state that has more spies than nurses and more room in prisons than in hospitals;
- a state where the number of bureaucrats increases more quickly than that of workers;
- a state where people are compelled to lie;
- a state where people are compelled to steal;
- a state where people are compelled to commit crimes;
- a state that possesses colonies;
- a state whose neighbors curse geography;
- a state that produces superb jet planes and lousy shoes;
- a state where cowards are better off than the courageous;
- a state where defense lawyers are usually in agreement with the prosecution;
- a tyranny, an oligarchy, a bureaucracy;
- a society where vast numbers of people turn to God to comfort them in their misery;
- a state that gives literary prizes to talentless hacks and knows better than painters what kind of painting is the best;
- a nation that oppresses other nations;
- a nation that is oppressed by another nation;
- a state that wants all its citizens to have the same views on philosophy, foreign policy, the economy, literature, and morality;
- a state whose government determines the rights of its citizens but whose citizens do not determine the rights of their government;
- a state in which one is responsible for one's ancestors;
- a state in which some people earn forty times as much as others;
- a system of government that is opposed by the majority of the governed;
- one isolated country;
- a group of underdeveloped countries;
- a state that employs nationalist slogans;
- a state whose government believes that nothing matters more than its being in power;
- a state that makes pacts with criminals and adapts its worldview to these pacts;
- a state that wants its foreign ministry to shape the worldview of all mankind at any given moment;
- a state that is not very good at distinguishing between slavery and liberation;
- a state that gives free rein to proponents of racism;
- a state that currently exists;
- a state with private ownership of the means of production;

- a state that considers itself socialist solely because it has abolished private ownership of the means of production;
- a state that is not very good at distinguishing between social revolution and armed invasion;
- a state that does not believe that people under socialism should be happier than people elsewhere;
- a society that is very sad;
- a caste system;
- a state whose government always knows the will of the people before it asks them;
- a state where people can be pushed around, humiliated, and ill-treated with impunity;
- a state where a certain view of world history is obligatory;
- a state whose philosophers and writers always say the same things as the generals and ministers, but always after the latter have said them;
- a state where city maps are state secrets;
- a state where the results of parliamentary elections can always be unerringly predicted;
- a state where slave labor exists;
- a state where feudal bonds exist;
- a state that has a monopoly on telling its citizens all they need to know about the world;
- a state that thinks freedom amounts to obedience to the state;
- a state that sees no difference between what is true and what it is in its interest for people to believe;
- a state where a nation can be transplanted in its entirety from one place to another, willy-nilly;
- a state in which the workers have no influence on the government;
- a state that believes it alone can save mankind;
- a state that thinks it has always been right;
- a state where history is in the service of politics;
- a state whose citizens are not permitted to read the greatest works of contemporary literature, or to see the greatest contemporary works of art, or to hear the best contemporary music;
- a state that is always exceedingly pleased with itself;
- a state that claims the world is very complicated, but in fact believes that it is very simple;
- a state where you have to go through an awful lot of suffering before you can see a doctor;
- a state that has beggars;
- a state that is convinced that no one could ever invent anything better;

- a state that believes that everyone simply adores it, although the opposite is true;
- a state that governs according to the principle *oderint dum metuant*;
- a state that decides who may criticize it and how;
- a state where one is required each day to say the opposite of what one said the day before and to believe that one is always saying the same thing;
- a state that does not like it at all when its citizens read old newspapers;
- a state where many ignorant people are considered scholars;
- a state where the content of all the newspapers is the same;
- a state whose government wants to control all forms of social organization;
- a state where there are many decent and courageous people, but a study of the politics of its government will not allow you to discover this;
- a state that does not like it at all when its regime is analyzed by scholars, but is very happy when this is done by sycophants;
- a state that always knows better than its citizens where the happiness of every one of its citizens lies;
- a state that, while not sacrificing anything for any higher principles, nevertheless believes that it is the leading light of progress.

That was the first part. And now, pay attention, because we are going to tell you what socialism is. Here is what socialism is:

Socialism is a system that . . . But what's the point of going into all these details? It's very simple: socialism is just a really wonderful thing.

Totalitarianism and the Virtue of the Lie[1]

The validity of "totalitarianism" as a concept is occasionally questioned on the grounds that a perfect model of a totalitarian society is nowhere to be found and that in no country among those which used to be cited as its best examples (the Soviet Union, especially under Stalin, Mao's China, Hitler's Germany) has the ideal of the absolute unity of leadership and of unlimited power ever been achieved.

This is not a serious obstacle. It is generally acknowledged that most of the concepts we employ in describing large-scale social phenomena have no perfect empirical equivalents. There has never been an absolutely pure capitalist society, which does not prevent us from making a distinction between a capitalist and pre-capitalist economies, and the distinction is very useful. The fact that there is no such thing as total freedom does not make the distinction between free and despotic regimes any less cogent or intelligible. Indeed, the best examples of totalitarian societies were arguably closer to their conceptual ideal than any capitalist society was to its abstractly perfect description. (Among arguments purporting to do away with the concept of "totalitarianism," the most absurd says that the Soviet Union, for instance, is in fact a "pluralist" system because there are always cliques or particular groups vying for power and influence in the establishment. If this is a symptom of pluralism, then the concept is useless and indeed quite meaningless, since all political regimes throughout history have been "pluralist" in this sense.)

There is no single cause we could hold responsible for the emergence of a system that wants the state to have total power over all areas of human life, to destroy civil society entirely, and to extend state owner-

[1] Reprinted from 1984 *Revisited*, ed. by Irving Howe (New York: Harper and Row, 1983).

ship over all things and all people. To be sure, power has always been sought by people as a value in itself, and not only as a means to gain wealth or other goods. This does not mean, however, that the phenomenon of totalitarianism may be explained by the thirst for domination inherent in human nature. Ambitions of power and struggles for it are quasi-universal, whereas the inner drive toward totalitarianism is not. Most of the despotic regimes we know in history were not totalitarian; they had no built-in tendency to regulate all realms of human activity, to expropriate people totally (physically and mentally) or to convert them into state property. Whether or not the term is properly used to describe some historical epochs in ancient China, or czarist Russia, or in certain theocratic societies and religious groups, or some primitive communities, modern totalitarianism is inseparably linked with the history of socialist ideas and movements. This does not mean that all the varieties of socialism are totalitarian by definition. European versions of totalitarianism – Russian Bolshevism, German Nazism, Italian Fascism – were bastard offshoots of the socialist tradition; yet in bastard children, too, a similarity to the parents is preserved, and can be clearly perceived.

The socialist idea emerged in the early nineteenth century as the moral response of a few intellectuals to social misfortunes brought about by industrialization – the misery and hopelessness of working-class lives, marked by crises, unemployment, glaring inequalities, the dissolving of traditional communities. In many respects the socialist critique of these characteristics of post-revolutionary societies clearly converged with the attacks coming from reactionary romanticism and from emerging nationalist ideologies. Socialism was essentially about "social justice," even though there has never been any agreement about the meaning of this vague term. All versions of socialism implied a belief in social control of production and distribution of material goods (not necessarily in the abolition of private property or in a controlled economy run by the state). All predicted that social control would secure the welfare of all, prevent waste, increase efficiency, and eradicate "unearned income" (another concept for which there has never been a satisfactory definition). Most of them were not explicitly or intentionally totalitarian, and some strongly stressed the value of cultural freedom.

Yet in those versions of socialism that relied upon the power of the state to achieve a just and efficient economy, intimations of a totalitarian philosophy can be found at least with hindsight. Marxism was repeatedly attacked in the nineteenth century, especially by anarchist writers, as a program for unabashed state tyranny. Historical developments perfectly bore out this assessment. Paradoxically, however, the despotic nature of Marxian socialism was to some extent limited by that component of the doctrine which was prominent in its late nineteenth-century version, and eventually entirely discredited (rightly so) as superstitious wishful thinking: the notion of historical determinism, some of whose elements Marx had taken up from Hegel and the Saint-Simonians. For the Marxists of the Second International, the determinist faith acted, on the one hand, as a source of their ideological confidence and, on the other, as a warning that the laws of history cannot be violated. This was a natural basis for an evolutionary concept of socialism, and it played this role in "centrist" Social Democratic orthodoxy. The crisis of the socialist idea that revealed itself at the very beginning of the twentieth century was expressed in, among other signs, the (not quite unjustified) contention that if Socialists relied upon "historical laws" and expected the "economic maturity" of capitalism to nurture the revolution, they could just as well bid farewell to all socialist hopes. There were those for whom revolutionary will and the political opportunity to seize power were all that counted, and they produced two totalitarian versions of socialism: fascism and Bolshevism (Domenic Settembrini emphasizes the essential similarity of Lenin's and Mussolini's ideological approaches very convincingly).

In both forms of totalitarian socialism – nationalist and internationalist – social control of production for the common good was stressed as essential. The model developed in the Soviet Union, China, and other communist countries proved to be more consistent and more resilient than the fascist or Nazi varieties. It carried out the total nationalization of the means of production, distribution, and information, pretending thereby to have created the foundation of the Great Impossible – all-encompassing universal planning. It is clear, indeed, that a fully consistent totalitarian system implies complete state control of economic activity; therefore it is conceivable only within a socialist regime. Fascism and Nazism did not attempt wholesale nationalization (their tenure was relatively short; the Soviet Union waited twelve years before incorporating agricultural production and the peasants themselves into state property). To this extent they were less totalitarian, insofar as they left segments of society economically less dependent on state power. However, this does not at all imply that they were any "better" in human terms; indeed, in various ways Nazism was more barbarous than Bolshevism.

In both cases the overriding ideology stressed the idea of social justice and proclaimed that some chosen parts of mankind (a superior race or nation, a progressive class or vanguard party) had the natural right to establish uncontrolled rule by virtue of historical destiny. And in both, the seizure of power was carried out under slogans that appealed to and incited envy as the driving revolutionary force. As in many (but not all) revolutionary movements, what was justice in doctrinal terms was, psychologically and in practice, the pragmatism of envy. The immediate aim was to destroy the existing elites – whether aristocratic or meritocratic, plutocratic or intellectual – and to replace them with a parvenu political class. Needless to say, egalitarian ideological ingredients, insofar as they played any role at all, could not long survive the seizure of power.

It is self-evident that no modern society can dispense with a principle of legitimacy, and that in a totalitarian society this legitimacy can only be ideological. Total power and total ideology embrace each other. The ideology is total in a much stronger sense, at least in its claims, than any that religious faith has ever achieved. Not only does it have all-embracing pretensions, not only is it supposed to be infallible and obligatory; its aim (unattainable, fortunately) goes beyond dominating and regulating the personal life of every subject to the point where it actually replaces personal life altogether, reducing human beings to replicas of ideological slogans. In other words, it annihilates personal life. This is much more than any religion has ever prescribed.

Such an ideology explains the specific function and specific meaning of the *lie* in a perfect totalitarian society, a function so peculiar and creative that even the word itself, "lie," sounds inadequate. The crucial importance of the lie in the communist totalitarian system was noticed long ago by Anton Ciliga, in his *Au pays du grand mensonge,* published in 1930; it took the genius of Orwell to reveal, as it were, the philosophical side of the issue.

What does the staff of the Ministry of Truth, where Orwell's hero works in *1984,* do? They thoroughly destroy the records of the past; they print new, up-to-date editions of old newspapers and books; and they know that the corrected version will soon be replaced by another, re-corrected one. Their goal is to make people forget everything – facts, words, dead people, the names of places. How far they succeed in obliterating the past is not fully established in Orwell's description; clearly they try hard, and they achieve impressive results. The ideal of complete oblivion may not have been reached, but further progress is to be expected.

Let us consider what happens when the ideal has been effectively achieved. People remember only what they are taught to remember today and the content of their memory changes overnight, if needed. They really believe that something that happened the day before yesterday, and which they stored in their memories yesterday, did not happen at all and that something else happened instead. In effect, they are no longer human beings. Consciousness is memory, as Bergson would have put it. Creatures whose memory is effectively manipulated, programmed, and controlled from outside are no longer persons in any recognizable sense and therefore no longer human.

This is what totalitarian regimes unceasingly try to achieve. People whose memory – personal or collective – has been nationalized, become state-owned and perfectly malleable, totally controllable, are entirely at the mercy of their rulers; they have been deprived of their identity; they are helpless and incapable of questioning anything they are told to believe. They will never revolt, never think, never create. They have been transformed into dead objects. They may even, conceivably, be happy and love Big Brother, which is Winston Smith's supreme performance.

This use of the lie is interesting not only politically but epistemologically as well. The point is that if physical records of certain events and their recollection in human minds are utterly eradicated, and if consequently there is absolutely no way anybody can establish what is "true" in the normal sense of the word, nothing remains but the generally imposed beliefs, which, of course, can be canceled again the next day. There is no applicable criterion of truth except for what is proclaimed true at any given moment. And so the lie really becomes truth, or at least the distinction between true and false in their usual meaning has disappeared. This is the great cognitive triumph of totalitarianism: it can no longer be accused of lying, because it has succeeded in abrogating the very idea of truth.

We can thus see the difference between the common political lie and its totalitarian apotheosis. The lie has always been employed for political purposes. But the trivial lies and distortions used by politicians, governments, parties, kings, or leaders are far removed from the lie that is the very core of a political system, the heart of a new civilization. The former are generally used for specific purposes, as an instrument to achieve specific goals. The normal political lie leaves the distinction between truth and falsity intact. The history of the Church provides a number of falsifications, distortions, and legends fabricated for well-defined ends. Constantine's contribution was a forgery that legitimated the Church's claims to political supremacy. It was exposed by a great ecclesiastical scholar and eventually recognized for what it was; so were many other legends that Catholic and Protestant historians have examined and dismissed. The commemoration of the Three Kings was a contrivance to bolster the doctrine whereby the Church claimed supremacy over the secular powers. But the Church has not rewritten the Gospel of St. Matthew in order to justify the legend; anyone can consult the text and see that it contains no hint that the three wise men who visited the infant Jesus were actually monarchs. The story remains alive as an innocent bit of folklore. Nobody knows who inserted the *Comma Johanneum* into the text of the Gospel; this was an unpleasant problem, to be sure, but eventually Catholic editors of the New Testament came to recognize the insertion.

During the last few centuries Catholic and Protestant cultures have produced a large number of outstanding historians who, far from employing various sorts of *pia fraus* to embellish the annals of the

Church, have done pioneering work in subjecting Church documents to critical examination. They have produced many works of lasting value (and where are the communist historians who are worthy of such respect?). The Church purified itself of forgeries and gained by it. But its forgeries were aimed at specific targets – unlike the modern totalitarian lie, the ultimate goal of which is the total mental and moral expropriation of people.

The destructive work of totalitarian machinery, whether or not this word is used,[2] is usually supported by a special kind of primitive social philosophy. It proclaims not only that the common good of "society" has priority over the interests of individuals, but that the very existence of individuals as persons is reducible to the existence of the social "whole"; in other words, personal existence is, in a strange sense, unreal. This is a convenient foundation for any ideology of slavery.

So far I have been discussing an ideal totalitarian society, of which existing ones are (or were) only more or less successful approximations. Later Stalinism (and Maoism) was a reasonably fair approximation. Its triumph consisted not simply in that virtually everything was either falsified or suppressed – statistics, historical events, current events, names, maps, books (occasionally Lenin's texts) – but that the inhabitants of the country were trained to know what was politically "correct." In the functionaries' minds, the borderline between what is "correct" and what is "true," as we normally understand this, seems really to have become blurred; by repeating the same absurdities time and again, they themselves began to believe or half-believe them. The vast and profound corruption of the language eventually produced people who were incapable of perceiving their own mendacity.

To a large extent this form of perception seems to survive, despite the fact that the omnipresence of ideology has been somewhat restricted recently. When the Soviet leaders maintain that they "liberated Afghanistan," or that there are no political prisoners in the Soviet Union, it is quite possible that they mean what they say: they have confounded their linguistic abilities to such an extent that they are incapable of using any other word than "liberation" for a Soviet invasion and have no sense at all of the grotesque distance between language and reality. It takes a lot of courage, after all, to be entirely cynical; those who lie to themselves appear among us much more frequently than perfect cynics.

A very small and innocent anecdote. In 1950, in Leningrad, I visited the Hermitage in the company of a few Polish friends. We had a guide (a deputy director of the museum, as far as I remember) who was obvious-

2 The adjective "totalitarian" was used in a positive sense by Mussolini and Gramsci but never by Soviet ideologists or, to my knowledge, by the Nazis.

ly a knowledgeable art historian. At a certain moment – no opportunity for ideological teaching must be lost – he told us: "We have in our cellars, comrades, a lot of corrupt, degenerate bourgeois paintings. You know, all those Matisses, Cézannes, Braques, and so on. We have never displayed them in the museum but perhaps one day we will show them so that Soviet people can see for themselves how deeply bourgeois art has sunk. Indeed, Comrade Stalin teaches us that we should not embellish history." I was in the Hermitage again, with other friends, in 1957, a time of relative "thaw," and the same man was assigned to guide us. We were led to rooms full of modern French paintings. Our guide told us: "Here you see the masterpieces of great French painters – Matisse, Cézanne, Braque, and others. And," he added (for no opportunity must be lost), "do you know that the bourgeois press accused us of refusing to display these paintings in the Hermitage? This was because at a certain moment some rooms in the museum were being redecorated and were temporarily closed, and a bourgeois journalist happened to be here at that moment and then made this ridiculous accusation. Ha, ha!"

Was he lying? I am not sure. If I had reminded him of his earlier statement, which I failed to do, he would simply have denied everything with genuine indignation; he probably would have believed that what he told us was "right" and therefore true. Truth, in this world, is what reinforces the "right cause." The psychological mechanism that operates in minds appropriately trained and put through a totalitarian mincer is a matter for professor Festinger to analyze according to his principle of cognitive dissonance.

Lying as a matter of political expediency is itself not a particularly interesting phenomenon and scarcely worth investigation, so long as the lie is just a lie pure and simple, devised for a specific purpose: a minister says that he did not sleep with a girl, but in fact he did; a president claims he was not aware of what his subordinates had been doing, but in fact he was. Nothing mysterious and nothing exciting in such facts; they are ordinary by-products of politics. In totalitarian systems lying is interesting not because of its extent and frequency but because of its social, psychological, and cognitive functions. For example, it would be very superficial to imagine that the lie as it appears in the Soviet press is just an amplification and intensification of the normal political lie. Certainly, if one wishes to collect political lies, any issue of *Pravda* ("Truth") or *Literaturnaya Gazeta* will do. Each issue is full of outright lies, suppressions, and omissions; and in each case the purpose they serve is obvious. They become remarkable only when seen within the grand machinery of the education designed to build the New Civilization.

The cognitive aspect of this machinery consists in effacing the very distinction between truth and political "correctness." Its psychological function is important in that, by training people in this confusion and injecting them with the belief that nothing is true in itself and that anything can be made true by the decree of authority, it produces a new "socialist man," devoid of will and of moral resistance, stripped of social or historical identity. The art of forgetting history is crucial: people must learn that the past can be changed – from truth to truth – overnight. In this manner they are cut off from what would have been a source of strength: the possibility of identifying and asserting themselves by recalling their collective past. It is not that there is no teaching of history (though apparently there was hardly any in Mao's China; no books were available except for Mao's works and technical manuals); rather, people know that what they are taught today is both "objectively" true and true for today only, and that their rulers are masters of the past. If they get accustomed to this, they become people without historical consciousness, thus without the ability to define themselves except in relation to the state; they are non-persons, *perduta gente*.

This mental and moral sterilization of society is, however, blistered with dangers. It works so long as the totalitarian regime, in dealing with its subjects, requires only ordinary passive obedience. If, in a moment of crisis, it requires personal motivation as well, the machinery fails. Stalinism was brought to such a crisis during the war with Germany, when the only way to mobilize the mass of Russians for defense was virtually to forget Marxism-Leninism and to use specifically Russian historical symbols and national feelings as an ideological weapon. An ideal totalitarian society consisting of malleable objects is strong in relatively stable conditions but very vulnerable in unstable ones. This is one of the reasons that a perfect totalitarian regime (or "the higher stage of socialism") can never be built.

No matter how much has been done to realize the great ambition of totalitarianism – the total possession and control of human memory – the goal is unattainable. This is not only because human memory is highly intractable. Nor is it because the human being is an ontological reality: to be sure, human beings can be immobilized by coercion, but they will always strive to regain their rights at the first opportunity. Even in the best of conditions the massive process of forgery cannot be completed: it requires a large number of forgers who must understand the distinction between what is genuine and what is faked (the crudest example would be an officer in a military office of cartography, who must have unfalsified maps at his disposal in order to falsify the maps). The power of words over reality cannot be unlimited since, fortunately, reality imposes its own unalterable conditions. The rulers of totalitarian countries wish, of course, to be truthfully informed, but time and again they fall prey, inevitably, to their own lies and suffer unexpected defeats.

Entangled in a trap of their own making, they attempt awkward compromises between their own need for truthful information and the quasi-automatic operations of a system that produces lies for everyone, including the producers.

In short, since totalitarianism implies the complete control by the state of all areas of life and the unlimited power of an artificial state ideology over minds, it can achieve its goals only if it succeeds in eliminating the resistance of both natural and mental reality, in other words, in canceling reality altogether. Therefore, when we talk about totalitarian regimes, we do not have in mind systems that have reached perfection, but rather those that are driven by a never-ending effort to reach it, to swallow up all channels of human communication, and to eradicate all spontaneously emerging forms of social life. In this sense all Soviet-type regimes have been totalitarian, but they have differed from each other in their degree of achievement – in the distance that separates their real conditions from the inaccessible ideal.

It is fair to say, first, that in Central and East European communist countries, this distance has always been greater than in the Soviet metropolis: totalitarianism there has never achieved the Soviet degree of efficiency. And, second, in the Soviet Union itself we have observed a growth of this distance – a backward movement from totalitarian perfection. We cannot pretend, however, to know the exact meaning of this process or to foretell its future course.

This slow but real regressive movement of Soviet totalitarianism has nothing to do either with a lack of totalitarian will within the system and its ruling class or with any "democratization" of the regime. It consists in some reluctantly given, or rather extorted, concessions to irresistible reality. (Back in the early fifties, Soviet ideologists even managed to hamper the development of military technology by their obscurantist attacks upon "cybernetics.") For obvious reasons, totalitarian states – fortunately for the fate of mankind, but unfortunately for the generations who live in their darkness – are inescapably and irreparably inefficient in economic management. Hence all economic reforms in communist countries, to the extent that they yield any results, go in the same direction: partial liberation of market mechanisms – in other words, partial restoration of "capitalism." The omnipotence of ideology proved disastrous in many areas subjected to its rule, so its power had to be restricted. The crisis of legitimacy is patent, as is the desperate quest for reshaped ideological foundations. As a result, the state ideology becomes more and more incoherent and meaningless.

This does not mean that we can expect a gradual corrosion, which step by step will lead to a miraculous mutation and transform the totalitarian society into an "open" one. At least, no historical analogies are helpful in making this sort of prediction. As long as the built-in totalitarian drive, supported by the powerful vested interests of privileged classes, operates in the Sovietized territories, there is little hope for the kind of progress that one day would imperceptibly cross the line separating despotism from democracy. The examples of Spain and Portugal are not very useful here, both because of the different international environment in which their transition took place and because they had never been very close to totalitarian perfection. Indeed, if the day came (let us give free rein to our fantasies and try to imagine it) when the Soviet political system were roughly similar to that of Spain in the last ten years of Franco's rule, this would be hailed by enlightened liberal opinion in the West as the greatest triumph of democracy since Pericles, and no doubt as ultimate proof of the infinite superiority of "socialist democracy" over the bourgeois order.

Still, a relatively nonviolent collapse of totalitarianism is imaginable. The frail hope for such a development has so far been nourished most strongly by the example of Poland in 1980–81. Among the Soviet dependencies, Poland has notoriously been less consistent than others in its totalitarian progress, all the monstrosities of Stalinism notwithstanding. My strong impression is that in the early postwar years, committed communists (still in existence then, though no longer in the sixties and later) in Poland were intellectually less corrupt but more cynical than was the case in other countries. By "cynical" I do not mean that they did not believe in the communist idea, but that they had little "false consciousness": they knew that what the Party wanted to convey to the "masses" was a pure lie, but they accepted and sanctioned it for the sake of the future blessings of the socialist community.

Nevertheless, despite all the efforts of the rulers, despite the overwhelming burden of organized mendacity, Poland's cultural continuity has not been broken. Throughout the post-war decades any relaxation of political conditions, whatever historical accidents might have brought it about, immediately pushed the suppressed historical identity of the Poles to the surface and revealed the glaring and incurable incompatibility between communism and Poland's deeply rooted traditional, national, religious, and political patterns. History books, whether printed in Poland or smuggled in from abroad, have always (if they were not tainted with official mendacity) enjoyed enormous popularity, not only among Poland's intelligentsia but – especially in recent years – among workers and young people.

The Polish "Solidarity" movement, in its brief months of existence, seems to have opened a new, unexplored avenue: a way in which an inefficient and clumsy totalitarian system might conceivably be propelled toward a hybrid form that would include genuine elements of pluralism. The military dictatorship has temporarily crushed the organized form of this movement, but it has failed to destroy the hope. Indeed, the fact that the communist tyranny no longer even tries to assert its legitimacy, and that it has been compelled to appear without ideological disguise, revealing its true nature in acts of naked violence, is in itself a spectacular symptom of the decay of a totalitarian power system.

Communism as a Cultural Force[1]

There is a Polish joke about a little girl who is told at school to write an essay entitled, "Why I love the Soviet Union." Uncertain of the answer, she asks her mother: "Mummy, why do I love the Soviet Union?" "What are you talking about," cries her mother, "the Soviets are criminals, nobody loves them, everybody hates them!" She asks her father. "What sort of rubbish are you talking now," he says, growing angry, "they are the oppressors whose troops are occupying our country, the whole world loathes them!" Distressed, the girl asks several other adults the same question, but receives the same reply from all of them. In the end she writes: "I love the Soviet Union because nobody else does."

I would like to proceed in more or less the same manner as the girl. I would like, namely, to consider a question that is seldom seriously considered (except in communist propaganda, but even there its authors don't take it seriously): communism as a source of cultural inspiration in this century. Anthropologists generally use the word "culture" in a neutral, non-value-laden sense, to denote the various systems of communication particular to a given society: law, tradition, educational institutions, the mechanisms of power, religious belief, art, family relationships, sexual norms, etc.; and all these are things that can of course be described without any value judgments and without presupposing that some cultures are higher or lower than others. In this sense of the word, Mayakovsky's poems are as much a part of communist culture as the lifeless jargon of a hack from any provincial propaganda department; so

1 Originally a lecture delivered at the Congress of Polish Culture Abroad, London, September 1985, this essay, translated from the Polish by Philip Cavendish, appeared in *Survey* 29, no. 2 (Summer 1985), under the title *Communism as a Cultural Formation*. The English text has been substantially revised for this edition by Agnieszka Kolakowska.

77

are the pictures produced by Maoist artists (which still have a long way to go before they attain the standards of American comic strips), just as much as the classics of Chinese painting. But I have in mind "culture" in a much more limited sense, and one that does presuppose certain value judgments. I have in mind, namely: (1) works that are original works of literature, art, or scholarship in the humanities, not attempts to copy already existing models; and (2) works of which it is safe to say that they have been absorbed into, and become integral elements of, that culture which is co-extensive with what we traditionally call the "Christian world," and which grew out of Greek, Roman, Jewish, and Christian roots (Russia, even if in its politics it is perhaps closer to its Tatar traditions, does to a great extent belong to this sphere).

My question, then, is the following: how do we explain the fact that international communism, both where it was a ruling ideology and where it only aspired to power, has proved, at certain historical periods, culturally so fertile – able both to inspire works of genuine worth, still considered part of European civilization, and to attract such a significant following among the cultural elite, including some truly outstanding individuals? The question is worth considering because the destructive and anti-cultural function of communism is very well known to us all; indeed, and more importantly, there is good reason to believe – and this is what makes the question particularly interesting – that it was built into the system from the start. This aspect of communist rule has been widely described, so there is no need to go into it here. It is worth noting, however, that communism, in contrast to other tyrannies, past and present, performed its culture-destroying function not only, and not even mainly, by negative means, such as censorship, repression, and prohibitions. Traditional tyrannies are less destructive insofar as their aim is limited to suppressing political opposition and eradicating from cultural life such elements as could pose a threat to their authority. As a rule such tyrannies limit their goals: they want to remain undivided and indestructible, but not necessarily to extend their control over all spheres of life. They can thus tolerate cultural expression if it is politically indifferent.

Communism, on the other hand, from the beginning conceived of itself as an all-embracing system of power; it seeks not only to eliminate threats to its existence but also to regulate all spheres of collective life, including ideology, literature, art, science, the family, even styles of dress. Such an ideal state of total control is of course extremely difficult to achieve; nevertheless, we can recall a time when the drive to achieve it was very strong, and ideological norms were established for everything: from the only correct view of the theory of relativity through the only correct kinds of music to the width of trousers that uniquely satisfied the requirements of socialist life. The most impressive results in this drive toward omni-regulation were achieved by the People's Republic of China; the Soviet Union during the last years of the Stalin era also did very well, though its results were not quite so outstanding. A partial retreat from this ideal was imposed by the pressures of reality; the abandonment of ideological criteria in the natural sciences was one such example. Other laws proved too troublesome to enforce, for instance those that concerned modes of dress. In most of the Soviet Union's European protectorates, and particularly in Poland, regulation never achieved such levels; not, however, because the principle itself was abandoned, but rather because the extent to which it can be implemented depends on the strength of the apparatus of power when confronted with the natural tendencies of social life. In this regard Poland was for many years, and indeed still is today, closer to the model of a traditional tyranny than to that of a totalitarian regime, for its ruling apparatus concentrates mainly on negative means of control, such as censorship and repressive measures against the opposition and people it considers politically suspect; it does not attempt, or does so very feebly and ineffectually, to impose ideological norms on cultural life. This is not, needless to say, because of any benevolent intentions on its part, merely because of its weakness.

This, however, is not what I want to discuss here; on the contrary, the object of my interest is communism as a culturally active force. That it was such a force seems unquestionable. Talented writers like Mayakovsky, Yesenin, Babel, Pilnyak, Fadeyev, and Ehrenburg; outstanding film directors such as Eisenstein and Pudovkin; avant-garde painters such as Malevich, Dejneka, Rodchenko, and for a short while even Chagall – all these, and a significant part of the intelligentsia, identified themselves ideologically with the Bolshevik revolution of 1917. The later fates of this quite considerable body of artists and writers were varied, as we know: some killed themselves, others were killed by executioners; a few prostituted their talents to the new tyrant or ended their days idle and embittered. In the 1920s communism also attracted a number of Western intellectuals, including members of the literary and artistic avant-garde: Aragon, Eluard, and Picasso were Communist Party members all their lives, as were many other people of unquestionable distinction in France, Italy, and Germany. Even in countries where communism never established itself as a political force of any significance, such as the U.S. or Great Britain, the number of intellectuals, writers, and artists who at some stage, for varying lengths of time, had been, if not CP members, then Trotskyite or Stalinist sympathizers, is impressive. The same can be said of the intelligentsia in Mexico and Brazil. In inter-war Poland, where the political influence of communism was marginal (although more noticeable in the trade-union movement) and naturally checked by its associations with a country that was an age-old enemy, it still managed to attract a certain number of genuine artists: Broniewski, Jasienski, Wandurski, Wat, Zegadlowicz, and Kruczkowski, or intellectuals like Stefan Czarnowski (in the later years of his life), Nowakowski, and Natalia Gasiorowska. In the first decade after the Second World War the communist government enjoyed the support of a considerable number of writers and artists, many of them outstanding. The same was true in Czechoslovakia and Hungary.

There is no need to multiply examples and names; the list is long. It is indisputable that in certain historical conditions communism not only exerted a powerful attraction for a great number of artists, but also inspired many works of art which had a major impact on the artistic and intellectual life of this century. Thus it was not only a distinct form of civilization, one that devastated and continues in its attempts to devastate Europe's historical continuity, destroying spiritual expression wherever its influence reaches, but also a source of energy which inspired that expression.

The least plausible and most naive way of explaining this is by generalizations of the type, "People are easily deceived, easily corrupted and intimidated, and this is the secret of communism's success." Dismissing the history of communism with such formulas is as easy as it is futile, even counter-productive, because it makes important historical phenomena impossible to understand. Furthermore, such formulas have the advantage that they can be applied to anything we don't like or are outraged by; their all-explanatory power betrays their uselessness. The history of communist culture is not so easily accounted for; it consisted of social processes which should be analyzed as such, not as the suspect motivations of individuals. If the question could be disposed of so simply, it would be impossible to explain why communist governments today, with all the instruments of deception, corruption, and intimidation still at their disposal, have entirely lost not only the ability to stimulate artistic and intellectual creativity, but also the power to attract cultural elites; and that they lost this ability not only within their sphere of power but also outside it, in Europe and America. How is it that Stalin could build up such support among intellectuals while present regimes, less cruel and bloodthirsty, cannot? Why do various other revolutionary and despotic regimes lack this ability? Fascism and Hitlerism were pure destroyers of culture and left nothing but desolation in their wake; and although they aroused the sympathy of a few members of Western cultural elites (Heidegger, Ezra Pound, Celine, and Knut Hamsun to name the best known), they proved extremely weak in this respect when compared with Stalinism.

In only one important discipline did communism prove completely barren, and that is philosophy. Official Soviet philosophy has left nothing of note; its history could be studied only as an example of the inevitable debasing of the intellect when it is reduced to being a servile instrument of the Party. Lukács and Bloch, two genuinely interesting thinkers who are still studied, are only partial counter-examples. Lukács is worth reading as a rare example of an outstanding thinker who throughout his life, despite conflicts and disagreements, put his intellect at the service of a tyrant; his books inspire no interesting thought and are considered "things of the past" even in Hungary, his native country. The only components of Bloch's thought that might conceivably be of some interest are those that have little connection with communism, or even with Marxism. In Poland and Czechoslovakia, too, the philosophy produced by the spirit of communism is a rubbish heap – though to archeologists even rubbish heaps can be of interest.

Communism has a centuries-old history. Even in its earliest guise – the utopian literature of the Renaissance and the Enlightenment (often religiously inspired, invoking the Apostolic community of goods which condemned private property as a sin) – it betrayed its incurable contradictions. These utopias were at the same time egalitarian and despotic; they promoted the ideal of perfect equality, but also rule by an enlightened elite to safeguard this equality. Communism, which came on the scene not just as a literary genre but as a political movement, had its roots in the Jacobin Left. Here the contradiction between equality, considered the supreme and absolute value, and freedom, was even more prominent: the ideal society was to be at the same time strictly egalitarian and despotically governed – a squaring of the circle. In the nineteenth century, the century of Marx, which witnessed the birth and growth of the modern socialist movement, communism did not find fertile soil in which to flourish. It had developed some theoretical offshoots, but it scarcely existed as a political movement; the First International was far from being its organ; Marx himself, despite his theoretical authority, was insignificant as a political activist; and the socialist parties of the Second International, although sometimes in conflict and split into factions, in their overwhelming majority (and this included Marxists) believed in the legitimacy of democratic institutions and in cultural freedom. Social criticism in the nineteenth-century novel was strongly developed and sometimes very sharp, but it had no connection with communism.

Modern communism in the proper sense was born at the beginning of the twentieth century, in the form of Lenin's faction. Until the First World War its influence within the socialist movement was nugatory outside Russia; the fact that it was a completely new ideological and political phenomenon, not merely a tactical or doctrinal faction within a movement, went unheeded for a long time, and gradually began to become apparent only after 1910. The movement made no secret of its embryonic despotism; its totalitarian potential was present at birth. If it managed, in time, to harness the revolutionary wave in Russia and establish itself on its crest, this was, admittedly, owing to an exceptional series of historical accidents, but not only to these. It was also thanks to an ability that later, in more developed form, became the keystone of Soviet success: the ability to absorb and assimilate all major social grievances and turn them to its advantage.

From the very beginning, ideologically as well as tactically, communism was a parasite. It efficiently exploited all social ills, attaching itself to causes that were not only important but also worthy, and supported by much of an intelligentsia nurtured on the ideals of enlightenment and humanism. Communism before the First World War not only defended workers' interests, but also exposed national oppression, took on board the aspirations of poor peasants, and protested against censorship. In short, it allied itself, in a non-doctrinaire fashion, with all potential sources of opposition to czarist autocracy and tried to channel them all in one direction. There was almost no communist involvement in the February revolution or the overthrow of the czar, and absolutely nothing communist in the slogans of the October Revolution: "peace" and "land for the peasants." The dominant ideology of the masses in the revolutionary process was not communism but anarchy, expressed in the slogan: all power to the soviets (councils). The Bolsheviks took over this slogan, then dropped it (when most of the soviets were Menshevik), and then adopted it again in order to exploit the anarchist utopia to smash still-existing government structures and impose their own rule on a demoralized and disorganized society. Lenin openly admitted that the Bolsheviks won because they adopted the Socialist Revolutionaries' agrarian program. The third slogan which, together with "peace" and "land for the peasants," played an important role in the disintegration of the former state was the "right to self-determination." We all know how this program turned out: "land for the peasants" meant mass expropriation of the peasantry and chaining peasants to the land on principles similar to those of feudal servitude; "peace" meant building the most militarized empire on earth, unequalled in aggression and insatiable in its greed for conquest; and "self-determination" meant the systematic stifling of all national aspirations and traditions.

Many intellectuals, however, saw Bolshevism not so much as a collection of policies to alleviate immediate social grievances, however severe, but as a global sort of utopian technology, the beginning of a new world, a new era, in which all human problems would be resolved and all misery eradicated once and for all. The most urgent problem was of course that of peace and war, and the connected issue of internationalism. World communism as we know it today is the product of the First World War. We Poles have a natural tendency to see that war in the light of one of the greatest events in our history, the re-emergence of an independent Polish state after years of subjugation. This outcome, however, had not been among the aims of any of the powers that launched the war. The war itself was an appalling slaughter of millions, and the longer it lasted the clearer it became that it was indeed, as left-wing socialists claimed, an imperialist war – a conflict between ruling elites carried out by the people. It would be hard to overestimate the role played by anti-war feeling in the sympathetic attitude of European intellectuals toward Bolshevism during the early 1920s. The Bolsheviks reaped the harvest from the disaster suffered by the Second International in 1914, when it became clear that international workers' solidarity, the ideological backbone of the socialist movement, was an empty slogan that disappeared without trace as soon as it was put to the test. The USDP, the German social-democratic anti-war faction set up in 1917, was thus a natural incubator of communism; and for the European writers who joined communist parties or sympathized with them at that time – like Arnold Zweig, Bertolt Brecht, Henri Barbusse, Romain Rolland, Anatole France, Jaroslav Hasek, to name the best known – the horror of war was the main motivation. Communism was the promise of a world without wars. It exploited the human desire for peace, which has become one of the most powerful social emotions of this century. Before the war, the communists were little more than a minor sect, even in Russia; in the period between the first and second Russian revolutions, the influence of Marxism and communism declined sharply among the Russian intelligentsia, and many distinguished intellectuals launched violent attacks on the historical and philosophical dogmas they had recently supported. It was not without reason that, at the 1934 Writers' Congress, Maxim Gorky, by then a wholly devoted Stalinist, described the years 1907–17, a great era in the history of Russian poetry, as "the most disgraceful and shameful decade in the history of the Russian intelligentsia."

But other motives played their part. There was the fascination with barbarism that is sometimes found among intellectuals; what fascinated here was the absolute beginning of a new era, a break with the past, freedom from the shackles of a bygone age. In Russia as in the West, this ethos of a culture unbound and unembedded, the (illusory, needless to add) freedom from inherited tradition, the cult of youth unhampered by the burdens of history, the desire to shock, to *épater la bourgeoisie* – all this, too, made the Bolsheviks attractive. They represented the radically New; they were the hammer that would smash the dragging, restricting weight of the past, responding to the call of the *Internationale*: "du passé *faisons la table rase."* For Blok and for Mayakovsky, for the French Surrealists, for the Futurists, this was an important aspect of the attraction. Its presence at that time as one of the factors of communism's magnetic powers is perhaps explicable by the historical circumstances. The real end of the nineteenth century, the real beginning of a new era in all areas of human experience, was the First World War. The Bolsheviks appreciated this more clearly and sooner than anyone else, and were thus able, for a time, to carve out a place for themselves in European culture as the embodiment of this new era – which in turn contributed to lending a semblance of authenticity, however short-lived, to communist civilization.

The first half of the 1930s brought new social upheavals which the communists succeeded in exploiting: the Great Depression, the triumph of National Socialism in Germany, and later the Spanish Civil War and the turbulent events in China. These were all burning, tragic issues. The Great Depression, with its millions of unemployed, its misery and despair, was a perfect opportunity for communism, which now presented itself as the promise of a society without unemployment and insecurity, and also as the most energetic enemy of the fascist cancer which seemed to be devouring Europe (also by exploiting the miseries of the time). At a time when millions were dying from the Soviet government's artificially induced famine in the Ukraine, from cold, torture, and exhaustion, from execution in Stalin's prisons and camps, or during the various stages of transportation, a significant number of Western intellectuals saw the Soviet state as a bastion of peace and revolutionary humanism, as the harbinger of a new world in which people would be equal, free from insecurity, and confident of the future. Among those who sympathized or identified themselves with communism were people like André Malraux, Walter Benjamin, Theodore Plivier, Jean-Richard Bloch, Theodore Dreiser, John Dos Passos, and Upton Sinclair. Leon Feuchtwanger and Romain Rolland greeted the macabre farce of the Moscow Trials as a triumph of justice.

Here, too, it is futile to bemoan human naiveté and blindness; here, too, social and cultural processes are at work which must be analyzed as such and explained. The Popular Front in the 1930s was of course a form of Soviet manipulation, but it was not merely manipulation: to the extent that it was effective, this was because its slogans reflected the real hopes, fears, and experiences of Europe. Fascism was not a communist-invented bogeyman, but a very real, and deadly, threat to civilizations and nations; although it fed off the same social diseases as communism, it attracted people of an entirely different sort, and it had almost no cultural vitality. The shaky and sometimes timid policies of the Western powers in the face of this threat were skillfully exploited by the communists; anti-fascism could be, and indeed was, a culturally inspiring force. The social upheavals resulting from inflation and the Depression were very real. The two-year Molotov-Ribbentrop pact must have come as a shock to many people, certainly, but the later course of the war soon blotted this embarrassing stain, and from 1941 to 1945 the Soviet colossus once again adopted, with some success, its role as the world's main protector from Hitler's barbarity; and it used its military successes as a strong base on which to build a new ideological invasion of Europe. After the war it adopted, also with some success, the role of ideological herald of decolonization.

Similar processes can be observed in the case of the Polish cultural elite: those of its members who came out in unequivocal support of the communist regime after the war tended mostly to come from socialist or left-liberal rather than communist backgrounds, and their allegiance was determined largely by their negative attitudes toward pre-war Poland, especially in the most recent years, after the death of Marshal Pilsudski. We tend, understandably, to idealize this pre-war period, because it was a time when Poland, for all its failings, was independent. Moreover, its failings seem insignificant when compared to those of the new "progressive" regime: press restrictions and censorship were minimal in comparison with the systematically destructive effects of the progressive muzzle imposed on Polish culture by the communist regime, and pre-war acts of police illegality pale beside the lawlessness which prevails in the People's Republic of Poland. But that part of the intelligentsia which in 1945 or 1946, after the horror of war and occupation, identified itself, with greater or lesser enthusiasm, with the new regime, saw things differently. Those who remembered the Brest trial, the Bereza concentration camp, the repellent wave of virulent anti-Semitism, and the oppressive clericalism, saw communism as a continuation of the Enlightenment: as a force that would combat the chauvinist and clerical current in the Polish tradition which it regarded as poisonous and pernicious. (Here, too, they were continuing a certain tradition, for this was a current that had been combated since at least the seventeenth century – long before the formation of the intelligentsia in the modern sense of the word – by the more critical and cosmopolitan segments of the educated Polish nobility.) Similarly, the social reforms announced by the communists reflected many of the traditional demands of the non-communist Left in Poland.

To say this is not to excuse anything, least of all the role of the intelligentsia in the massive communist lie. But communism is – to repeat a banal observation – a historical phenomenon of immense importance which needs to be explained; it is not enough simply to condemn the gullibility and corruptibility of its followers. If communism successfully exploited genuine social grievances, many of them the preoccupation of both liberals and socialists in Europe, this does not mean that it resolved these problems in any way, or even that it tried to resolve them. On the contrary, it brought disaster in all the social, cultural, national, and international issues it championed. The only ostensible exception was an issue which the Soviets endlessly trumpet as their great achievement: the issue of unemployment. I say ostensible because unemployment in the Soviet Union was eliminated by a system of forced labor; and indeed, there has never been unemployment among slaves. Hitler, too, triumphed over the plague of unemployment. However, in democratic societies unemployment remains a very real and thorny problem. In conditions of great unemployment, the promises of communism begin to seem attractive, and the hope flourishes that many people will be prepared to exchange their freedom for the security of slaves.

Communism was a gigantic façade, and the reality concealed behind it was the sheer drive for power, for total power as an end in itself. The rest was merely instrumental – a matter of tactics and some necessary self-restrictions to achieve the desired end. But the façade was more than mere decoration: it was communism's only means of survival; its respiratory system. It was also the ineradicable residue of the tradition of the Enlightenment and nineteenth-century socialism, of which communism was indeed a deformed descendant. As with all descendants, however deformed, some inherited traits are always visible, and in communism, too, these were evident. The rationalism, contempt for tradition, and hatred for the mythological layer of culture to which the Enlightenment gave birth developed, under communism, into the brutal persecution of religion, but also into the principle (practiced rather than directly expressed) that human beings are expendable: that individual lives count only as instruments of the "greater whole" or the "higher cause," i.e., the state, for no rational grounds exist for attributing to them any special, non-instrumental status. Thus rationalism was transformed under communism into the idea of slavery. And romantic and early socialist strains – the search for a lost community and human solidarity, the protest against social disintegration caused by the industrial revolution and urbanization – developed, under communism, into caricature: solidarity imposed by force, in an attempt to create a fake, merely ostensible unity – the unity of despotism.

Nevertheless, both the rationalist and the Promethean phraseology, as well as the phraseology of solidarity, were highly visible in the language of communism from the outset, testifying to its links, however deformed, with the tradition of the Enlightenment and Romanticism. They also lent the communist ideology a certain pathos, and this in turn, since it was certainly authentic in the minds of adherents, inevitably lent communism a semblance of truth. In the period of communism's ideological nascency this was, of course, an advantage, but it also had its dangers. For the façade, to the extent that it was taken seriously within the movement, tended inevitably to take on an independent life of its own and to question its own purely instrumental role; and taking the façade seriously also meant confronting it with the reality of the political movement, or the state. This is how communism was able, indeed forced, constantly to produce its own internal critics, heretics, and apostates, who appealed to the original sources – ever-present in the ideological jargon – in order to expose the poverty of the reality. This phenomenon is almost entirely absent from other totalitarian movements, where the gap between the façade and reality was small – as a rule the ideology made its true intentions brutally plain – and the ideological tradition frail. Hitler could have been Stalin's equivalent, but there was no Nazi Marx or Engels, not even a Lenin, to back him up. He replaced them with an artificial, invented genealogy.

Thus communism was forced, to use its own phrase about the bourgeoisie, constantly to produce its own grave diggers. In the intellectual and moral criticism which eventually brought about the bankruptcy of the communist ideology, a particularly important and effective role was played, as we know, by former communists and left-wing socialists – people who not only were well acquainted with its political mechanisms and psychology, but had also "internalized" them, finding no adequate substitute for their experiences. Arthur Koestler, Ignazio Silone, Boris Souvarine, and Bertram Wolfe were all communists; George Orwell was a left-wing socialist. Starting with Milovan Djilas, the role of former communists in the ideological disintegration of the European Peoples' Democracies in the 1950s and 1960s was tremendous. In Poland, the names in this category are legion. Similarly in France.

But there is an important distinction to be made here. When we speak of the attractive power of the communist idea and of its cultural fecundity, we can have in mind one of two things: the work, in general and as a whole, of artists, writers, and intellectuals who identified or sympathized with communism; or specifically those of their works which bear the distinct stamp of communist ideological inspiration. The problem is that many outstanding artists and writers with communist sympathies either did not leave behind any work which unambiguously testified to their political leanings, or made only indirect reference to communism in their work. Sometimes their work dealt with causes which, while championed by communism and in line with communist ideology, were not identifiable as communist by their content alone; one could defend them without being either a communist or a fellow-traveler. Aragon was undoubtedly an outstanding poet, whose place in French literature is assured; but we can distinguish between his poetry and his mendacious Stalinist apologetics, or propaganda novels. Some of Pablo Neruda's poetry is distinctly and recognizably communist, while nothing in the work of the Mexican muralist Siqueiros, a first-rate artist, betrays the fact that he, too, was a thoroughly committed Stalinist. Theodore Dreiser was a communist sympathizer who toward the end of his life joined the Communist Party, but his novels belong to the rich tradition of American social criticism rather than to communist propaganda. In the pre-war poetry of Wladyslaw Broniewski, the lyrical is easily distinguished from the political, but even the latter contains some things worthy of note: political poems which – unlike his post-war eulogy to Stalin – do somehow testify to the fact that communism was able, at a certain period, to absorb the energies arising from genuine social conflicts, not just from the history Soviet imperialism. Similar distinctions can be made in the case of most of the artists mentioned above.

There have been – and I stress the past tense – some specifically communist works of art, literature and thought, unambiguous in their political content, that have nevertheless endured as part of our cultural heritage. But one can safely say that the longer the communists have been in power, the fewer such works there have been. Genuinely original work inspired by communist ideas, work of any real worth, virtually disappeared in the Soviet Union in the 1930s. This was owing not only, perhaps not even chiefly, to purges and killings, but above all to the growing stranglehold of a totalitarian system that left no room for individual expression, which was replaced with the obligatory agit-prop pap. This effectively eliminated those vestiges of authenticity that still remained in communist ideology. A certain amount of good writing did emerge from the Second World War, but the best of it was inspired by patriotism rather than communism: it depicted the horror of the war from the point of view of people who, in desperate circumstances, fought for their own life and for the life of their country, not for the triumph of the revolution. In Poland and other Soviet protectorates, post-war art inspired by the communist ideal produced very little of lasting value; socialist realism in art and literature was a stillbirth. Similarly, post-war writers who had seriously adopted the communist faith did not fully enter the national literature until they had forsaken it.

This is, I admit, a rough-hewn and summary account. It ignores transitional stages, possible exceptions, and works of art in which various ideological strains were mixed. But there is no space here to discuss individual lives and works in detail. If there were any communist-inspired works whose artistic merits are worth serious consideration, it remains indisputable that very soon after the communists came to power, everything of any cultural worth that was being produced in the countries of the Soviet bloc arose either in spite of the communist ideology or parallel to it, by-passing it, as it were.

It should be said, however, that when an ideology aims to be all-embracing and all-powerful, to work alongside it or parallel to it is to work against it. Work that simply ignores ideology, doctrine, and the authorities is tolerated, to be sure – even, to some extent, in the Soviet Union. But this is a symptom of the ideology's senility and decrepitude, not an intentional tribute paid to liberal values. Internal criticism of communism has practically ceased to exist; it has become socially superfluous. Communism no longer produces its own critics who appeal to its own doctrinal assumptions; every critical remark is aimed at principles, not at their supposed deformations. Neither in Western Europe, nor in the United States, nor in communist countries, are there any culturally significant artists who are inspired by communism. The collapse has been total and is certainly irreversible. Only in Latin America, with its enormous social problems, poverty, backwardness, and glaring inequalities, has communism retained something of its former appeal. In the Soviet Union, however, the only ideology with any signs of vitality is not communism but imperialism. In short, communism as a cultural force in the sense I have outlined here – as a force capable of producing works of enduring cultural value – has ceased to exist in the civilized world. Clearly it is still a political and military power capable of terror and conquest, and of mobilizing those forces in the Third World which hope to achieve power as cousins of the great empire. But it can no longer spread its influence through the intermediary of intellectual elites.

To say this is not to explain how communism came into being and was able to establish itself as such a powerful focus of ideological identification for so many people, including a considerable number of intellectuals. That would require a separate analysis, which I do not intend to undertake here. I will only repeat that the process cannot be explained by talking about stupidity or terror; that is a crude simplification of the problem. We might equally well explain the rise and success of Islam by saying that the Arabs were stupid, and this was why, instead of believing in Christ, they chose to believe in the false prophet Mohammed. In any case, I do not think the rise and spread of communism is causally explicable in the same way as drought or floods are explicable. Viewed in retrospect, all great historical events seem to have been determined by circumstances, and this holds true also for the sudden eruption of great religious movements. With hindsight we can always find causes. But the fragility of such explanations becomes evident when we consider that if they really laid bare all the mechanisms and sufficient conditions of historical change, we would be able to predict them. But we cannot. Communism was born as a quasi-religious movement, i.e., as the ideological expression of the need for ultimate salvation. This need is probably a permanent and ineradicable element of all civilizations, but its presence alone does not explain why, at certain times and in certain places, it comes to the fore in the form of intense historical convulsions, engulfing enormous numbers of people and leading to unexpected and violent upheavals which overturn the existing order. Communism, which grew out of a desperate need for ultimate salvation, for a new era, is an instance of such a convulsion. The product of the tradition of the Enlightenment, emerging at a time when educated elites had largely forsaken their traditional faiths, it took the (inconsistent) form of a secular religion; and the psychological mechanisms thanks to which it was able to advance were similar to those that underlay the vitality of those traditional faiths in their most dynamic periods. The missionary force of its militant atheism was driven by a similar mechanism. However, its doctrinal form was a caricature of religion, for communism demanded both blind obedience and the recognition that it was a rational interpretation of the world. But it could not have both; and, floundering between these two inconsistent demands, it brought about, within the sphere of its influence, the collapse of both rationalism and religion. Its ideological bankruptcy was at the same time a defeat for the Enlightenment, of which it was the ultimate and most consistent – and therefore also the most self-destructive – expression.

Again, none of this explains the genesis of communism. At best, it explains the authenticity that initially characterized its message, and thus the reasons for its brief success as a catalyst in cultural life. But why history should have chosen those particular times and places to realize the self-destructive potential of the Enlightenment – this we do not know. Every powerful and significant social movement is the result of a combination of circumstances, among them the mentality of a particular age, the political and economic conditions, and the psychology, energy and initiative of the individuals involved. No one can claim to possess a method of quantifying all these historical circumstances and measuring them on a single scale which would provide a causal explanation of historical events. There is little doubt, however, that this particular convulsion is drawing to a close, and the loss of its ability to mobilize culturally active forces is the outstanding symptom of this decline. Communism is becoming more and more visibly a question of brute force, and it would be untrue to say that this is all it ever was. As to the form this decline will take, and the timescale in which it will happen, we can only consult the fortune-tellers.

What Is Left of Socialism?[1]

Karl Marx – a powerful mind, a very learned man, and a good German writer – died 119 years ago. He lived in the age of steam; he never saw a car, a telephone, or electric light, to say nothing of later technological devices. His admirers and followers used to say, and some still do, that this doesn't matter, and that his teaching is still perfectly relevant to our time because the system he analyzed and attacked – capitalism – is still here. That Marx is worth reading is certain. The question is, however, whether his theory truly explains anything in our world, and whether it provides grounds for any predictions. The answer is no. Another question is whether or not his theories were ever useful. Here the answer is, obviously, yes: they operated successfully as a set of slogans that were supposed to justify and glorify communism and the slavery that inevitably goes with it.

When we ask what those theories explain or what Marx discovered, we may ask only about ideas that were specific to him, and not about commonsense platitudes. We should not make a laughingstock out of Marx by attributing to him the discovery that in all non-primitive societies there are social groups or classes with conflicting interests that lead them to fight with one another; this was known to ancient historians. Marx himself did not pretend to have made this kind of discovery; as he wrote in a letter to Joseph Weydemeyer in 1852, he had not discovered the class struggle but rather had proved that it leads to the dictatorship of the proletariat, which in turn leads ultimately to the abolition of classes. It is impossible to say where and how he "proved" this grandiose claim in his pre-1852 writings. To "explain" something means to sub-

---

1 Written in Polish. Originally published as "Po co nam pojecie sprawiedliwosci spolecznej?" in *Ksiaska dla Jacka [Kuronia]*, Fundacja Nowej: Warsaw, 1995, and in daily newspaper "Gazeta Wyborcza," 1995, nr. 105, May 6–8. English version appeared as "What Is Left of Socialism," published in *First Things*, 2002, Nr. 126.

sume events or processes under laws; but "laws" in the Marxist sense are not the same as laws in the natural sciences, where they are understood as formulas stating that in well-defined conditions, well-defined phenomena always occur. What Marx called "laws" are, rather, historical tendencies. There is thus no clear-cut distinction in his theories between explanation and prophecy. Besides, he believed that the meaning of both past and present may be understood only by reference to the future, of which he claimed to have knowledge. Hence, for Marx, only what does not (yet) exist can explain what does exist. But it should be added that for Marx the future *does* exist, in a peculiar, Hegelian, manner, even though it is unknowable.

All of Marx's important prophecies, however, have turned out to be false. First, he predicted growing class polarization and the disappearance of the middle class in societies based on a market economy. Karl Kautsky rightly stressed that if this prediction were wrong, the entire Marxist theory would be in ruins. It is clear that this prediction has proved to be wrong; rather, the opposite is the case. The middle classes are growing, whereas the working class in Marx's sense has been dwindling in capitalist societies as technological progress has increased.

Second, he predicted not only the relative but also the absolute impoverishment of the working class. This prediction was already wrong in his lifetime. It is worth noticing that in the second edition of *Capital* Marx updated various statistics and figures, but not those relating to workers' wages; those figures, if updated, would have contradicted his theory. Not even the most doctrinaire Marxists have tried to cling to this obviously false prediction in recent decades.

Third, and most importantly, Marx's theory predicted the inevitability of the proletarian revolution. Such a revolution has never occurred anywhere. The Bolshevik Revolution in Russia had nothing to do with Marxian prophesies. Its driving force was not a conflict between the industrial working class and capital, but rather was carried out under slogans that had no socialist, let alone Marxist, content: *Peace* and *Land for Peasants*. Needless to add that these slogans were to be subsequently turned into their opposite. What in the twentieth century perhaps comes closest to the working class revolution were the events in Poland of 1980–81: the revolutionary movement of industrial workers (very strongly supported by the intelligentsia) against the exploiters, i.e., the state. And this solitary example of a working class revolution (if indeed it may be counted as such) was directed against a socialist state, and carried out under the sign of the cross, with the blessing of the Pope.

Fourth, Marx predicted the inevitable fall of the profit rate, a process that was supposed to lead ultimately to the collapse of the capitalist economy. Like the others, this prediction proved to be simply wrong.

What Is Left of Socialism?

Even according to Marx's theory, this could not be an inevitably operating regularity, because the same technical development that lowers the part of variable capital in production costs is supposed to lower the value of constant capital. Therefore the profit rate might remain stable or increase even if what Marx called "living labor" declines for a given unit of output. And even if this "law" were true, the mechanism whereby its operation would cause the decline and demise of capitalism is inconceivable, since the collapse of the profit rate can very well occur in conditions in which the absolute amount of profit is growing. This was noticed by Rosa Luxemburg, who invented a theory of her own about the inevitable collapse of capitalism, which proved no less wrong.

The fifth tenet of Marxism that has turned out to be wrong is the prediction that the market will hamper technical progress. The exact opposite has quite obviously proved to be the case. Market economies have proved extremely efficient in stimulating technological progress, whereas "real socialism" turned out to lead to technological stagnation. Since it is undeniable that the market has created the greatest abundance ever known in human history, some neo-Marxists have felt compelled to change their approach. At one time, capitalism appeared horrifying because it produced misery; later, it turned out to be horrifying because it produces such abundance that it kills culture.

Neo-Marxists deplore what is called "consumerism," or the "consumerist society." In our civilization there are indeed many alarming and deplorable phenomena associated with the growth of consumption. The point is, however, that what we know as the alternative to this civilization is incomparably worse. In all communist societies, economic reforms (to the extent that they yielded any results at all) invariably led in the same direction: to a partial restoration of the market, that is to say, of "capitalism."

As for the so-called materialist interpretation of history, it has provided us with a number of interesting insights and suggestions, but it has no explanatory value. In its strong, rigid version, for which there is considerable support in many classic texts, it implies that social development depends entirely on the class struggle, which ultimately, through the intermediary of changing "modes of production," is determined by the technological level of the society in question. It implies, moreover, that law, religion, philosophy, and other elements of culture have no history of their own, since their history is the history of the relations of production. This is an absurd claim, completely lacking in historical grounds.

If, on the other hand, the theory is taken in a weak, limited sense, it merely says that the history of culture must be investigated in such a way as to take account of social struggles and conflicting interests, and that political institutions depend in part, at least negatively, on technological development and on social conflicts. This, however, is an uncontroversial platitude which was known long before Marx. Thus the materialist interpretation of history is either nonsense or a platitude.

Another component of Marx's theory that lacks explanatory power is his labor theory. Marx made two important additions to the theories of Adam Smith and David Ricardo. First, he stated that in relationships between workers and capital, it is the labor force, rather than labor, that is sold; secondly, he made a distinction between abstract and concrete labor. Neither of these principles has any empirical basis, and neither is needed to explain crises, competition, and conflicts of interest. Crises and economic cycles are understandable by analyzing the movement of prices, and the theory of value adds nothing to our understanding of them. It seems that contemporary economics – as distinct from economic ideologies – would not differ much from what it is today if Marx had never been born.

The tenets I have mentioned are not chosen at random: they constitute the skeleton of the Marxian doctrine. But there is hardly anything in Marxism that provides solutions to the many problems of our time, mainly because they were not urgent a century ago. As for ecological questions, we will find in Marx no more than a few romantic platitudes about man's unity with nature. Demographic problems are completely absent, apart from Marx's refusal to believe that anything like overpopulation in the absolute sense could ever occur. Neither will the dramatic problems of the Third World find help in his theory. Marx and Engels were strongly Eurocentric; they held other civilizations in contempt, and they praised the progressive effects of colonialism and imperialism (in India, Algeria, and Mexico). What mattered to them was the victory of higher civilizations over backward ones; the idea of national determination was to Engels a matter for derision.

What Marxism is least capable of explaining is the totalitarian socialism that appointed Marx as its prophet. Many Western Marxists used to insist that socialism such as it existed in the Soviet Union, deplorable as it might be, had nothing to do with Marxist theory and was best explained by specific conditions in Russia. But if this is the case, how is it that so many people in the nineteenth century, especially the anarchists, predicted fairly exactly what socialism based on Marxist principles would turn out to be – namely, state slavery? Proudhon argued that Marx's ideal was to turn human beings into state property. According to Bakunin, Marxian socialism would consist in the rule of the renegades of the ruling class, and would be based on exploitation and oppression worse than anything previously known. According to the Polish anarcho-syndicalist Edward Abramowski, if communism were by some miracle to win in the moral conditions of contemporary society, it would result in class division and exploitation worse than what existed at the time (because institutional changes do not alter human motivations and moral behavior). Benjamin Tucker said that Marxism knows only one cure for monopolies, and that is a *single* monopoly.

These predictions were made in the nineteenth century, decades before the Russian Revolution. Were these people clairvoyant? No. Such predictions could be made rationally, and the system of socialized serfdom inferred from the things Marx anticipated. It would be absurd, of course, to say that this was the prophet's intention or that Marxism was the efficient cause of twentieth-century communism. The victory of Russian communism resulted from a series of extraordinary accidents. But it might be said that Marx's theory contributed strongly to the emergence of totalitarianism, and that it provided its ideological form. It anticipated the universal nationalization of everything, and thus the nationalization of human beings. To be sure, Marx took from the Saint-Simonists the slogan that in the future there would be no government, only the administration of things; it did not occur to him, however, that one cannot administer things without employing people for the purpose, so the total administration of things means the total administration of people.

None of this means that Marx's work is not worth reading; it is a part of European culture, and one should read it as one reads many classics – just as one should read Descartes's works on physics even though it would be silly to read them as a textbook about how to do physics today. Even in the former communist countries, the current repugnance for Marx and Marxist texts might pass; even there they will eventually be read as remnants of the past. One of the causes of the popularity of Marxism among educated people was the fact that in its simple form it was very easy; even Sartre noticed that Marxists are lazy. Indeed, they enjoyed having one key to open all doors, one universally applicable explanation for everything, an instrument that made it possible to master all of history and economics without actually having to study either.

Does the demise of Marxism automatically mean the end of the socialist tradition? Not necessarily. Everything, of course, depends on the meaning of the word "socialism," and those who still use it as their own profession of faith are usually reluctant to say what they mean, apart from empty generalities. And so some distinctions have to be made. The trouble is that the desire to detect "historical laws" has led many people to conceive of "capitalism" and "socialism" as global "systems," diametrically opposed to each other. But there is no comparison. Capitalism developed spontaneously and organically from the spread of commerce. Nobody planned it, and it did not need an all-embracing ideology, whereas socialism was an ideological construction. Ultimately, capitalism is human nature at work – that is, man's greed allowed to follow its course – whereas socialism is an attempt to institutionalize and enforce fraternity. It seems obvious by now that a society in which greed is the main motivation of human action, for all of its repugnant and deplorable aspects, is incomparably better than a society based on compulsory brotherhood, whether in national or international socialism.

The idea of socialism as an "alternative society" to capitalism amounts to the idea of totalitarian serfdom; the abolition of the market and overall nationalization can yield no other result. The belief that one can establish perfect equality by institutional means is no less malignant. The world has known pockets of voluntary equality, practiced in some monasteries and in a handful of secular cooperatives. However, equality under compulsion inevitably requires totalitarian means, and totalitarianism implies extreme inequality, since it entails unequal access to information and power. Nor, practically speaking, is equality in the distribution of material goods possible once power is concentrated in the hands of an uncontrollable oligarchy; this is why nothing remotely close to equality has ever existed in socialist countries. The ideal is therefore self-defeating. We know very well why the idea of all-encompassing planning is economically catastrophic; Friedrich von Hayek's criticism on this point has been amply borne out by evidence from the experience of all communist countries without exception. Socialism in this sense means that people are prevented by repression from engaging in any socially useful activity except on orders from the state.

However, the socialist tradition is rich and varied; it includes many varieties apart from Marxism. Some socialist ideas did indeed have a built-in totalitarian tendency. This applies to most of the Renaissance and Enlightenment utopias, as well as to Saint-Simon. But some espoused liberal values. Once socialism, which started out as an innocent fantasy, became a real political movement, not all of its variants included the idea of an "alternative society," and of those that did, many did not take the idea seriously.

Everything was clearer before the First World War. Socialists and the left in general wanted not only equal, universal, and obligatory education, a social health service, progressive taxation, and religious tolerance, but also secular education, the abolition of national and racial discrimination, the equality of women, freedom of the press and of assembly, the legal regulation of labor conditions, and a social security system. They fought against militarism and chauvinism. European socialist leaders of the period of the Second International, people like Jaurès, Babel, Turati, Vandervelle, and Martov, embodied what was best in European political life.

But everything changed after World War I, when the word "socialism" (and to a large extent "the Left") began to be almost completely monopolized by Leninist-Stalinist socialism, which skewed most of these demands and slogans to mean their opposite. At the same time, most of these "socialist" ideals were in fact realized in democratic countries with market economies. Alas, non-totalitarian socialist movements suffered for decades from ideological inhibitions and lacked the courage to denounce and fight consistently against the most despotic and murderous political system in the world (apart from Nazism). Soviet communism was supposed to be a kind of socialism, after all, and it embellished itself with internationalist and humanist phraseology inherited from the socialist tradition. Leninist tyranny thus succeeded in stealing the word "socialism," and the non-totalitarian socialists were complicit in the theft. There were some exceptions to this rule, but not many.

Be that as it may, socialist movements strongly contributed to changing the political landscape for the better. They inspired a number of social reforms without which the contemporary welfare state – which most of us take for granted – would be unthinkable. It would thus be a pity if the collapse of communist socialism resulted in the demise of the socialist tradition as a whole and the triumph of Social Darwinism as the dominant ideology.

While acknowledging that a perfect society can never be attained and that people will always find reasons to treat each other badly, we should not discard the concept of "social justice," much as it may have been ridiculed by Hayek and his followers. Certainly, it cannot be defined in economic terms. One cannot deduce from the expression "social justice" the answer to questions about what particular taxation system is desirable and economically sound in given conditions, what social benefits are justified, or what is the best way for rich countries to aid the poorer parts of the world. "Social justice" merely expresses an attitude toward social problems. It is true that more often than not the expression "social justice" is employed by individuals or entire societies who refuse to take responsibility for their own lives. But, as the old saying goes, the abuse does not invalidate the use.

In its vagueness, "social justice" resembles the concept of human dignity. It is difficult to define what human dignity is. It is not an organ to be discovered in our body, it is not an empirical notion, but without it we would be unable to answer the simple question: what is wrong with slavery? Likewise, the concept of social justice is vague, and it can be used as an ideological tool of totalitarian socialism. Yet the concept is a useful intermediary between an exhortation to charity, to almsgiving, and the concept of distributive justice; it is not the same as distributive justice because it does not necessarily imply reciprocal recognition. Nor is it simply an appeal to charity, because it implies, however imprecisely, that some claims may be deserved. The concept of social justice does not imply that there is such a thing as the common destiny of mankind in which everybody takes part, but it does suggest that the concept of humanity makes sense – not so much as a zoological category but as a moral one.

Without the market, the economy would collapse (in fact, in "real socialism" there is no economy at all, only economic policy). But it is also generally recognized that the market does not automatically solve all pressing human problems. The concept of social justice is needed to justify the belief that there is a "humanity"– and that we must look on other individuals as belonging to this collectivity, toward which we have certain moral duties.

Socialism as a social or moral philosophy was based on the ideal of human brotherhood, which can never be implemented by institutional means. There has never been, and there will never be, an institutional means of making people brothers. Fraternity under compulsion is the most malignant idea devised in modern times; it is a perfect path to totalitarian tyranny. Socialism in this sense is tantamount to a kingdom of lies. This is no reason, however, to scrap the idea of human fraternity. If it is not something that can be effectively achieved by means of social engineering, it is useful as a statement of goals. The socialist idea is dead as a project for an "alternative society." But as a statement of solidarity with the underdog and the oppressed, as a motivation to oppose Social Darwinism, as a light that keeps before our eyes something higher than competition and greed – for all of these reasons, socialism – the ideal, not the system – still has its uses.

The Heritage of the Left[1]

Long shelves can be filled with books written by ex-communists, be they writers, intellectuals or philosophers, like Ignazio Silone, Arthur Koestler, Boris Souvarine, Henri Lefebvre, Edgar Morin, Annie Kriegel, Pierre Daix, Dominique Desanti, or by former apparatchiks and leaders like Ruth Fischer, André Marty, Charles Tillon, Milovan Djilas, Wolfgang Leonhard, to name only a few.[2] (We can leave aside a number of spies.) Some of their books are autobiographical, some analytical or historical. However, in all of them the authors have tried to come to grips with, to explain and to understand the phenomenon of communism, and their own past commitment to it. These books constitute an important part of the political life of our century. The often quoted prediction of Ignazio Silone that the struggle between communists and ex-communists would be decisive in the future may have been an exaggeration, but it contains a kernel of truth: ex-communists did indeed play a significant role in bringing communism to ruin.

It would be difficult to think of books of this kind written by Leftists – whether European or American. I mean books that explain and analyze, in historical or psychological terms, the Leftists' own misguided commitments, wrong beliefs, and false hopes. It seems that these people jumped from one fellow-travelership to another without explanation

---

1 Reprinted from *Balkan Forum* 4 (1994).
2 To mention only a sample of their works: Koestler, *Darkness at Noon*; Souvarine, *Stalin, a Critical Survey of Bolshevism*; Kriegel, *Un autre communisme? Aux Origines du Communisme Français, Les Communistes Français, Les Grands Procès dans les systèmes communistes*; Djilas, *The Fall of the New Class: A History of Communism's Self-Destruction, The New Class: An Analysis of the Communist System; Memoir of a Revolutionary*; Leonhard, *Die Revolution Entlässt Ihre Kinder*. Editor's note.

and without thinking about the past. The Soviet Union doesn't look quite so good anymore? We have the glory of a new socialism being built in China and the immortal thoughts of Chairman Mao. Something wrong with China, too? There is Cuba, the great hope of a people fighting the imperialist dragon. Fidel also not quite perfect any more? Then let's look for something else. There was not much else to be found, though, at least in the positive sense. There were some admirers of Pol-Pot and Khomeini among Leftist intellectuals (there is no limit to human stupidity), but admittedly only a few.

So there was a never-ending search for a good, noble cause, and once a good cause was abandoned for any reason it was immediately forgotten, and a new cause was found. For a long time there were, of course, genuinely good negative causes but fewer and fewer, it seemed: Franco's Spain (cross off), Salazar's Portugal (cross off), Pinochet's Chile (cross off), apartheid in South Africa (cross off). The worst tyrannies in Africa were mentioned only to the extent that one could, however implausibly, blame Western democracies for their existence.

Why is it that, while communists tried so obstinately to analyze communism and their own involvement with it, such analyses are so unusual among Leftists? Communism was a serious business, and committed communists meant business. They knew what they were after; theirs was real power politics on a world-scale. Very often they lied, of course, but they were usually lucid in going about it. Communists felt personally responsible for an impersonal Great Cause. Leftists, on the other hand, enjoyed a purely mental commitment without responsibility. Communist leaders appeared to have no great respect for their progressive helpmates; the latter were flattered and used, but they were not treated seriously, and for good reason. Communists were hawks; Leftists were irritated butterflies. This might be a reason why communists, once they had abandoned their creed and their parties to become social-democrats or liberals (or left politics for good), only rarely or temporarily joined the ranks of the Left.

Almost any cause, even a good cause, can testify to this comfortable irresponsibility of Leftists. There were, no doubt, serious political, moral, and military reasons for the U.S. to withdraw its troops from Vietnam, and the horrible "mistakes" committed in the course of that war are hardly disputed today. But the Great Reason that was most loudly and most systematically invoked – the belief that once North Vietnam was taken over, South Vietnam would be "liberated" – never existed. However nasty and corrupt the South Vietnamese regime may have been, one did not need to be clairvoyant to know that its communist successors would bring upon the Vietnamese people incomparably worse horrors and calamities. Didn't the Leftists of the 1970s know what Asiatic

The Heritage of the Left

Stalinism meant? Most of them probably didn't, but theirs was not an excusable ignorance; they preferred not to know. Are there any books written by Leftists or former Leftists analyzing this experience without lying? I cannot say with certainty that there are *none*, but I have never come across such an analysis. The Chinese "great leap forward" produced many millions of corpses and the "great cultural revolution" many millions more. Have the former adulators of the Great Chairman come up with their own examination of the monstrosities the Leftists pretended not to have noticed? Have the enthusiasts of the great oppressor of Cuba done so? (Again, I have not heard of such an analysis, but I am prepared to admit my mistake if I am wrong.) Progressive people, when confronted with evidence showing that they were supporting regimes based on slavery, torture, and mass slaughter, normally would reply: "A fabrication of the CIA!" And later, when the evidence became too overwhelming even for them, they just forgot about the whole business.

We can remember the time, admittedly not very recent but not very remote either, when, if you said that there were concentration camps in the Soviet Union, you were automatically labeled a "cold warrior." And since a cold warrior was wrong by definition, it followed logically that there were no concentration camps in the Soviet Union. When the glory of the Soviet Union faded, new lights appeared and at every stage we saw the same pattern: adore the despots and then escape and forget.

There was, however, one Great Cause that has persisted more or less intact throughout the past decades in the Leftist mentality: the loathing of democratic countries. Allegiances changed, but if there was something enduring in Leftist politics, it was this: in any conflict between a tyrannical and democratic country, the tyrants were right and democracy wrong: the U.S. *versus* the Soviet Union, the U.S. *versus* Cuba, Israel *versus* Syria. Even in the case of Argentina under military dictatorship *versus* Britain the tyrants were right. To show this there was no need to argue that one or another tyrannical regime was the most glorious achievement of mankind; it simply so happened that in any conflict with democracy, the tyrants were right.

Tony Judt makes this remark in his book *Past Imperfect. French Intellectuals 1944–1956* (University of California Press, 1992). His book deals with an earlier period than that referred to above, but the basic patterns are the same. Indeed, France during those years was the main source of the *gauchisme* that was later to spread throughout the Western, democratically governed world. My wife read this book before I did and said: "Look, we must have read a lot of this stuff in the 1950s and then it did not strike us as something extraordinary; read today it looks almost unbelievable."

The focus of the book is neither communists nor liberals, nor conservatives, but precisely the *gauchistes*, the *engagés* spokesmen of Progress. Judt's purpose is not simply to depict the mass of long-forgotten absurdities but to understand and explain them against the background of French history before and during World War II. French reactions to political show-trials in Eastern Europe are investigated with particular attention. Along with the most famous figures, like Jean-Paul Sartre and, on the Catholic side, Emmanuel Mournier, a large number of both famous and lesser-known writers and intellectuals appear on the pages of this interesting report.

While the Third Republic, its political establishment and its bourgeoisie, were, Judt says, attacked in the 1930s both by the Left and by the Maurrasists, there were some idols of the past, like Proudhon or Péguy, that were common to both movements. The horrors of World War I were still relatively fresh in people's minds and unconditional pacifism was strong, but the attractive force of communism was not, at least compared to the years after World War II. In any case, the Third Republic was considered irredeemable and neither Leftist nor Rightist critics regretted its demise. "To take a stance against Pétain at this early stage would not only have required considerable foresight, not to speak of courage; it would also have meant a willingness to defend, albeit in some modified form, the very values with which the deceased Republic had been associated" (p. 25). For some time a hope (which later on was to seem incomprehensible) of a national renewal built upon the ruins of the discredited democracy was widespread among the Left. These illusions were not long-lasting, however, and were soon replaced by another, and even shorter-lived, illusion of French society working in unity, after the war, for progress and social justice. The glory of the Soviet Union's huge war effort contributed enormously, of course, to the strength of French communism. To non-communist Leftists like Sartre, "Revolution" became a "categorical imperative," an "*a priori* existential requirement," Judt says, but it was an empty slogan, void of content and not supported by any analysis. The Liberation soon brought bitter disappointment, and the Resistance was inevitably transformed into a legend. Enormously inflated stories about the recent heroic past were naturally welcome; no one wanted to talk about the mass collaboration with the Nazis. It took many years before some people dared speak the truth – a truth known to everyone but conveniently forgotten. It was now anti-Americanism which offered itself as a natural continuation of the anti-Nazi resistance and which was warmly embraced by many intellectuals as a place for safe and comfortable heroism.

A digression is in order here. People who, like the present author, lived through the German occupation in Poland, later read French memoirs of the war years that seemed to describe a fairy-tale world. The French during the war continued to attend theaters, published without inhibition books and journals censored by the Germans, and gave each other literary prizes; high schools and universities functioned. Life was poorer, to be sure, but its continuity was not broken.

After the War, those who had been Pétainists for only a short time were busy condemning, with sanctimonious fury, those who left Marshal Pétain somewhat later. (There were, of course, cases of obviously horrible collaboration; but even Brasilliach, Judt says, was ultimately sentenced to death for his revolting opinions.)

Everything in French intellectual life, both during and after the war, was clouded in ambiguities. This is no doubt true of many political circumstances, but rarely has such ambiguity been used as a philosophical instrument to justify particular political choices. Merleau-Ponty, the great analyst of ambiguity, managed to avoid the worst, and those who, amid political ambiguities, preserved their lucidity and decency, like François Mauriac and Raymond Aron, were able to do so because they both clung to the simple distinction between good and evil (as opposed to the distinction between the politically "correct" and "incorrect"). Sartre did much to make this distinction meaningless. The case of Mounier's group and its self-inflicted blindness was perhaps more disturbing because of their Christian credentials. They declared that there was no point in condemning the "excesses" of Stalinism because democracy is not innocent either, or they went so far as to actually approve judicial-political murders in Eastern Europe as necessary costs on the path to the kingdom of justice.

Unlike communists, who simply denied everything that was known about the monstrosities of "really existing socialism" (the term was not yet in circulation), Leftist fellow-travelers admitted the facts to some extent, but justified them by appealing to the historical meaning of Stalinism, including its worst aspects. They assured their readers that socialism was growing despite "certain excesses." Some vilified the victims of show-trials, while others reflected sadly on the damage such trials inflicted on the reputation of socialist countries. But even those who were clearly uncomfortable with this display of cruelty still believed that there was no other option but to support communism in the East and its Western outposts. (Anti-Semitism, so prominent in the last period of Stalinism in the Soviet Union and Czechoslovakia, was not mentioned at all; but Israel was viciously attacked as a tool of imperialism.) Whatever the rulers of communist countries did, they were on the Left and thus they were friends. Moral indignation was reserved for Spain or colonized Algeria, that is to say, for crimes supposedly perpetrated by "capitalism" as such. At best some (albeit few) Leftists condemned the atrocities of communism because in their view it was no longer communism but the same old capitalism restored. Thus defensive strategies varied among intellectuals, but there was always a way of defending and glorifying the "land of the great lie" (the title of Ciliga's book) if the will to believe was there. Communism proved extraordinarily successful in instilling in intellectuals the belief in the necessity of global and indivisible choices: either you opt for socialism and justice, in which case you must support the Soviet Union unconditionally, or you take the side of capitalist exploiters and oppressors. Today it seems incredible that this primitive and mendacious view of the world could have been so easily swallowed by so many people who took pride in their sophisticated philosophical education, and had indeed been educated at the École Normale or the Sorbonne.

It is pointless, however, to lament human blindness or wickedness (whichever word is more appropriate in any given case). The history of intellectuals who flattered despots is a long one, and it was well known before communism appeared; but the comparatively massive support intellectuals gave to the communist tyranny requires a more specific explanation. Naturally, aspects of human character and various cultural issues played a role: hatred of the bourgeois milieu, which was, for the great majority of French intellectuals, their own; latent national pride and envy, expressed in a rabid anti-Americanism; the belief (not entirely irrational) in the imminent victory of communism in Europe and the need to make sure one was on the winning side; all forms of ideological blindness; the cult of strength and violence, so common among intellectuals who were political leaders *manqués*; the genuine desire, however misguided in its practical expression, to support the cause of the exploited. But there always remains something still to be explained. The Leftism of the 1940s and 1950s was an appendix, wrapped in the specific language of French culture (and perhaps expressing the West's suicidal impulse), to the world-wide phenomenon of communism. And communism cannot be explained away by the base intentions of individuals. Despite all that we know about it, it still awaits an explanation in historical terms. The Bolshevik revolution may have been – and I believe it was – an accident, but the fact that it established itself and began to spread like cancerous tissue is still intriguing. The anthology of all the absurdities ever uttered by Sartre or Mounier[3] seems endless; one reads it today with mingled horror and amusement. Judt, in the last chapters of his book, depicts very well the peculiar French intellectual tradition against the background of the grotesque Leftist phraseology. He is less convinc-

---

3 See, for example, his *Communisme, Anarchie et Pérsonnalisme*, 1966. Editor's note.

ing in insisting that this tradition, whether or not accompanied by Marxism, is still very much alive; he seems to display a certain anti-French bias here. One cannot blame him for not attempting to explain the entire phenomenon of communism. Perhaps it is too early.

Genocide and Ideology[1]

The Holocaust can be viewed from different perspectives: as the bloodiest chapter in the extraordinary history of the people of Israel or as an aspect of twentieth-century nationalism and totalitarianism. My remarks deal with the latter. I have nothing new to say about the history of the Holocaust, and I am not going to discuss the relevance of the massacre of Jews to the present state of the "Jewish question," in particular to the situation of the state of Israel. I do not deny the validity of such reflection, of course; on the contrary, this is probably almost the last moment when such questions can be discussed within the framework of living memory, and not as a matter of scholarly inquiry. In ten or fifteen years the world will be ruled by people for whom the Second World War will be a closed chapter of the past; the link between these events and the existence of the state of Israel will be forgotten, and political decisions will no longer be in the hands of people who were witnesses to or victims of the atrocities of those years. But that is not my subject on this occasion.

A short self-introduction is not out of place in discussing a topic which can hardly be treated in a strictly scholarly and dispassionate manner. I am not a Jew or of Jewish origin myself. I spent the war in Nazi-occupied Poland as a boy, from the age of twelve to seventeen. I lived in various places, including Warsaw. I remember the destruction of the Warsaw Ghetto, which I saw from outside; I lived among Poles who were active in helping Jews and who risked their lives every day trying to save those few who could be saved from the inferno. Most of the time

1 Originally a lecture delivered at the University of Seattle in November 1978, on the fortieth anniversary of Kristallnacht, and sponsored by the Institute for the Study of Contemporary Social Problems. Reprinted from *Western Society after the Holocaust*, edited by Lyman H. Letgers (Boulder, Colo.: Westview Press, 1983).

I lived with Jews who were hiding from their hangmen. As you know, about 6 million Polish citizens perished in the genocide, about half of them Jews or Poles of Jewish descent. I, as well as everyone I knew in this period, had and still have a clear sense of a community of victims, and I admit that our memory does impose a bias on our analysis of these events.

We sometimes wonder what it was that was so horrifyingly new in the massacre of European Jews in the Second World War. Genocide is clearly not an invention of the twentieth century, let alone of the Nazis, aside from the more efficient technique they developed of killing people and of transporting them to slaughter. Neither is ideological genocide, by which I mean mass extermination that the exterminators justify not simply by their need to have more room for themselves or to enrich themselves, but by an elaborate "philosophy," implying that the victims *deserve* annihilation for metaphysical, historical, or moral reasons. As far as I know, the mass slaughter of Anatolian Armenians during the First World War was not supported by any ideological considerations; neither were the massacres of Indians in North America. In the history of European conquest in South America in the sixteenth and seventeenth centuries, we might occasionally find a kind of "philosophical" argument for slaughter, to the effect that Indians were not properly human beings endowed with souls; yet this theory (soon denied by the Church) was seldom referred to, and even if adopted it did not provide a reason for mass killing. It could only yield the conclusion that in moral terms killing was indifferent. On the whole it seems that these massacres were not ideological and that the killers did not bother much about constructing theories to lend their actions legitimacy. They were after wealth and power; they knew what these were. At best, the total "otherness" of their victims in terms of religion and culture helped the conquerors to overcome any inhibitions they may have had. The same may be said of most of the atrocities committed throughout the early stages of colonization, whether or not they deserved the label of "genocide" (a word which is obviously impossible to define with perfect precision[2]).

But Nazis cannot claim to have been the inventors of ideological genocide either. Mass extermination in religious wars of the past falls into this category, no matter what other reasons – more or less sophisticated than the victims' incorrect opinions about divine grace and the Holy Trinity – were invoked. The massacre of the Cathars in Southern France at the beginning of the thirteenth century might deserve the name of ideological genocide. But heretics had a choice, at least theoretically:

---

2 On the definition of genocide, see V.N. Dadrian, "A Typology of Genocide," *International Review of Sociology* 2 (1975).

they could have converted to the orthodox doctrine, repented and renounced their errors. The Jews had no such option. Jewishness being hereditary, one could not (according to the doctrine) get rid of it; one was incurably corrupted and irrevocably condemned. Of the two components of the Nazi ideology which are relevant to this discussion – the innate superiority of the Germans and the intrinsic and incurable evil of Jewishness – neither was new.

We know of various attempts to trace the origin of this ideology back to German Romanticism, or even further back. Thomas Mann and George Lukács may be mentioned in this context or, in America, Peter Viereck. Even more effort has been devoted to explaining the historical background of the phenomenon of Nazism in terms of the economic, social, and emotional conditions in Germany after World War I. Some authors, mostly former Marxists, went further in philosophico-historical explanations and tended to the view that Nazism, far from being a monstrous accident, was a typical symptom of a general totalitarian trend, of which the Soviet system was another striking example, and that both announced a new political formation which, cruel and inhuman as it might be, was a natural product of tremendous changes in technological development. This gloomy outlook may be found in the writings of Bruno Rizzi, Friedrich Pollock, and James Burnham. To them the specific Nazi ideology seemed of little importance; the general economic and political features of the new order being, as it were, fatefully preordained in the very nature of recent technical development, it *was* a matter of chance, or of contingent local tradition, which ideological shape the system would take in a given country – communist in Russia or Nazi in Germany. The particular ideology itself had no more than an instrumental function in mobilizing the resources for tasks which, however burdensome, were imposed by history.

We may set aside this last problem and state generally that, fortunately, there are no compelling reasons to accept this sinister prophecy: no grounds for believing that irresistible historical forces lead the world unavoidably to a totalitarian order. We may admit that some aspects of technological change seem to favor such a development (e.g., the increasing shift of important decisions to central powers), but others counteract it (e.g., the technological and economic inefficiency of totalitarianism), and it would be presumptuous to maintain that we can predict the outcome of the clash between these opposite tendencies on the global scale.

However convincing the explanations of Nazism in terms of economic and cultural history might be, it is difficult to resist the impression that there was something demonically new in this ideology, and that its temporary success was to a large extent owing to the personal contribution of Hitler himself (and, of course, of Rosenberg). His creativity should not be underestimated or reduced to a simple expression of preexisting trends that merely produced him as their necessary instrument. It might well have been the case that the militarization of the German economy was a solution to the country's problems, and that an official pseudo-religion involving worship of the state and dreams of power were likely to emerge as an auxiliary device. But the specificity of Nazi ideology is not properly accounted for by such considerations. This is owing perhaps to the natural reluctance of the human mind to admit that crucial historical events, events which changed the course of world affairs, were produced by mere chance and by a series of unpredictable coincidences, not by an intelligible sequence of necessities. And although it might be true that the result of the First World War made a second one very likely, possibly even inevitable, there was no preordained necessity in the rise and the victory of Nazism – nor, for that matter, in the fact that the Third Reich ultimately lost the war. Nazism was a creation of the human mind, not of impersonal historical forces, and its doctrine was not a fortuitous and passive instrument in the achievement of goals that were ready-made independently of this doctrine. However miserable intellectually and however abominable morally, the Nazi ideology was real not only in the sense that people actually believed in it, but also in the sense that it effectively influenced its leaders' behavior as an independent variable.

This is particularly true in the case of anti-Semitism. It has been repeatedly pointed out by historians that the extermination of Jews in the last phase of the War was actually harmful to the Reich in terms of warfare, since the *Endlösung* required huge transportation resources that were badly needed for military purposes, and Jewish slave labor could usefully have been employed. Nonetheless, it continued, for ideological reasons. Nazi anti-Semitism was ideologically supported not only by specific accusations like those found in traditional Christian anti-Semitism. Essentially, the Jews were guilty of being Jews and therefore doomed to destruction. They were the embodiment of evil and simultaneously an abstract symbol of evil: whatever was touched by Jewishness was evil, and, conversely, whatever was evil seemed to be of Jewish origin. Plutocracy, communism, liberalism, pacifism, liberalism, avant-garde art, and the theory of relativity – all these were Jewish. The Holocaust was not only a cunning way of achieving objectives that were set up independently of it; it was a goal in itself, an act of great historical justice, a definitive victory over evil.

In this context I would like to call attention to a book published in Poland under the title *Conversations with a Hangman*. The author, Kazimierz Moczarski, was an officer of the Polish Underground Army fighting against the Nazi occupation. He was also involved in organizing help for the Warsaw ghetto fighters before and during the 1943 uprising. Like many soldiers who had fought in the non-communist anti-German underground, he was imprisoned after the war by the Polish communist authorities, savagely tortured, and eventually sentenced to death. He was not executed, however, and was released in the late 1950s. During his ordeal in prison he spent nine months in one cell with SS Gruppenführer Jurgen Stroop, the hangman of the Warsaw ghetto. (Stroop himself was subsequently sentenced to death by a Polish court and executed in 1952.) After his release Moczarski wrote this fascinating book relating his long conversations with the Nazi criminal in a Warsaw prison. It is perhaps a unique document, the best portrait we have of a genuine Nazi who persisted to the end in his macabre creed: he believed that the reason the Nazis had lost the war was that they had been *too good*, not resolute enough in uprooting all the poisonous tendencies in Germany.

It is in this sense that the Nazi genocide may have been an ideological genocide of a new kind. But it leads us nowhere to say that this ideology was a product of madness or of paranoia. There are no paranoiac states or mass movements, and the Nazi doctrine, though perhaps exceptional in its open barbarity, was not at all exceptional in the degree to which it outraged reason.

We now come to the main question I am purporting to discuss: what is the legacy of Nazi ideology in today's world? What changes in the contemporary clash of ideas may be reasonably attributed to the record and outcome of National Socialism?

In discussing this I would dismiss the marginal phenomena of contemporary Nazism in the literal sense. The small groups of fanatics here and there who still use the Nazi symbols and the phraseology of Hitler's Germany seem to me unimportant; hideous as they are, they have no future and no more role to play, and the amount of attention they attract in the press is disproportionate. The very fact that they use Nazi symbols reveals their hopeless position. Indeed, I believe that what remains of the Nazi heritage is not any direct or even indirect continuation of this ideology, but rather certain transformations which, as a result of the collapse of Nazism, have occurred in the postwar ideological struggle as a whole.

A remarkable aspect of Nazism was its overtness. It had very few elements of a mendacious façade. It displayed its goals openly and uttered them aloud: to erect a German superstate, to destroy the Jews, and to transform Poles and other Slavs into slaves after exterminating their educated classes[3] and thus annihilating their culture. This program

3 The extermination of the Polish educated classes was part of the

was put into effect, and its executors in the army, the SS, police, and the Party scarcely needed what is called "false consciousness": they did what the ideology explicitly expected them to do, however ridiculous the justifications of this ideology as a race theory may have been.

Though the physical extermination of Jews was not explicitly required in *Mein Kampf* or in other representative ideological documents, the implications were perfectly clear, as we know. In *Mein Kampf* Hitler states "merely" that the Jews are devils, pernicious bacilli, a plague, vampires, parasites, and irredeemable enemies of the human race; that they hate all culture and try to destroy everything sublime and beautiful; and that "the Jews' instinct toward world domination" will die out only with them.[4]

In a speech in the Reichstag a few months before the beginning of the war (January 30, 1939), Hitler announced that if the Jews succeeded in provoking a war the outcome would be the annihilation of their entire race.[5] There was nothing equivocal in pronouncements of this kind, and yet they were not taken at face value at the time, or even later, when the massacre was already in progress: the reports from the Polish Underground were simply not believed in the West, so that in Western countries, in spite of the information available, hardly anyone had a clear idea, before the end of war, of what was in fact going on under the Nazi occupation. And it was only much later that people started asking themselves why Hitler's threats had not been taken seriously.

The importance of this aspect of Nazism is brought into relief when it is confronted, as it often has been, with another ideology of a totalitarian state: with communism in its Stalinist period. Although analogies of this kind can often be convincing, one difference between Nazism and Stalinism is neither negligible nor secondary: in contrast to Nazism, Stalinism was all façade. It exploited – quite successfully – all the ideological instruments of the socialist, humanist, internationalist, universalist tradition. It never preached conquest, only liberation from oppression; it never extolled the state as a value in itself, only stressed the necessity of reinforcing the state as an indispensable lever to destroy the enemies of freedom; and it promised, in conformity with Marxist doctrine, the abolition of the state in the perfect world of communism. It

---

"Ausserordentliche Befriedungsaktion und Sonderaktion Krakau" led by H. Frank. As a result of these "actions" about 700 university professors, 16,500 school teachers, 5,000 medical doctors, and over 5,000 lawyers, politicians, priests, and men of letters were executed. Editor's note.
4   *Mein Kampf*, English translation (London, 1939), p. 539.
5   *The Speeches of Adolf Hitler*, edited by N.M. Baynes, Vol. 1 (London, 1942), p. 741.

preached equality, democracy, self-determination for all nations, brotherhood, and peace.

The presence or the absence of a powerful ideological façade may have been responsible for both the strengths and the weaknesses of each of these two orders. The fact that Stalinism was able to present itself as the legitimate heir of socialist dreams and values, as the embodiment of the old revolutionary humanism, was clearly its strength. Thanks to the skillful manipulation of words it was able – even when its oppressive and terrorist aspects were at their peak – to attract a large number of intellectuals and thus to enhance its world-wide influence. The fact that thousands of outstanding minds fell prey to Stalinist delusions and joined the cause of communism in good faith (whether briefly or for a long time) cannot be dismissed with melancholy comments on human naiveté; it deserves attention as the most striking example of the power of ideology in our century. But that same power was vulnerable to internal dangers which were bound to become manifest in due course. Those who took the façade seriously – as very many did – and assimilated the art of seeing all events and facts, however inconsistent with the proclamations of the system, through the glass of ideology so that they were able to condone the horrors of Stalinism, sooner or later were caught up by the independent force of their beliefs and finally had to confront the doctrine with the reality. Time and again, in people's minds, the façade tore itself away from the reality, took on a sort of autonomous life, and was turned against the reality. Time and again, communists used communist phraseology to attack the communist system. So it might be said that the ideology, mendacious though it was, carried the germs of its own self-destruction, and that communism, thanks to its ideological contradictions, was capable of producing its own critics.

Not so with Nazism. The high degree of convergence between its real and its avowed aspirations made it stronger in one sense and weaker in another – at least so it seems in retrospect. Because of its self-confessed genocidal ideology it had no chance of becoming an intellectual movement of any size or of producing cultural achievements of any value. Though it is true that the resistance of intellectuals to Nazism was astonishingly poor in Germany, their active involvement in building the new culture was very poor as well. In contrast to communism, which for a certain period proved fruitful in various domains of culture,[6] Nazism was entirely sterile. It turned out to be pure cultural vandalism. In literature, art, or philosophy it brought nothing but devastation, and what it left can today be counted as nothing but the decline of the human spirit.

It succeeded in attracting very few outstanding intellectuals, and the

---

6   I discuss this issue in my "Communism as a Cultural Force," included in this volume.

most famous of them, Martin Heidegger, adhered to the ideology for barely one year. Here was nothing remotely comparable to the ideological prowess of communism. And it naturally selected people according to "characterological" criteria much different from those typical of communism when it was alive as a faith; the only virtues it was capable of mastering and of attracting were of a military nature: *Blut und Ehre*. On the other hand this spiritual poverty and the relative lack of a false façade was not without its advantages. It prevented Nazism, except for a few episodes at the beginning, from ideological splits: Nazism produced few heretics and seldom nurtured the germs of its own ideological dissolution.

It seems clear that the downfall of Nazism and its all-but-unanimous condemnation throughout the world greatly contributed to an important shift in the ideological aspect of postwar political struggles, and that we are still witnessing the impact of those events, including the way "the Jewish problem" is approached and anti-Semitism articulated. This seems to me to be common sense, though I admit that it would be difficult to prove – as in all cases where we try to grasp the meaning and the causes of large-scale social phenomena. It is arguable that racial and national hatred in all parts of the world is more powerful and more threatening than it was before the Second World War, and that anti-Semitism is in quite good health. So is the cult of, and the need for, a "strong state." But this is probably not because of the continuing impact of Nazi ideology. On the contrary, this ideology, or rather the fact that it has been discredited, changed the way such hatreds and aspirations are expressed.

There are surely multiple reasons for the general growth of nationalism and for its particular form as state nationalism. Among them are the enormous growth of the economic role of the state under various political regimes and, at the same time, the emergence of a large number of new states with no tradition and no remotely homogeneous ethnic or cultural background. Alongside the nationalism of distinctive ethnic groups which affirm their right to build states of their own, we see the phenomenon of nationalism without a nation, or nationalism focused on a state that has no ethnic unity. But it is worth noting that national movements and political bodies, including those that accept the label of "nationalism," almost never phrase their grievances and claims in terms of a nation's right to dominate other people; they do not talk of natural superiority, of *Lebensraum*, and the like. Not only are all national aspirations expressed in terms of an indisputable right to self-determination or of the right to regain possession of lost territories, but the very idea of conflict with another nation is very carefully avoided. Mussolini and Hitler were not afraid of revealing their imperial goals; they did not hesitate to admit that they were pursuing a policy of conquest, as they considered themselves entitled and called to do by virtue of the natural superiority of their peoples or by the laws of history. Hardly anyone does this today. Nationalist ideologies that expressly condemn the idea of human rights and praise war as the seminary of the highest human values, that preach the inequality of men, appeal to instincts that go against reason, and scoff at the concept of justice, are marginal phenomena in political life. (Mao Tse Tung was an exception in explicitly dismissing the concept of human rights.) Racial and national hatred, imperial aspirations, and totalitarian regimes and movements flourish under the cover of humanitarian, pacifist, and internationalist slogans. The concepts of national sovereignty, progress, and justice turned out to be useful in justifying all manner of internal repression and expansionist policies, including cases of what may properly be called genocide in postwar history (like the massacre of communists in Indonesia and the recent mass slaughter in Cambodia).

This applies to anti-Semitism as well. The patterns of anti-Semitism clearly changed after the horrors of Nazism. Explicitly anti-Jewish right-wing movements and ideologies, although they exist, are feeble and marginal. And apart from them, the concept of anti-Zionism is quite sufficient to absorb most of the traditional anti-Semitism. Of course, it would be very unfair to say that all those who oppose Zionism are anti-Semites. After all, there are Jews who are opposed to Zionism on political or religious grounds: old socialists who on principle reject all political ideas and movements based on national sentiments, and religious Jews who believe that Judaism is essentially a religious, not a political, idea. But while it is manifestly untrue that all anti-Zionists are anti-Semites, it is true, on the other hand, that virtually all anti-Semites call themselves anti-Zionists; one very seldom comes across people who define themselves as hostile to Jews as such, or who openly advocate their destruction. This has contributed to the erosion of the inherited political patterns and divisions.

Before the war Zionism in Europe was opposed most strongly by segments of the Jewish socialist movement; in various countries anti-Semites rather favored the emigration of the Jews they wanted to get rid of. Today anti-Semitism has found a comfortable outlet in the form of anti-Zionism, and the latter has been adopted in the West both by communists and by various leftist sects. Thus a good deal of the anti-Semitic tradition is on the side of the political spectrum that calls itself the Left. Again, it may not follow that all leftist anti-Zionists are in fact anti-Semites, but to be an anti-Semite and to call oneself an anti-Zionist today will very likely mean being on the side of progress, freedom, equality, and universal human happiness. Government-sponsored anti-Semitism – called anti-Zionism, of course, yet very poorly disguised – reappeared endemically throughout postwar history in European communist countries (in the Soviet Union, Poland, Czechoslovakia, and Romania). It has been particularly virulent in the Soviet Union, and it led to the remarkable situation where being a Jew is compulsory and forbidden at the same time. It is compulsory in that if you had Jewish ancestors you have no right to define yourself as a Russian or a Ukrainian, and Jewish nationality is written in your internal passport by the police authorities whether you like it or not. And it is forbidden in that Jews have no right to cultivate their separate cultural tradition even in the miserably limited form allowed to other nationalities. In Poland the official Soviet anti-Semitism of the last years of Stalin's rule (the campaign against so-called "cosmopolitans") was not followed on any significant scale, but in the turbulent years 1956–57 some factions in the ruling party started exploiting anti-Semitic slogans for their own purposes. But the great anti-Semitic campaign was launched by the party leadership in 1967, after the Six-Day War, and again it had a background in the conflict of party cliques vying for power. Given the intensity and the omnipresence of anti-Semitic propaganda for quite a long period, the results must have appeared disappointing to its organizers, though the poison certainly was not harmless.

It may be said that, on the whole, the ideological effects of the Holocaust were not the same in East European communist countries as they were in the West. In Poland, where a good deal of the slaughter during the war actually took place, the Holocaust is mentioned in such a way as to efface or disregard the special character of what happened to the Jews. This was not the case in the first years after the war: then the Holocaust was discussed and depicted in many memoirs, novels, books, and films. In recent years, however, official propaganda, while devoting a lot of effort to keeping the memory of Nazi atrocities alive, has stressed the universal character of genocide and – except for a few special and politically motivated occasions – avoided recalling the massacre of the Jews as a separate and unique story. The same rule is much more consistently and thoroughly observed in the Soviet Union, where specific references to Jews are hardly ever made when the horrors of war are mentioned. The general tendency is to induce people to forget that there was anything special about Jews in Nazi genocidal policy. It is true, of course, that millions of Poles and Russians were victims of the genocide, yet it is also true that the case of Jews was special, and the deliberate refusal to mention it is only one of many examples of how the history of the last war is being falsified in the official communist version.

Meanwhile, popular anti-Semitism in the Soviet Union, unceasingly encouraged and reinforced by state propaganda, displays features very similar to traditional anti-Semitic prejudices that can be traced back to the destruction of the second temple. Party leaders are paid back for their anti-Semitism with the familiar accusation that they are Jews themselves and that communist rule is in fact the oppression of the Russian people by the Jews. This tendency can be noticed to a certain extent in some factions of the Soviet nationalist underground movement, and it is expressed in the accusation that the Bolshevik revolution was in fact the work of foreigners – Poles, Georgians, Latvians, and above all Jews. Thus the same patterns we know from the history of socialist anti-Semitism (Jews identified as bankers, usurers, and capitalists, socialist ideas mixed with anti-Jewish stereotypes) return in popular discontent against the communist system: this time the communist power is identified with Jewishness. This characteristically incoherent search for national innocence recurs time and again. In Poland, during the anti-Semitic campaign of 1968, the Jews were accused simultaneously of undermining Soviet-Polish friendship and of having been responsible for the atrocities of Stalinism.

How is this deliberate verbal confusion, together with the impressive growth of Orwellian language and the above-noted changes in patterns of ideological struggle, to be assessed? Are racist and chauvinist tendencies more threatening or less once they are wrapped in universalist, humanitarian, and pacifist phraseology? Do political slogans purposely designed to arouse national and racial hatred, anti-Semitism in particular, carry more or less danger when they are so transformed? This question may be put in a general way: is it as a whole better or worse if hatred is called love, slavery freedom, oppression equality?

The answer is not obvious. On the one hand, racism and anti-Semitism seem to be more vulnerable when they appear in full light, as in the Nazi movement, and better protected if their expressive forms are elusive and embellished with humanist ornaments. But the question can also be looked at from another angle. More hypocrisy in ideological expression generally displays more respect for those universalist values and thus attests to their increasing recognition. If movements more or less similar to Nazism cannot now openly employ the same ideology, this bears witness to the fact that the downfall of Nazism was more than military.

So it is not at all clear what sort of practical morals we can draw from the frightening experience of Nazism forty years later, and what is now the real meaning of the slogan "never again" which resounded throughout all Europe after the fall of Hitler's Reich. Given the lavish use of political mimicry, and the trivial truth that history never repeats itself, the question of how we are to identify political and ideological phenomena which carry dangers similar to Nazism is bound to be controversial. The word "fascism" has become a word of abuse devoid of content: who is not occasionally called "fascist" by political enemies? Consequently the lessons we should learn from the Holocaust are by no means easy to set forth, though at first glance the opposite seems to be the case. Should we be wary of people wearing the swastika and worshiping Hitler? They are pathetic remnants of the past. Should we be alert to anti-Semitism? Yet anti-Semitism articulated as such is a marginal phenomenon, and anti-Zionism gives a respectable abode to the non-articulated kind. And it would be exaggerated to say that the Ku Klux Klan poses an enormous threat to humanity. Should we point out the perils of nationalism? But all of us, depending on our political allegiances, sympathize with some national movements and despise others. Throughout the world, ideologies and parties which define themselves as "left" support nationalist movements and label them as "progressive," even the most extreme of them, if on an international plane they happen to be damaging to the United States, to any Western European country, or to Israel.

Thus there seem, regrettably, to be few clear and practical lessons we could learn from the history of Nazism – except, of course, the general recognition of democratic values and of human rights. Yet for this purpose the negative material we can collect from recent history is also only too abundant.

The Third Reich was an exquisite example of the ideological state, i.e., of a state supposed to be ruled by one *Weltanschauung*, the truth of which was guaranteed by the higher wisdom of those in a privileged cognitive position. Nazi philosophers were entirely right in terms of their doctrine when they concentrated their attacks on Descartes and the skeptical tradition.[7] What they wanted to destroy was the belief in universal standards of cognition and the universal character of truth. Nazism had an "epistemology" of its own, primitive though it may have been. It was based precisely on the abolition of universal criteria of truth and on the belief that some segments of mankind – the supreme race and its leaders – have a deeper insight which no arguments based on ordinary logical criteria could invalidate. The claim that absolute knowledge is stored in the better part of mankind and immune to the scrutiny of universal criteria of rationality – a claim that can justify anything – is obviously a prescription for despotism, no matter how this privileged part is identified – in racial, political, religious, or class terms. And the

---

7   See S. Tyrowicz, *Swiatlo wiedzy zdeprawowanej: Idee niemieckiej socjologii i filozofii 1933–1945*. (*The Light of Corrupted Knowledge: German Sociology and Philosophy 1933–1945*, Poznan, 1970.)

reason Nazism was so shocking in the Western world was not that such claims had been made – they were not unusual, after all – but that they were applied with such consistency, in the very center of Europe, in a country which in terms of technical, scientific, and cultural achievements belonged to the most advanced part of civilization.

For years people kept repeating the same question: how was it possible that the same cultural setting which produced Thomas Mann and Einstein also produced Himmlers and Eichmanns? The shock came not just from Nazi atrocities but, more specifically, from the fact that they seemed to have emerged from the same civilization we all belonged to, which suggested that there was something essentially sick in the very foundation of this civilization. Marxists tried to argue that Nazism was a natural and inevitable product of capitalism – not a particularly strong claim when confronted with the liberating potential of Stalinism and with the fact that democratic institutions are so strongly and clearly connected with the market economy. Catholics, in their turn, devolved the main responsibility on the atheism of the National Socialist philosophy and argued that an attempt to forget God could not have failed to yield such results – again, a doubtful argument, considering that a clear positive correlation between a society's religious fervor and its respect for democratic values is by no means a well-proven sociological fact, to say the least. If it were so, some theocratic states of the past, or contemporary traditional Islamic states, should be models of democracy. Catholic critics are right, however, in pointing out that the cult of a nation, or of a state, or of a nation-state, as a supreme and absolute value carries a powerful totalitarian potential and, if consistently upheld, provides the justification for all imaginable violations of individual rights, including genocide if needed.

Many great Germans of the past were occasionally singled out as spiritual ancestors of Nazism, including Hegel, Fichte, and Luther; and Lukács seemed to believe (in *Die Zerstorung der Vernuft*) that all of German philosophy from Schelling onwards, with the sole exception of Marxism, had been, as it were, teleologically propelled by an urge to pave the way for Hitler.

There is, however, something artificial in reconstructing such pedigrees. It seems safe to say that no ideology, and certainly no ideology with all-embracing claims, is immune to the danger of being used as an instrument of oppression and slavery, and this includes religious systems, socialist and anarchist ideals, national doctrines, and all sorts of high-minded utopias. To be sure, some are better adapted to such use and some less so, and Nazism was obviously unusual in this respect. Yet if we judge various world views by their ostensible content alone, few seem less suited than Christianity to serve oppressive purposes, and yet

Christianity turned out to be quite serviceable when needed. Evil can catch hold of any ideology, no matter how well designed, and turn it into its tool. Except for the virtue of tolerance, there are hardly any values which by force of their content, intrinsically, could not be employed for evil purposes, and the virtue of tolerance itself has been repeatedly attacked for protecting evil and lies from destruction and thus for being self-defeating. This is, as we know, a matter of persistent controversy: should tolerance be extended to people preaching and practicing intolerance, in particular to racist and totalitarian movements? This is a question of the best strategy for defending democratic values, the absolute strategy – i.e., one that involves no cost – being impossible here or anywhere else. To suppress intolerant movements and ideas for the sake of tolerance is self-defeating, and not to suppress them is also self-defeating; this simply amounts to saying that as long as movements against tolerance exist, their very existence makes a state of perfect tolerance impossible – an apparently tautological assertion. A democratic order enjoying strong support and functioning with reasonable efficiency can survive while allowing intolerant movements, however abominable, to express themselves; the idea that it must stifle freedom of speech in order to maintain it can easily be expanded into a more general theory stating that we have to establish tyranny in order to prevent a tyranny from being established. After all, the saying "we shall know freedom once more only when we have destroyed the foes of freedom"[8] is actually a quotation from Hitler.

Yet to tolerate totalitarian movements within a democratic society means just that: to tolerate them, and nothing more; it does not, or at least ought not to, imply that public institutions should treat them in the same way they treat movements and ideas within the democratic spectrum. In other words, a constitution which is committed to defending democratic values cannot at the same time pretend, without self-contradiction, to be indifferent to these values: it cannot treat ideologies and activities committed to their destruction on a par with all others. This is admittedly easier to state as a general rule than to convert into practical measures that would be sheltered from abuses. Nevertheless the self-protection of democracy is simply abandoned if its enemies enjoy the same kind of respect as its defenders. And if, on the other hand, totalitarian or racist movements are powerful enough to tear apart the legal fabric of a democratic society, this does not prove that democratic principles have lost their validity or turned out to be inconsistent. What it does prove is either that democracy was incapable of mobilizing its resources to defend itself, or that in some circumstances consistent

---

8 *The Speeches of Adolf Hitler, op. cit.*, vol. 1, p. 8.

nationalism and jingoism have enormous totalitarian potential. Once national values are declared supreme, there are no rights of individuals that could be defended if they happen to clash, or even just appear to clash, with the ideal of a strong nation, and there are no limits to mendacity and repression. Nazism was the most splendidly consistent example of national values exalted as the source and the measure of all others.

This last moral might appear trivial, but if we take it seriously it is perhaps less trivial than it appears. It cannot teach us which side we should take in today's conflicts, but it does at least teach us what kind of ideas, however adorned with humanist phrases, we should treat with the utmost suspicion. The history of the Holocaust is equally important viewed from both sides: the suffering of the victims and the depravity of the hangmen. The intensity of evil may not have been unique or unparalleled in history, or, for that matter, in our century, yet its ideological justification was apparently unique. Those who reject the content of this ideology – and there are very few who do not – must not avoid a question that reaches beyond Nazi doctrine: to what extent are they ready to justify evil for the sake of ideological values of any sort? Those who believe that such limits cannot be defined or who simply refuse to define them are in the proper sense the spiritual heirs of Hitler.

The Devil in History[1]

Leszek Kolakowski in an Interview with George Urban

George Urban: My mental image of Leszek Kolakowski has two, as I see it, complementary faces: your attitude to Marxism, and your attitude to the Church. Let me try to approach your interpretation of Marxism indirectly, through some of the parables you have written about the Old and New Testament. What induced you as a young Communist philosopher to publish a book under the title *Conversations with the Devil*?[2]

Leszek Kolakowski: This book was not meant to be a political statement. It contains various cautionary tales, each taking its cue from some episode in Holy Scripture. In each, in one way or another, the Devil makes his appearance, but my stories were not designed to offer some philosophical equivalent of a *roman à clef*: My purpose was mainly to underline the significance of the awesome paradox whereby good results may flow from evil, and evil results from good. That these two can thus support each other is a shattering fact about human experience. But these problems may be discussed in terms broader than those offered by politics.

Urban: You may very well not have intended these parables to contain clues to your philosophical-political thinking, but for the critical reader they are, as I see it, indubitably there. It is a significant fact about your

1 This is a shortened version of the interview that was published in *Encounter* (January 1981); has been reprinted in *Stalin and Stalinism: Its Impact on History and the World*, George Urban, ed. (Cambridge: Harvard University Press, 1986).
2 *The Key to Heaven: Edifying Tales from Holy Scripture to Serve as Teaching and Warning, And Conversations with the Devil* (New York: Grove Press, 1972); a new edition reprinted as *Tales from the Kingdom of Lailonia and The Key to Heaven* (Chicago: The University of Chicago Press, 1991).

writings that you should be so much preoccupied by Scripture – *Conversations with the Devil* is a companion piece to your *The Key to Heaven*. And if I were asked to render a layman's reading of these cautionary tales I would say that your purpose is not only to lay bare the nature of evil, but to identify it in the framework of two "churches" – that of Christianity and that of Marxism-Leninism-Stalinism.

Kolakowski: I did not, as I say, intend to write political stories in disguise, though in some cases I probably did. However, I spent many years studying Christian sects and heresies, especially those of the sixteenth and seventeenth centuries, and one can't do that without observing certain analogies which occur in all ideological thinking and all bodies in which such thinking is enshrined. Nevertheless, I am ready to concede that, seen from our present perspective, one can see the analogies you have in mind.

Urban: Let me try to transfer your "awesome paradox" (whereby good can flow from evil and evil from good) from daily experience to our understanding of history. Where does "the devil," so to speak, enter history, or our understanding of it?

Kolakowski: It is part of Hegelian historio-philosophy that historical events turn the intentions of historical actors into their opposites, but this is, as I say, also our run-of-the-mill daily experience. Marx and Engels had much to say about this problem. Man, they contend, is – until the debut of a class-conscious proletariat – an object of history. He is not only unaware of the history he is making but simply cannot be aware of it because he finds himself in the grip of a "false consciousness" which is not just a mental fact, reversible by a mental cure, but has social roots: social processes of his own making appear to man as forces governed by superhuman powers. This grand design of the dialectic – the intentions of the makers of history being turned into the reversal of these intentions – produces certain "laws" of history. These apparently operate from the inception of the division of labor until the mid-nineteenth century, when the arrival of the proletariat on the world scene happily coincides with the arrival of Marx and Engels as revolutionary social thinkers. From then on the proletariat, enlightened by Marxist thinking, serves as the appointed vehicle of the revolutionary dénouement of history. False consciousness is eliminated. History is no longer marred by the law of reversed intentions. The proletariat, now gripped by true consciousness, can and does translate its will into the desired results. The riddle of history is solved, man's alienation is ended, and the world moves into the era of classless society. Such, in simple outline, is the Marxist mythology.

Urban: I can detect not one but two "devils" in your story. The first, as you have said, is the genuine problem of the frustration of human intentions, which is an experience we all share.

Kolakowski: Yes, but it is, I must stress this, a great evil which has preoccupied me all my life and induced me to spend time contemplating Hegel's and Marx's answers to it, with all the latter's prophetic anticipations. The second "devil" is the Marxist assumption that with the debut of the proletariat as a perfectly conscious historical class the whole burden of past experience can somehow be declared null and void, and mankind consequently embarks on writing an entirely new history, history par excellence. Marx put this very graphically when he observed that the coming revolutions will draw their poetry from the future, not the past. Hegel had trained the searchlight of his thinking exclusively on the past and explicitly repudiated extrapolations into the future. Marx's orientation, on the other hand, was not only futuristic, but he believed that it is with the hoped-for results of the future that we have to judge the past, too. This compounds the evil. Marx's view is deeply rooted in the Utopianism of August Cieszkowski and Moses Hess, and thus partly in Christian millenarianism and Jewish messianism. We can, I agree, say that there are two devils in my account: first, history's stubborn inclination to frustrate and reverse human ambition and, second, Marx's chimerical notion that the revolutionary movement of the world proletariat will somehow abolish all ideological, social and economic contradictions of past society and usher in the golden age. In other words, I believe that the frustration and reversal of human foresight is a basic fact about the human condition.

Urban: Which is one way of believing in Original Sin.

Kolakowski: And I am also convinced that the claim that there is a technique for overcoming this condition, or a privileged class to carry out this technique, is dangerous and misconceived.

Urban: Every despotism worth its salt claims to have (as you have just implied) a "hot line" to God or the future. Hence their demand that the despot's orders be taken on trust: *Der Führer befiehlt, wir folgen* – "Stalin-the-genius is always right" – and so on. You have observed in several of your essays that in any theodicy Divine Providence is vindicated in spite of the existence of palpable evil – this, indeed, is the meaning of theodicy: "God, to test the faithful, now and again delivered St. Peter's See into the hands of the ungodly," you write in *Marxism and Beyond*. "So much greater, then, the merit of the faithful if they bow their head and listen to the Divine Voice, even though it issues from the throat of Balaam's she-ass . . ." If this is so, and if we take (for the sake of argument) Marxism as a substitute religion with claims similar to those of the genuine article, might a Communist not cogently reason that "the Law of History" or "Historical Necessity" sometimes delivers the leadership of the "workers' movement" into the hands of a Stalin? And might he not, further, insist that this, however, does not invalidate – but reinforce – his duty to subject himself to the orders of Stalin? Bukharin argued this kind of thing when he said (much to his later undoing): "It is not him [Stalin] we trust but the man in whom the Party has reposed its confidence."

Kolakowski: This has been the standard Communist argument. Time and again I have heard old Communists say: it is better to make mistakes with the Party than to be right against the Party. They were mostly blissfully unaware of any trace of a "theodicy" in their attitude and, from a strictly Communist point of view, there was undoubtedly something very sound in what they were saying. Without this dogged and Utopian loyalty to the cause in spite of its evils, the Communist movement would not have survived. Such attitudes now hardly exist. In Russia and Eastern Europe they expired with the last ideologically motivated Communists, though in the West one encounters freak survivals of the species. But while their commitment lasted, these men would not be shaken from their unquestioning allegiance – no mistakes, wrongs, and crimes of the Party could dent their conviction that the unity of even a guilty Party was a thousand times more important than frivolous considerations of "morality" and the like.

Urban: The existence of evil for a truly believing Christian reinforces his commitment to God, for if God were all-good in his earthly manifestations, a Christian's love of God would be a mere commercial transaction: returning love for love. But when he loves God through evil, his faith and loyalty have stood the supreme test. This is the sort of argument (echoing Luke 6:32) we repeatedly encounter in your writings, and I would, on the strength of it, take my analogy with Communism a step further by suggesting that a truly committed Communist loves Stalin, including Stalin's murderous deeds, because his faith in the cause, like the Christian's love of God, demands that he should will the means if he truly wills the ends. What I'm saying is that an unforgiving and unjust Party has a gruesome magnetism of its own.

Kolakowski: Your analogy is only partly valid. Christianity does not claim that God's justice will prevail in our life in this world, that merit will be rewarded and wrongdoing punished. It holds that God's ways are inscrutable, that we cannot comprehend them by intellectual cognition alone. Christianity teaches that we must trust God's justice in spite of manifest evil and wait for justice to be done on the Day of Judgment.

Communism, by contrast, claims to be offering a scientific and empirically verifiable explanation of the whole of reality. It is not a religion but a caricature of religion which incidentally confirms the theologians' observation that the Devil is an ape of God.

Whether a committed Communist has to love the wrongdoings of a Stalin on the analogy you suggest seems to me more open to question. Undoubtedly most fully loyal Communists approved of and even loved Stalin's misdeeds if they were at all ready to concede that these were misdeeds. But many preferred to believe that nothing may be called a misdeed as long as it arguably serves the good cause. In either case, the analogy stands to the extent that a caricature, too, is an image – albeit an overdrawn one – of reality.

Urban: You have argued in *Main Currents of Marxism* that Marx's theory that the proletariat possesses a special type of historical awareness – "cognitive privilege" – inevitably leads to the Stalinist kind of dictatorship. How does the first lead to the second?

Kolakowski: I did not say that it was inevitable, but that the Leninist version of Marxism, though not the only possible one, was quite plausible. Very briefly: Marx alleges that the working class carries, simply because it is the working class, a kind of privileged knowledge, "revolutionary consciousness," of the course of history (this interpretation of his words was – correctly, I believe – strongly argued by Lukács). But this cognitive privilege, while it may have existed as something much to be desired in the minds of Marx and Engels, has to this day failed to materialize in the minds of the workers. Lenin (and before him Kautsky) thought that this little practical difficulty could be overcome by adding a supplement to Marx's theory: since the proletariat was incapable of spontaneously generating "revolutionary consciousness," it had to be instilled from without. This was to be done by the "vanguard" of the proletariat, the Communist party; and the Party – now sole repository of the true purpose of history – is vested with the right, indeed the duty, to discard the immature, empirical consciousness of the masses and lead them, through revolution, to the classless society. And Lenin added – which is an important point – that what the workers could produce of themselves was a bourgeois consciousness, since in a capitalist society only two basic forms of consciousness could exist.

The implication of this theory is that the Party knows better what lies in the genuine interests of society, and what constitutes the will of society, than society itself, and once the spirit of the Party is incarnated in the will of one man, Marxism-Leninism comes to mean the dictatorship of one man over the proletariat. Thus Marx's hypothesis that the working class has a privileged knowledge of the final purpose of history culminates in the assertion that Comrade Stalin is always right.

Urban: Wouldn't the theodicy, Marxist-style, in that case still apply? Suppose we equate the "Historical Mission" of the Proletariat, as conceived by Marx, with Divine Providence, and the despotism of Stalin with palpable evil – wouldn't Marx's vision (God's love) still be vindicated under the injunction: do what Stalin orders you to do because his sin is *felix culpa* in the service of a higher good? Repeatedly you stress in your books that a Christian loves God because he has faith, not because he expects to be rewarded. The act of believing is the whole justification of faith. The more God appears to be evil, the more the Christian reaffirms his faith in Him. Stalinism is then – I would infer by way of a parallel – a special manifestation of Marxism, and a believing Communist simply reaffirms his faith in Marx's vision by obeying and supporting Stalin.

Kolakowski: I must enter a correction. Christianity teaches that God can test the faithful by letting them suffer, but He cannot show Himself to be evil. And the analogy does not hold good for another reason: Stalinism is not an incidental evil which somehow superimposed itself on an otherwise benign vision. On the contrary: the tyranny of one man, the worship of a personalized ideology and the power-structure derived from it, is the perfect embodiment of the spirit of Communism. Stalin's rule is the rule of Communism *par excellence*. All other variants of Communism-in-power are half-baked, diluted, timorous, immature or senile by comparison. Since the death of Stalin, Soviet Communism has not been able to regain its health, though as far as the institutional framework is concerned, the legacy of Stalinism survives intact.

Urban: If the institutional incarnation is intact, why could Stalinism not survive Stalin?

Kolakowski: Because, under Stalin, the police-terror, the purges and massacres affected too many members of the apparat. That they affected the people at large would not have mattered, because the population as such is of no importance in the Soviet system, but the continuing insecurity of the apparat was intolerable. Nobody was safe. Members of the Central Committee and the heads of Stalin's various satrapies could be imprisoned and executed with as little fuss and on as little evidence as the man in the street. When Stalin died, the Soviet establishment took care not to saddle itself with another dictator of the stamp of Stalin.

Urban: I am interested in tracing the development of your attitude to the totalitarian element in Marxism. Some twenty years before you wrote *Main Currents of Marxism* (i.e., in your revisionist phase as a Communist), you suggested in a number of different formulations that for any worthwhile social change to be achieved one's targets have to be set way beyond the hoped-for change because mankind is slow and ruled by inertia. Hence, you argued, Utopian social thinking should not surprise us – we have to aim for outsized objectives and employ the rhetoric of inflated hopes in order to achieve modest results. Indeed you repudiated the caution of commonsensical objectors: "an excess of common sense may be inimical to an effective fight."

If all this is true (and here, too, you reflect the words of the New Testament, e.g., Luke 12:31), where would you draw the line between idealism and blindness, enthusiasm and suicide? Couldn't Stalinism and any dictatorship that claims to be working for social change (and which does not?) draw on your reasoning to justify its existence?

Kolakowski: I would endorse this line of thought now only with very great reservations. I still insist that often it is only by aiming for what is now impossible that we are likely to attain the possible. But any social Utopia which purports to offer a technical blueprint for the perfect society now strikes me as pregnant with the most terrible dangers. I am not saying that the idea of human fraternity is ignoble, naïve or futile; and I don't think it would be desirable to discard it as belonging to an age of innocence. But to go to the lengths of imagining that we can design some plan for the whole of society whereby harmony, justice, and plenty are attained by human engineering is an invitation for despotism. I would, then, retain Utopia as an imaginative incentive ("regulative idea" would be the Kantian phrase for it) and confine it to that.

Urban: Your emphasis, in the late 1950s and early 1960s, that Utopia is necessary but also necessarily unattainable, marks an important point in your revisionism. To call the Communist blueprint "Utopian" and to add in the same breath that the labor of mountains will give birth to a small mouse was, it seems to me, your way of striking an uneasy compromise between approval and complete rejection of the Marxist vision.

Kolakowski: I suppose it was, but this is now a long way behind me. A society without conflict is a figment of the imagination. Evil is continuous throughout human experience. The point is not how to make one immune to it, but under what conditions one may identify and restrain the Devil. We are not faced with a choice between a perfect and imperfect society; our options are between one sort of imperfection and another. Yet, in order to realize that gradations exist between the two, we have to keep alive a certain regulative idea of perfection as an ideal standard against which we can measure our failures and achievements.

Urban: Are you entirely happy with rejecting Utopia as a normative idea? You did (again, in your middle period) repeatedly observe that Utopia on the Left is a sort of self-fulfilling prophecy: "Utopia crosses over from the domain of . . . moral thought into the field of practical thinking, and itself begins to govern action . . ." In another instance you say that the Left can never renounce Utopia "because goals that seem unattainable now will never be reached unless they are articulated when they are still unattainable . . ."

I believe these are historically well-attested observations. I also believe that you are now right in stressing that the "blueprint type of Utopia" is dangerous. Yet our experiences with the Third World, for example, suggest one significant lesson, namely that the developing majority of mankind seems to want, and want desperately, a seamless type of Utopia of the kind you now reject. The magnetism for the Third World of the Marxist-Leninist type of vision of the perfect society has been overwhelming, even though, in most cases, it amounted to no more than a convenient label for a "quick fix" toward modernization.

Two questions follow. First, is it within the realm of the possible that the underdeveloped, undernourished, and under-housed majority of mankind will understand the perils of the "blueprint type" of Communist Utopia, that Arabs and Iranians will cease to see the West as their principal adversaries and shift their hostility to that mother and father of all blueprints – the Soviet Union? Second, if in the Third World some Utopian target-setting is an unavoidable necessity, can the Western democracies offer a kind of "Utopia for export" that might appeal? Could it be done without making nonsense of what democracy stands for?

Kolakowski: If some millenarian fever seizes a large part of society, little can be done. But millenarianism is not a normal condition. What people in the Third World would seem to seek is not paradise but the means to cope with misery and starvation, even though it is true that extreme despair may breed chiliastic illusions. The West has no "Utopia for export," as you put it, and it would be foolish to try to devise one. It can offer no instantaneous, patent answers to the problems of overpopulation, the ungovernability of giant cities, soil-erosion, and similar calamities. What it can do is offer very complex, piecemeal, and uncertain advice, and show through irrefutable examples that totalitarian solutions are not only most unpleasant, but do not work in either the First, the Second, or the Third World.

Urban: You have stressed in your recent writings that socialism is the prerequisite for any fully effective totalitarian system, that dictatorships and despotisms of various ferocity can arise, and have arisen, in a variety of non-socialist environments, but that a fully totalitarian dictatorship must have socialism for its base. Wouldn't Sparta under the constitution of Lycurgus and Hitler's Germany (to take two random examples) rather challenge your theory, unless, of course, we grotesquely stretched the word "socialism" to cover certain Spartan and National Socialist institutions?

Kolakowski: The point where despotism differs from totalitarianism is the destruction of civil society. But civil society cannot be destroyed until and unless private property, including the private ownership of all the means of production, is abolished. As long as large numbers of people exist whose livelihood and conduct of life are independent from the state, your tyranny – hard and bloodthirsty though it may be – cannot be totalitarian. Stalin was fully aware of this when he decided to liquidate the independent peasants as a class. The totalitarian ideal could not be achieved without the collectivization of the peasantry – without the destruction of a class of people who constituted among them a large part of civil society and were not at the mercy of the state. Once this class had been liquidated at the cost of several million lives, the state, with its artificial ties embracing the whole of an atomized and terrorized society, became omnipotent. It is in this sense that I argued that a totalitarian society has the best chances of fulfilling the ideal in a socialist economy. At the end of the process the individual became the property of the state. This does not mean, though, that all forms of public ownership open the road to totalitarianism. There are many examples which show that civil liberties and democratic institutions can coexist with extensive nationalization.

No absolutely fireproof totalitarian system has yet been devised, but the Stalinist and Maoist models have come very close to translating the "entelechy" of totalitarianism into reality. Nazi Germany, on the other hand, and Fascist Italy were imperfect totalitarianisms (Mussolini's Italy, to be sure, much more imperfect that Hitler's Reich); Hitler was satisfied with the subordination of the existing forms of economic activity to the internal needs and imperial ambitions of the state, instead of expropriating and nationalizing all means of production. Nor have most of the Soviet Union's East European dependencies achieved the Soviet level of totalitarianism. In spite of all attempts to impose uniformity through pressure or – as in the cases of Hungary and Czechoslovakia – armed intervention, there are more and more cracks in the East European bloc of the Soviet empire.

Fortunately, much in the make-up of human beings resists the pressures of totalitarian control. Family life, emotional and sexual relationships, individual and collective memory, art and literature, escape to a certain extent the impact of the system. This holds, as we now know, even for the most regimented society we have yet seen: Communist China where, under Mao, a great effort was made either completely to destroy family life and personal relations, or to subordinate them to the goals and ideology of the state – so much so that the Maoists under the Cultural Revolution exceeded anything the Soviet system under Stalin managed to achieve in terms of the *Gleichschaltung* of the individual. Yet the spirit of liberty survived.

Urban: How much continuity was there between the Leninist and Stalinist types of totalitarianism? Scholars are strongly divided on this issue, some arguing that the link was weak or indeed that Stalinism was *sui generis*, while others believe that Stalinism was the logical end-product of Leninism and even Marxism.

Kolakowski: The Stalinist kind of totalitarianism issued directly from Leninism and that – albeit less directly – from Marxism.[3] I cannot here go into a detailed discussion of this problem, but let me simply say this without offering evidence: I do not think that Stalinism was a necessary and unavoidable product of Marxism. But that is not saying enough. To make my position clear I would pose the question differently: "Was the Stalinist ideology a legitimate interpretation of the Marxist philosophy of history?" And my answer to that question is yes. I can address myself in even stronger terms to the same problem by asking: "If one made a thorough attempt to translate the principal values of the Marxist kind of socialism into practical politics, would something like the Stalinist system be likely to emerge as the result?" And my answer to that question, too, is yes.

3 See the author's article, "The Marxist Roots of Stalinism," included in this volume. Editor's note.

Urban: You have spoken of the atomization of Soviet society. Where do the confessions made at the Moscow show-trials fit in? It is, on the face of it, surprising that whereas Hitler and Mussolini were content to have their enemies arrested and executed without exacting from them confessions in praise of the system, Stalin had his victims bribed or tortured to the point where they extolled the glory of the man and the power that were sending them to the gallows.

Kolakowski: Being the model dictator he was, Stalin was anxious to have his victims annihilated morally as well as physically. It was not enough for everyone to see that Stalin's victim was rightly hanged or shot; it was just as important to show that the victim himself recognized the rightness of being hanged or shot.

Urban: It was nevertheless surprising that so many could be made to indict themselves so abjectly and consistently over so long a period. I happened to be a daily ear-witness to the trial of Laszlo Rajk in 1949. It taught me a lesson that I ought to have learned before but didn't, viz., that it is one thing to offer cool historical or psychological explanations from the detachment of one's ivory tower, and quite another to experience day by day, blow by blow, the slow unfolding of a web of wildly unlikely and contradictory lies and fabrications. I could sense well enough how these men had been reduced to the state they were in. But I could not quite see why a victorious world power would need this kind of evidence to support its legitimacy.

Kolakowski: Enough is by now known about the ways in which false confessions were obtained for us not to have to say any more about them. Stalin's manifest objective was to show that there was no mercy. The people arrested, tortured, and executed in the 1948–52 period may or may not have had sympathies with some of Tito's policies, but that was not the point. The point was to drive it into the heads of every man, woman, and child that the slightest deviation by deed or thought was to be punished by death, and not an easy kind of death at that. There were to be no martyrs.

Going back to the 1935–38 "show-trials," one could conceivably understand why Stalin needed the false witness of the Old Bolsheviks, especially those who were brought to public trial (most of them were not). But why did he insist that those hundreds of thousands of small people, who were never given a trial but simply shot, should also go through the tortuous process of self-indictment and adulation of the Bolshevik system? No one was going to read about their confessions, so why do it?

The explanation, as I see it, is simple: Stalin wanted to make all those hundreds of thousands of people accessories to his crimes, accessories, moreover, to crimes committed against themselves, and thus accomplices in a general campaign of falsification. Even those who somehow survived the camps nevertheless acquired a subconscious interest in supporting the lie, because they had themselves assisted in creating it. This is, to my mind, the root cause of the neurosis of Soviet society.

Urban: You are, in fact, endorsing Alexander Zinoviev's reading of life in the land of "Ibansk" where truth and lie, farce and tragedy, are hopelessly interwoven.

Kolakowski: Yes, Zinoviev's *Yawning Heights* is a perceptive satire.

Urban: I still wonder whether we have fully explained Stalin's need of *morituri te salutant*. I am inclined to feel that by exacting praise from the dying, Stalin wanted to create a special kind of monument to himself – one that would somehow inscribe in capital print in the annals of history that he alone was Lenin's true reincarnation: revolutionary, theoretician, and "builder of socialism."

Kolakowski: One might say that Stalin was obsessed by a demonology of sorts which went way beyond his political needs. He *had* to demonstrate, again and again, the power of ineradicable evil: now it resided in Trotskyism, now in Leftist Deviation, now in Rightist Deviation, in Titoism, in Zionism, whatever. In every case Stalin put up a symbol of absolute evil which the Party was then directed to fight and vanquish. Of course, this cultivation of enemies did have its practical uses – it kept the Party and the bureaucracy in a state of mobilization and enforced unity. But the demonology was undeniably there.

Urban: Why did Hitler or Mussolini not need this eschatological justification through the medium of show-trials and false confessions?

Kolakowski: The lie plays an important but different role in Nazism – it has to do with straightforward propaganda: e.g., you tell the public that you have a decisive weapon when in fact you haven't and so on. In Nazism there was a high degree of convergence between the Nazis' actual goals and their avowed goals. They stated more or less openly what they wanted: national glory, the extermination of the Jews, the partial extermination of some of the Slavic nations to make room for German ambitions, the creation of a Nazi world empire, and so on. These were genuine goals and the Nazis always said that they would pursue them as, in fact, they did.

Communism, on the other hand, and especially Stalinism, hides behind a false façade. Stalinism had to pay lip service to the old socialist tradition. It had to talk about internationalism, social justice, freedom, equality, and the like because the framework of socialism and the vocabulary in which it was couched were its only title to legitimacy. Therefore the lie in Communist practice was, and is, a much more heinous thing than it was in Hitler's system, because the Stalinist practice of nationalism, slavery, and genocide is the complete negation of the avowed aims of the Soviet system. Hitler didn't, as far as his goals were concerned, lie very much to the world, but the world believed his truth to be too Satanic to be credible. Stalin lied to the world and, for a very long time, the lie succeeded.

Urban: You have spent many years thinking and writing about Stalinism. I can consequently well understand your preoccupation with the Devil . . .

Kolakowski: The Devil is part of our experience.[4] Our generation has seen enough of it for the message to be taken extremely seriously. Evil, I contend, is not contingent, it is not the absence, or deformation, or the subversion of virtue (or whatever else we may think of as its opposite), but a stubborn and unredeemable fact.

Urban: It is an intriguing and much-discussed question whether the Satanic element in Bolshevism inheres in the Russian tradition or stems from Marxism-Leninism alone. Alexander Solzhenitsyn and Vladimir Maximov are the best-known spokesmen of the view that the evils of the Soviet system are ideological rather than Russian, while the list of those who believe that some form of centralized despotism is endemic in Muscovite political culture includes Hugh Seton-Watson, Ronald Hingley, Robert C. Tucker, and Richard Pipes. It is against Richard Pipes, and especially against his book, *Russia under the Old Regime* (1974), that Solzhenitsyn's principal attacks are directed. Richard Pipes's method of using certain Russian proverbs to underpin his argument "affects me in much the same way as I imagine Rostropovich would feel if he had to listen to a wolf playing the cello," Solzhenitsyn wrote in the Spring 1980 issue of *Foreign Affairs*. Indeed, he claimed that American scholars

4 See the author's essay "Politics and the Devil" in *Modernity on Endless Trial* (Chicago: The University of Chicago Press, 1991). Editor's note.

demonstrate a "fundamental misunderstanding of Russia and the USSR," and that their presentation of pre-revolutionary Russia echoes arguments of Soviet propaganda. Where do you see the origins of the Satanic element in Bolshevism?

Kolakowski: Stalinism resulted from the coincidence of a variety of factors. I would not deny that Russia's particular tradition bears the brunt of responsibility for it. Yet, for several decades before the 1917 Revolution Russia was the scene of a clash between Slavophile and Westernizing forces. The Westernizers were powerful in Russian culture, including political culture in the second half of the nineteenth century. Both the Bolshevik and Menshevik currents of Russian Social Democracy (as it then was) represented Westernizing types of political thinking; and it was only after the Revolution that they were swamped and swallowed up by the old Tatar and Byzantine tradition in the shape of Leninism and then Stalinism.

Yet this explanation alone does not satisfy. That the cultural de-Westernization of Russia under Leninism and Stalinism was something that happened within the ideological framework of Marxism cannot be dismissed as insignificant or accidental. We cannot say that the Marxist-Leninist-Stalinist element was unimportant in the process. I would, therefore, define my position as being somewhere between Solzhenitsyn's and Pipes's, closer to Pipes than to Solzhenitsyn, but differing from Pipes in the sense that for me the impact of Marxism is important in its own right. I don't see Soviet Marxism merely as a latter-day incarnation of traditional traits in Russian culture. Otherwise it becomes very hard to explain why pre-revolutionary Westernizing socialists and liberals were so easily disarmed and defeated. What, we must ask, was it about Marxist ideology that enabled it to push Russia back, at one terrible blow, to the Tatar tradition in the name of "socialism"? And I am saying this fully aware of the fact that, by now, very few (if any) Soviet leaders are seriously guided by ideology. They nevertheless adhere to the intellectual framework and vocabulary of Marxism and Leninism because without it their title to rule would be non-existent.

But, while we are on Solzhenitsyn's text, let me make some further points that need stating although they are only loosely connected with the question at hand. Solzhenitsyn is certainly right in stressing two things: first, that the oppressiveness of the Soviet regime far exceeds that of czarist Russia in its last two decades; second, that Soviet rule is no less destructive of Russian national culture than it is of the culture and traditions of other nations and nationalities in the Soviet empire, even though Russian is used as the lingua franca of the state.

What, then, explains the Revolution and the ensuing tyranny? Speaking as a Pole, we Poles may rightly argue that the Communist system was imposed on us by foreign tanks, and that in the absence of the Soviet threat the system would instantaneously fall apart. But this is not an argument the Soviets can use: they have no Big Brother breathing down their necks; they are sovereign as a State; their system was launched and is being kept alive by domestic forces alone.

It astonishes me that Solzhenitsyn is so eager to prove the innocence of the czarist regime. No Pole can swallow that; nor can any member of those many non-Russian peoples whose forefathers lived under czarist rule. Solzhenitsyn alleges in the article you quote that although Alexander I entered Paris at the head of his forces, he did not annex an inch of European soil. This is only true on the supposition that the Poland of the time had already been part and parcel of Russia on the strength of divine law as interpreted by Catherine II!

Religious freedom? Does Solzhenitsyn forget the history of the Uniates, whose ruthless persecution began under Catherine and was then continuous in czarist history (with especial ferocity under Nicholas I) until its consummation under the Soviet regime?

Our fathers saw the Russian czars as hangmen, and rightly so. What reason would the Poles (or any of the other oppressed nations in the czarist empire) have had to support a man like General Denikin, whose avowed purpose during the Civil War was the restoration of the old empire? We have learned from bitter experience exactly what Lenin meant when he promised "self-determination" to the subject nations of the czarist empire. Yet the lies of Lenin and those of his successors cannot be used to whitewash the czars who did not even bother to make such promises! Victims for 130 years of fierce Russian oppression, the Poles cannot share Solzhenitsyn's image of the czarist regime as one of fatherly concern. They have lost too many of their men to the czars' hangmen.

Urban: Let me pick up your point about ideology. You said that very few Soviet leaders are seriously guided by it – yet they adhere to the rhetoric because ideology is their only title to legitimacy. This is strikingly illustrated by various passages in Veljko Micunovic's *Moscow Diary* (1980), where Khrushchev's attempts to lure the Yugoslavs back into the "camp" are shown to take the form of appeals and reminders of Marxist-Leninist solidarity, a shared revolutionary heritage, and so on. The Yugoslavs, in Micunovic's presentation, do not ultimately fall for the bait, but neither do they entirely avoid making concessions to the rhetoric. The ideological framework was, and is, important.

Kolakowski: Moscow's only title to Yugoslav allegiance was "socialism." This was as true for Hungary in 1956 as it was for Czechoslovakia in 1968 and Afghanistan in 1979. That, in reality, Moscow's concern was Soviet hegemony does not diminish the importance of the rhetoric of ideology. In fact, it makes it more significant as a handy and effective tool.

Urban: Critical observers of Marxism, and later of Leninism and Stalinism, have been telling us all the way from *Landmarks* (1909) to Melvin J. Lasky's *Utopia and Revolution* (1976) that the appeal to revolutionary ideology has more to do with our chiliastic expectations than our reason. Lasky, for example, attributes these expectations to two general factors, each deeply embedded in the human psyche. The first he summarizes in the statement: man "is born *in extremis* and dies *in extremis*, and his liveliest moments of joy, pleasure, and excitement are in the extreme emotions of sex, affection, and combat." The splendors and miseries of Utopia are, on this showing, merely refined projections of an "anthropological *leitmotif*." The second factor is man's inborn quest for "newness," and Lasky shows this too to be a potent force in projecting forward images of the Golden Age and perfect polity. "The recurrent passion for the new," he writes, "is the cry of the human animal spirit for rebirth, for energy, surprise, and adventure; it reasserts historical man's need for a sense of differentness and otherness, and his heartfelt hope of fresh purpose and fulfillment."

My final questions, then, are twofold: would you agree that Marxism and Leninism spring from such anthropological roots? And, second, would you say that the proper intellectual locus of Communist ideology is somewhere under the rubric of "Faith"? That future curricula will teach it as a form of religion, and with the same skeptical curiosity as today's deal with the intricacies of "homoiousian" versus "homoousian" in medieval theology?

Kolakowski: It is the case that Marxism as an ideology is a modern variant of apocalyptic expectations which have been continuous in European history. Other contemporary versions, such as the vision of Jehovah's Witnesses, are extremely weak by comparison. I subscribe to the expectation that once the Marxist variant disappears – as it will – those human energies and aspirations which have temporarily assembled under the aegis of Marxism will take on a new disguise – but this is, of course, speculation.

However, if we appeal to "anthropological roots," we implicitly assume that similar phenomena must have accompanied human thinking since the dawn of civilization – which induces me to introduce another distinction.

Many religious forms of worship did well without apocalyptic expectations. All of them, however, put great stress on the notions of Rebirth and a New Beginning. In most cases the locus of Rebirth is "out there," in Heaven, whereas the idea of a Messiah who promises to bring total renewal on earth is a very peculiar and modern version of soteriology. Religious messianism expected Renewal from divine intervention, whereas modern secular Utopias expect it to flow from the application of human knowledge and social engineering.

Secular Utopias cling to the framework of religious eschatology – descent into Hell, absolute break, the arrival of a New Time – but, because they have abolished the idea of man's dependence on divine judgment and divine rule, they lapse into incoherence. And, not unnaturally, the final source of this incoherence is the desperate hope that one can reach the Absolute within the finiteness of human existence, that one can abolish the past, bring forth a "New Man" and so on. All these things can, of course, be done, but only in caricature: we can cancel out the past by falsifying history, and we can produce a "New Man" by totalitarian coercion. But these will be travesties.

Yes, to answer your last question, we are dealing with Faith, but I attach to this word no pejorative meaning. What is wrong with modern Utopian fantasies, including Marxism, is not that they are centered on Faith, but that they are centered on Faith pretending to be knowledge, a *fides mala fide*, if I may say so.

Having spent much time studying the history of religious heresies, I am far from taking a disparaging view of the early Christian controversies about "homoousia." There were serious issues at stake – nothing less, in the final analysis, than the divinity of Jesus Christ and thus of the legitimacy of the Church. This was a fundamental issue.

In any case, the quarrel of sixteenth-century theologians as to the form in which Jesus's body is present in the Eucharist seems to me a great deal more stimulating and worthwhile than Marxist squabbles about the presence of "value" in commodities.

What Is Wrong with God?

A Layman Pronounces upon the *Catechism*[1]

The *New Catechism of the Catholic Church*,[2] the product of six years of labor by a special commission, contains 2865 paragraphs and comprises, together with indexes, 676 pages. Thus one cannot possibly hope to discuss all its important new teachings in a short review.

As expected, the *Catechism* does not, and was not supposed to, contain any doctrinal novelties, be it in matters of theology or in the social teaching of the Church. It is, however, a codification of a number of Church documents, proclamations, encyclicals, and pontifical letters issued in the last several decades. Therefore the question that concerns us is not so much one of innovations in the *Catechism* but rather the spirit of the whole.

The journalists who first wrote about the *Catechism*, doubtless without having read it, reported the following exciting scoops: according to the *Catechism*, one should not drive while drunk (indeed, this does not appear in the sixteenth-century version of the catechism), nor should one evade paying taxes, nor should one consult horoscopes (the Church has condemned astrology from ancient times). This is typical of the way in which the ignorant idly leaf through important documents. There is, of course, some slight updating, but in every case it clearly follows from the traditional commandments and rules, and there is no need to go into it in detail. If, for example, one should not lie, then clearly it follows that one should not lie on television. A fairly uncomplicated deduction and a fairly unsensational commandment.

It was also predictable that the *Catechism* would provoke attacks and criticism from Catholic progressives, who would accuse the Church of

1 Translated from the Polish by Zbigniew Janowski from "Laik nad Katechizmem sie wymadrza" in PULS, 62, No. 3 (London, 1993).
2 *Catéchisme de l'Eglise Catholique* (Paris, 1993).

betraying the spirit of the last Vatican Council. Again, the text of the *Catechism* provides no grounds for such charges. In any case, the critics who level them should support them by adducing quotations from both documents. But it seems that, on the contrary, the *Catechism* is in perfect accord with the teachings of the Second Vatican Council, whose documents are cited constantly, especially *Gaudium et Spes* and *Lumen Gentium*. Unless, of course, the progressives expected that the new *Catechism* would do away with the celibacy of the clergy, abolish the dogma of Papal infallibility, allow the practice of homoerotic love, introduce a liberal democratic order into the constitution in the Church, and demand the immediate expropriation of the Brazilian bourgeoisie.

The novelty lies not so much in what the *New Catechism* contains as in what it leaves out. There are no condemnations of other forms of Christianity or non-Christian religions. There is a canonical definition of heresy (2089) – to which, for mysterious reasons, there is no reference in the index – but no definition of a heretic (a definition which, in accordance with Canon Law, cannot be entirely deduced from the notion of heresy). The entry in the index refers the reader to a single passage (465) which contains only a brief mention of the Christological heresies of the first centuries, and is thus of purely historical interest. One passage (406) mentions "the first Protestant reformers," who claimed that Original Sin entirely annihilated human freedom. The part which asserts the traditional doctrine of the Holy Trinity contains a fairly long chapter devoted to that most mysterious person of the Trinity – the Holy Spirit; but although the cult of the Holy Spirit is greater in Orthodox Christianity, there is no mention of the (only) dogmatic difference between the Roman and the Orthodox Church: the so-called *filioque* question (whether the Holy Spirit comes, as the Eastern Church teaches, only from the Father, or from both the Father and the Son). There are, however, frequent references to Byzantine liturgy. The *Comma Johanneum*, the most explicit founding text of the doctrine of the Trinity (1 John 5:7, 8) is not referred to: an indirect admission that — as Erasmus of Rotterdam already observed — it is a later interpolation.

It is worth noting that as far as references to pontifical documents are concerned, there is a gap here that stretches from the middle of the sixteenth century to the end of eighteenth (the *Catechism* mistakenly mentions Pius IV as the author of *Cum quorundam*; in fact its author is Paul IV, perhaps the worst tyrant and persecutor in the history of the modern Papacy, reformer and ascetic though he may have been). I am not sure how to account for these omissions. It is certain, however, that the most important post-Tridentine documents, throughout the seventeenth century and later, are condemnations of successive heresies and errors: of

Baius, of the Jansenists, of the Jesuit moralists, the Quietists, the Gallicans, Fénelon, Eybel, and so forth. So perhaps the *Catechism*'s silence on these questions is an attempt to purge Church doctrine of any "anathematizing context" (not a very graceful neologism, I'm afraid).

But although doctrinal conflicts with non-Catholic Christianity are practically absent from the *Catechism*, the issue of good relations and respect has its place. It is presented in the spirit of the *Unitatis Reintegratio*, which is cited where appropriate. Those who are born in non-Catholic Churches and "live in Christ, cannot be accused of the sin of schism or heresy"; they deserve brotherly respect. Moreover, "justified by the faith received at their baptism and united (*incorporés*) with Christ, they rightly bear the name of Christians" (818). (One dreads to think what the Tridentine Fathers would say about this.) As for Orthodox Churches, their communion with the Catholic Church "is so profound that it needs little more to be complete and permit a common celebration of the Lord's Eucharist" (838). In a number of places (781, 839) there are references to the people of Israel as God's people, the first to whom the Revelation in the Old Covenant was given and among whom Jesus, the Messiah of Israel, was born. The link with the Jewish people is stressed, although reference is of course also made to the fact that the Jews rejected the messianic message of Christ – who, although he profoundly revered the Temple of Jerusalem, changed the attitude toward Old Testament law and forgave sins himself (574–591). The Muslims are referred to briefly (841) as professors of the faith of Abraham, who are also included in the prospect of salvation. As for pagans (the word is not used, except in a quotation from St. Paul), the *Catechism* admits that they, too, seek an unknown God and that God wants their salvation as well. The principle that there is "no salvation outside the Church" does not mean that there can be no salvation for those who, through no fault of their own, are ignorant of Christ's Gospels and of the Church, but strive to do God's will according to their conscience. The *Catechism* also advocates "sincere respect for different religions, which sometimes bring the light of truth which enlightens all men" (2104).

All these themes are familiar from the Second Vatican Council or other pontifical documents of the past few decades. Among them is also the principle of religious freedom, interpreted to mean that no one may be forced to act against his conscience (160) or prevented from freely practicing religion within the limits of the law. But this "right to religious liberty" is "neither a moral license to adhere to error, nor a supposed right to error, but rather a natural right of the human person to civil liberty, i.e., immunity, within just limits, from external constraint in religious matters by political authorities" (2018). "The right to religious freedom can of itself be neither unlimited nor limited only by a 'public order' conceived in a positivist or naturalist manner" (2109).

Here, however, the *Catechism* allows an unfortunate ambiguity to creep in. If these general limitations imposed on religious freedom came down to saying that one may not justify acts forbidden by law by invoking religion, i.e., by claiming that one's religion allows them or demands them, no reasonable person would object. But the *Catechism* here invokes, although it does not cite, two important, albeit less than edifying documents: Pius IX's encyclical *Quanta cura* of 1864 (to which the famous "syllabus" of errors was a sort of appendix) and Leo XIII's encyclical *Libertas praestantissimum* of 1888. Both these documents clearly and unequivocally condemn religious freedom in the sense of freedom from state interference in the public practice of all religious cults, freedom to worship or to choose not to worship, and freedom from the imposition of the Catholic religion as the only state religion; the religious freedom they allow is that everyone in the state is free to worship God and follow His commands. In short, religious freedom in this sense is the lack thereof. And although, again, these documents, written at a time when liberalism was considered the arch-enemy of Christianity, are not quoted explicitly, but are merely referred to in footnotes to those paragraphs which deal with religious freedom, invoking them suggests – implicitly but undoubtedly – that the compulsory elimination of non-Catholic forms of religiosity (and of atheism) and the recognition of Catholicism not only as the state religion, but as the only acceptable religion, in short the total abolishment of toleration and religious freedom, would be a praiseworthy and desirable thing. All of which is clearly counter to the unequivocal ecumenical declarations in the *Catechism* and its rejection of "all forms of discrimination aimed at the fundamental rights of a person, regardless of sex, race, or color of skin, social condition, language or religion" (1935). This leads to a highly regrettable ambiguity which could easily be exploited in the propaganda of a state with an established state religion, even in an extreme form of such a state. *Dixi.*

It is hard to avoid associating this ambiguity with the Augustinian, "positive" concept of freedom, elements of which are present, although not prominently or emphatically so, in the *Catechism*. According to the Augustinian concept of freedom, I am free not because I can choose between good and evil, but only when I choose good. On the one hand, freedom in the *Catechism* is defined as the power to choose, to act or not to act; and it presupposes freedom of choice between good and evil (1731–1732): "Mortal sin is a radical possibility of human freedom, as is love itself" (1861). On the other hand, we read that "the more good we do, the freer we become. True freedom comes from doing good and justice. The choice of disobedience and evil is an abuse of freedom and leads to the slavery of sin" (1733); and "The more obedient we are to the promptings of grace, the more we grow in inner freedom . . ."(1742).

This is a dangerous ambiguity. According to the normal meaning of the word "freedom," I am free because of the very possibility of choice; in other words, I am free both when I choose good and when I choose evil. In the latter case I become evil, but I am still free, and therefore responsible for my actions. However, freedom in the "positive," Augustinian, sense, means freedom from sin. This implies that the fewer opportunities for sin the world offers me, the more my freedom flourishes. From this it naturally follows that all forms of constraint which limit my opportunities for sinning are not only beneficial to me but actually increase my freedom. This is why the Augustinian doctrine of freedom can serve as a good justification for a repressive regime. "True freedom," as opposed to ordinary freedom, freedom *tout court*, is – as we know from the recent past – an unfortunate phrase. The *Catechism*'s ambiguity on this point naturally awakens wariness and mistrust in all those who value freedom (not the "true" kind, but the ordinary kind) as a priceless treasure.

Apart from Biblical texts, encyclicals, and the declarations of various Councils, the *Catechism* also cites a number of Church Fathers – both Latin and Greek – and later Doctors of the Church, as well as Church writers (even some who were not canonized). The last of them chronologically, if I am not mistaken, is Cardinal Newman. But it is with some astonishment that one sees, under the heading "Church writers," the name of Cicero (cited once). This somewhat excessive ecumenism is doubtless the result of sloppiness.

The social teaching of the Church is laid out in the first and second sections of the third part, sections which deal respectively with man's vocation and the Ten Commandments. The moral principles naturally remain unchanged, but there are significant omissions and changes of emphasis. The *Catechism* stresses that the human person is the end and basic principle of all social institutions. A government is legitimate insofar as it acts toward the common good and uses means which are morally acceptable; within these limits various political systems are possible and acceptable. Despotic power is illegal. Citizens are encouraged to participate in public life and to exercise their right to vote. The *Catechism* also considers "excessive inequalities" between people and nations to be scandalous; it extols the virtue of solidarity and stresses the need to respect human dignity in all cases without exception. The teaching of the Church defends the right to property and unconstrained private enterprise, and also the right to emigration. However, it also insists on the right to health care, family allowances, and other institutions of the welfare state.

As before, the Church condemns theories which make profit the ultimate goal of economic activity. It also condemns totalitarian ideologies ("associated in modern times with 'communism' or 'socialism'" – this is the only appearance of these two words in the *Catechism* (2425); they do not appear in the index). In short, according to secular criteria, if we set aside the theological justifications of its teaching, the Church is close to social democracy: it advocates neither total liberalism nor a command economy. Strikes are acceptable if absolutely necessary, but recourse to violence by strikers is condemned. It is unbecoming for priests to participate directly in political activity; this is the task of lay Catholics. In comparison with the classical social encyclicals, the *Catechism* does not advocate a corporate state, although it does, of course, stress the importance of human solidarity.

The social doctrine laid out in the *Catechism* is necessarily general, since it is intended to be universal: it is a conceptual skeleton from which it would be hard to deduce detailed instructions in controversial matters, except in extreme cases. One cannot blame the authors of the *Catechism* for this. But one can say that, generally, the Church is more than ever before reconciled with the liberal-democratic order. One can hardly fail to notice that the essential document in the history of the Church's social teaching, *Rerum Novarum* (1891), is not mentioned at all, and the second most important one, *Quadragesimo Anno* (1931), is mentioned only once, in connection with a relatively minor matter. The social encyclicals of John Paul II are cited a number of times.

In connection with the Fifth Commandment, the *Catechism* says that in extreme cases capital punishment is not to be excluded; however, it condemns direct euthanasia (as well as abortion, of course), although it permits abstaining from extreme medical procedures for the dying if such procedures would be disproportionate to the results they could be expected to achieve. In such cases it also permits the use of painkillers even if they might accelerate death. Suicide, although still considered evil, does not automatically preclude salvation; God can save the suicide, and the Church should pray for him. Torture is condemned unconditionally. One passage even seems to contain a suggestion of self-criticism: in the past, the *Catechism* says, torture was applied without any protest from priests, who in their own tribunals applied the rules of Roman Law concerning torture. "These regrettable facts apart, the Church has always stressed the duty to show clemency and mercy" (2298). How this "apart" is to be weighed against the "always" we may leave for historians to ponder.

The code concerning sexual activity remains unchanged. It continues, among other things, to prohibit non-natural methods of contraception, artificial insemination outside marriage and pre-marital sex.

The *Catechism* is not, as I understand it, a collection of absolutely binding dogmas, like the Nicene Creed, but rather an interpretation of the Creed which the Church considers the most appropriate at a given moment. Because every *Catechism* is such an interpretation, not all its components must be considered binding *de iure divino*, and one can imagine that they might change in future. For example, abandoning the rule of celibacy for the clergy, or refusing absolutely and without exception to condone capital punishment, or relaxing the code concerning sexual activity, would not require any dogmatic revisions.

Nor is the *Catechism* a textbook of theology, although it is an interpretation of the Revealed Word, and in this sense a theological text; but the interpretation it offers is brief and to the point, with no lengthy discussion or historical detail.

In matters of theology, the most complex and controversial issues, and in modern times the most hotly debated, are those which concern predestination, grace, and free will. This is an area full of tortuous argumentation, dead-ends, and contradictory explanations, some of which beg the question. Let us recall the heart of the contention. Grace is by definition independent of merit. But two of the doctrines preached by St. Augustine and his followers, including theologians of the early Reformation, were fiercely contested.

First, grace, which justifies us – that is, makes us worthy of salvation – is irresistible ("efficient"). This means that those on whom it is bestowed cannot reject it; if they could, it would mean that man could thwart God's will. Second, grace is unmerited; it is bestowed upon some (in fact on very few) regardless of their behavior. After the Fall, no one can achieve merit by himself. Without divine aid, human will inevitably chooses evil; if it chooses good, it does so because of grace, which is independent of merit and irresistible.

According to Christian humanists, including the Jesuits, this doctrine makes God a capricious tyrant who metes out eternal salvation or damnation according to unfathomable rules that have nothing to do with our efforts. Moreover, it entirely eliminates the role of free will. This is morally as well as theologically dangerous, for it suggests that there is no point in our making an effort, since in the matter of our salvation nothing, literally nothing, depends on us. Jesuit theology, called Semi-Pelagian by opponents (the name was unknown in antiquity and does not appear in condemnations of Pelagianism), holds that while grace, which makes us capable of performing good deeds, is of course necessary for salvation, it is given to everyone equally, and that it is our will

147

which makes it efficient. Thus salvation is the work of two independent forces: God, the distributor of the necessary aid, and man, who makes the free choice between good and evil.

The decrees of the Tridentine Council on this matter left a margin of ambiguity which the followers of St. Augustine, as well as Jesuits and other Christian humanists, could exploit to their own ends, invoking them selectively. Pope Clement VIII wisely forbade theologians to engage in debates on these matters, but to little avail. Numerous later decrees, from the condemnation of Baius in 1567 to the condemnation of Quesnel in 1713, had a clear intent: the condemnation of the Augustinian doctrine (without, of course, mentioning the great Church Father by name) and the (gradual but undoubted) recognition of Jesuit Semi-Pelagian humanism.

Where does the *Catechism* stand on this crucial issue? Its general tendency is anti-Augustinian, but ambiguities remain. St. Paul's remark about Adam, *"in quo omnes peccaverunt"*, which was mistranslated in the Vulgate as "in whom all have sinned" and subsequently became the strongest Biblical support for Augustinian teaching on Original Sin, is rendered here (as in the more recent Catholic translations of the New Testament) as "inasmuch as all have sinned," which does away with the idea of inherited guilt. The *Catechism* talks about the mystery of the "transmission" of Original Sin and the resulting corruption of human nature (403–405), but does not talk about the guilt itself being inherited. It says that "by our first parents' sin, the devil acquired a certain domination over man, even though man remains free" (407). This can be reconciled with the Semi-Pelagian interpretation. Freedom of choice between good and evil is recognized (1732). Admittedly, "the merit of good works is to be attributed in the first place to the grace of God, then to the faithful" (2008), and our merits are "the gifts of divine grace" (2009 – of the many passages about grace, this one alone cites St. Augustine, although on other subjects the *Catechism* cites him abundantly), but there is no suggestion that grace acts irresistibly or that God bestows it only on some, leaving the rest of mankind at the mercy of their own corruption, which inevitably leads to Hell. It should be noted that God shapes our will, so that, when we have grace, we truly act as we want to act; thus we are not compelled, even though we do good from necessity. Freedom in this sense, however, is only a nominal freedom.

In other connected matters, too, the position of the *Catechism* is humanistic, not Augustinian. Children who die without baptism are entrusted to the mercy and goodness of God, who can save them (1261); while according to St. Augustine (but not St. Thomas Aquinas), infants who die before receiving baptism are for this reason alone destined to eternal torment in Hell, despite not being guilty of any real sin. In accordance with the teaching of St. Paul (whose ostensibly unambiguous text disciples of St. Augustine interpreted to mean the opposite), Jesus Christ died for all men without exception (605). Not only perfect contrition (*contritio*), which flows from love for God and regret at having offended Him, but also imperfect contrition (*attritio*), which flows from selfish motives, such as fear of damnation and shame, is considered a gift of God (1453). This distinction was not recognized before the Tridentine Council, and followers of St. Augustine rejected it as an unworthy innovation.

In sum, one can say that on this particularly important point the *Catechism* represents a further step toward freeing the Church from Augustinianism and embracing a humanist-Jesuit-Pelagian theology. *Gaudeamus*.

Jesus Christ – Prophet and Reformer[1]

When a historian deals with Jesus, he is interested above all in what can reliably be said about this man, in what we know about him for sure. He also wants to know about the antecedents of his teachings in Jewish culture, and how the image of the Jewish God changed from the Pentateuch to the late prophets, and whether Jesus the prophet can be taken as a continuation or crowning of those changes. He is interested in the results of research on the Qumran manuscripts and the light they have shed on the problem. These are topics that can be profitably discussed only by specialists, and they are not what I want to discuss here.

A historian of ideas may also want to situate Jesus in the whole history of Christianity, exploring, in his research on this inexhaustible topic, the boundless area of thought and events which grew up around the myth of Christ. Indeed, it is difficult, when speaking about Jesus the man, to shake off the twenty centuries of events through which we see him. The figure of Jesus is enveloped in the shadow of theology and in the thicket of theological controversies that surrounds every word of the Gospels. How can we ignore the vast areas of ambiguity, ostensible or real, with which the history of Christianity has weighed down the teachings of its founder? But this, too, is not what concerns me here.

A historian of religion may treat Jesus as an element in a certain mythological structure, which he might compare with others in order to bring out cultural differences and similarities. He may, although this is difficult, try to ignore the extent to which the figure of Jesus is enveloped in the shadow of the contemporary world and the presence of Christianity in it; he may aspire to the same degree of disinterestedness and objectivity, the same scholarly and aesthetic distance, that we display toward Egyptian or Greek myths. But this is also not what I want to attempt here.

1   Written in Polish under the title "Jezus Chrystus: Prorok i Reformator." First published in *Argumenty*, Nos. 51–52 (1965). Translated by Agnieszka Kolakowska.

Jesus Christ – Prophet and Reformer

Finally, a biographer may try to unravel the psychology of Jesus and put together a consistent psychological profile of the whole person – if he can free himself from all ulterior motives, whether apologetic and Christian or blasphemous and anti-Christian. But this, too, is not what interests me here.

What interests me is the purely philosophical point of view: a view, in other words, that is neither historical nor psychological nor that of the historian of religion. My aim is to attain enough mental freedom to read the canonical and apocryphal texts of the Gospels without recalling the commentaries, or even the Epistles of St. Paul; to read just the simple words, without reading any complex theological or philosophical speculations into them. I would like to summarize what the layman can discern in the figure and teaching of Jesus: the layman who professes no particular Christian faith, embraces no dogma and belongs to no church community, but who does feel himself to belong to the larger tradition of which Christianity is an essential part – the tradition of which Buddha, Socrates, Kant, and Marx are also a part. I do not want to reconstruct the psychological profile of Jesus. I am interested in his place within the European tradition as a whole: in how, and in which of its aspects, the mission he ascribed to himself became a component of the intricately woven tapestry which makes up our cultural heritage. And I am interested in this tradition independently of the Christological dogmas around which the Christian religious consciousness has been shaped.

Philosophers and Jesus

Jesus Christ was not, as we know, a philosopher. Textbooks on religious philosophy, even Christian textbooks, do not mention him, and modern philosophers rarely deal with him. However, some philosophers have done so, and it is worth mentioning some of their views in order to outline the various types of philosophical approaches to this extraordinary figure.

Of the great philosophers, Pascal, Kierkegaard, Hegel, Nietzsche, and Jaspers wrote about Jesus. For Hegel, he represented a phase of human historical self-knowledge; he was a concrete, sensory manifestation of that idea of God at which man arrives when he conceives of God as something in which he participates – something of which he himself is a manifestation, another form of being. Thus the person of Jesus is almost reduced to a stage of human self-consciousness in its relation to the absolute. This does not mean that Hegel makes Jesus unreal, stripping him of personhood and humanity; he acknowledges that Jesus is far more human than the Greek anthropomorphic gods. But he deprives Jesus of his peculiar extra-historical uniqueness; of that quality – that timeless exceptionality, at once singular and enduring – which established Christianity, and which is embedded in the belief that here was something supra-natural that irrupted into history from outside it.

Kierkegaard, on this issue as on others, developed his own view in opposition to Hegel, depicting Christ as always contemporary, and true for Christians only by virtue of this contemporaneousness. Christ, he said, is no more than a sterile item of historical information for us if we see him as the transmitter of a *past* revelation; he is the real Christian life for each individual only when that individual is able to make him *literally* contemporary, and thus to understand his invitation – "Come all ye who labor and are oppressed and I will comfort thee" – as addressed to him personally, always valid and spoken to him anew at every moment. For a Christian, Jesus is not just a messiah who appeared at a certain historical moment to teach dogmas or preach commandments in God's name. He is the personal embodiment of the permanence of Christianity in every individual Christian; an ever-vital counter-element of every existence; a presence in which each existence will seek the answer to its own frailty and its own wretchedness.

Pascal's attitude to Jesus, most evident in his attacks on deism and the "philosophers' God," was, despite all the differences, basically the same. For Pascal, the world manifests neither the complete absence nor the evident presence of a deity; it is not utterly abandoned by God, nor is it obviously under His protection. It manifests "the presence of a God who is hidden." This ambiguity of God's presence in the world is the ambiguity of our fate: the fate of those who are able to know God but who are permanently tainted by sin. It is through Jesus Christ that our knowledge of God becomes for us the knowledge of our own wretchedness, and we need this conjoined knowledge. We can learn each of these two truths – that God exists and that we are wretched – separately, but only the apprehension of Jesus as a person amalgamates them and contains them, necessarily, as one joint truth. By itself, our knowledge of our infirmity is a source of despair; by itself, our knowledge of God is merely speculative, theoretical, without value in our lives. But in the apprehension of Jesus we attain at once the full awareness of our fall and the hope of a possible cure; and it is this that constitutes Christian faith. Thus a purely philosophical Christianity, based on speculative proofs, is not possible. Nor is a purely historical one, based on what we know from the Bible. Jesus Christ appears to us not just in his dogmatic and his historical aspects, but as a real existence, a real redeemer; and it is through this presence, which is neither simply a fact nor simply a doctrine, that we become aware both of the darkness in which we live and of the way which leads out of that darkness.

Finally, Nietzsche's is also one of the "great" philosophical interpretations of the figure of Christ. Nietzsche is the greatest of those very few who have dared to proclaim themselves not only enemies of Christianity but enemies of Christ. For him, Jesus was someone who wanted to annihilate all the important values of life, who glorified his own inability to resist and who raised this weakness to the rank of a virtue. He robbed all values of their reality by transferring them to man's spiritual "interior," and he codified a morality for those who cannot defend their own rights and who seek comfort in their own passivity, making it a cause for pride.

These attitudes, briefly sketched, are three ways in which philosophers have approached the person of Jesus. Nietzsche addresses him as one prophet to another: as a true prophet to a false one. Hegel's approach is that of a historian of the spirit toward a certain historical phase. Pascal and Kierkegaard approach him as Christians who seek the supra-natural realities of their faith in its most personal values.

In some limited sense, Pascal's and Kierkegaard's approach may also be acceptable to those who are not concerned with the dogmatic content of Christianity. Not, of course, in the sense that they see Christ as a personal and historically unequivocal embodiment of the supra-natural world, to whom they could address their questions or worries, but in the sense that Jesus, like all great thinkers, prophets, reformers, and philosophers, has that peculiar contemporaneousness which can be achieved where universal values spring from one unique source. A philosopher, if he wants to go beyond the purely historical or purely factual point of view, will not approach a philosophical or religious tradition as a fact that is simply there to be understood, nor as a line of thought which is simply to be agreed or disagreed with; he will not view a cultural tradition as a cumulation of "truths," nor as a sequence of historically neutralized facts. He will try, rather, to bring out those of its values which are universal and yet enduringly linked to their author, inextricably bound up with their personal source. This duality is one of the more difficult elements of the philosophical approach to tradition. Jesus, on this approach, is reducible neither to a set of events (a set that would also comprise the content of his teaching) nor to a set of abstract values that could be viewed and assessed quite independently of the circumstances in which they came into being. We approach his teaching as, to use an ugly expression, "essentialized fact," or as a universal value whose content is linked to its historical origin.

Jesus's Main Prophecy

From a purely historical perspective, Jesus was a Jew from Galilee who believed in the Jewish God and believed that this God had entrusted him with a special mission of teaching. He was also someone of whom his disciples in turn believed that he could calm winds by his command, walk the waters of a lake, draw fish into nets, resurrect the dead, heal lepers, make the blind see again, drive out demons from the possessed, talk with Moses and Elias, multiply bread for the poor, and turn water into wine and wine into blood; they also believed that he fulfilled the promises of the Old Testament about the Messiah and that his mission was attested to by his resurrection. This Jesus, although he accepted the tribute of his believers, did not consider himself to be God; indeed he denied that he could be so considered. When he was called good he said that only God is good; he acknowledged that he did not know when the promised day would come; he said, "not what I will, but what thou wilt." In this sense one cannot say that Jesus made Christianity, if the belief in his divinity is counted among Christianity's fundamental precepts. It was Paul who began the deification process, and in the end, in spite of the opposition which still persisted among the pre-Nicene fathers, he prevailed; thus was the dominant understanding of Christianity definitively established, despite numerous "Arian" relapses. This Jesus considered himself, we may assume, a Jewish reformer, charged with a supra-natural mission as God's anointed, that is, as Christ, who brought from God – the same God in whom he and his listeners believed – the news of the approaching end of the world and an appeal to all to prepare themselves immediately for the final cataclysm. He was convinced that the end of the world was imminent – so imminent that he sometimes told his listeners and disciples that many of them would see the coming of God's Kingdom on earth with their own eyes. This coming would be preceded by famines, pestilence, and earthquakes, by falling stars and the eclipse of the sun, and would end with the visible descent of God's son from the heavens, surrounded by angels playing trumpets. The failure of these prophecies to be fulfilled did not weaken the belief of the disciples, who explained them differently. But the expectation of imminent catastrophe imposed an entirely new perspective on things: from that moment on, all worldly concerns disappear in the shadow of the apocalypse. Earthly realities, the whole multiplicity of things that are important in life, lose all meaning and all independent value. The material world is no longer important: it can still be, it still is, an object of duty, but it could not be an object of desire, for in its fragility it was approaching its end.

Jesus the Reformer

In this light, the precepts of the new teaching, and the extent to which it really was new, can be understood.

Readers of the Gospels have long been struck by certain inconsistencies in the personality of Jesus. He preaches peace, forgiveness, mercy, and desistance from resisting evil; but in his own behavior he is quick to anger and easily irritated, even by small things. He warns that he will deny knowing and send away even those who perform miracles, prophesy, and exorcize demons in his name, if they do not fulfill the will of God. He says that a terrible vengeance will befall cities which do not believe in him, and promises that on the Day of Judgment the fate of Tyre and Sidon will be more tolerable than that of Chorazin and Bethsaida, which disregarded his teachings in spite of his miracles. To Peter, when he expresses the hope that his Lord will not be killed, he says, "Get thee behind me, Satan." He curses a fig tree on which he finds no fruit and condemns it to wither away, although it is not the right time of year for figs. He drives out the money changers from the temple with a scourge. He proclaims that he brings not peace but a sword, that he will separate families, and that because of him in every house fathers shall bet set at variance against sons and daughters against mothers. His listeners say, "These are hard sayings." Opposition or skepticism rouse him to violent anger. He is unshakably certain of his mission, and it is only at the very last moment, as he is dying in torment, that he seems to burst out with a cry of despair to the God who has forsaken him. But even that cry of despair is a quotation from the Psalmist.

It may seem that the impulsive character of Jesus does not quite fit his teaching; some of his behavior seems to reveal the anger of the old Jewish God whose image he changes in his teaching (which was, in fact, in accordance with the intentions of earlier prophets). And indeed it is difficult to sum up in one word Jesus's attitude toward the Old Testament – a difficulty testified to by the endless disputes on the matter in the history of Christianity (did he abolish the Law of the Old Testament? supplement it? amend it?). The Sermon on the Mount begins with the statement that he does not want to destroy the law but to fulfill it; but what follows is hard to reconcile with that passage. When Jesus broadens the commandment against killing to encompass mere anger, and the commandment against adultery to encompass mere lust, we may consider him to be supplementing the laws, in the same spirit that guides the whole of his teaching: it is not actions that matter but the spirit from which they spring, not behavior but purity of heart and love of one's neighbor with no ulterior motive. But when he contrasts the principle of an eye for an eye with refraining from resistance to evil and turning the other cheek, he is no longer just supplementing the Old Testament: he is abolishing it, apparently without noticing. He certainly does not want to break the continuity of the Jewish creed; he wants to renew it and "internalize" it. He disregards the Jewish laws of ritual; he does not observe the Sabbath, nor perform ritual ablutions; he does not pay taxes to the Jewish cult, which outrages the orthodox. He represents a continuity with the late prophets, but evokes the rigorous laws of Deuteronomy as if deliberately to stress the contrast between his own teaching and the old tradition (which by then was of course partly out of date). The break in the continuity was achieved by his disciples, mainly in the Jewish Diaspora. But it was not just the news of his miraculous resurrection that created the break, but also his teaching, which can easily be formulated so that it no longer merely supplements the faith of Israel but transgresses it in a fundamental way. And indeed this is how St. Paul views the matter.

This is a crucial point, and it means that Jesus does not, in fact, so much replace some laws by others, complete them or amend them, as teach that laws are not needed at all, for love entails the command, and thus makes it superfluous; it is, so to speak, spontaneously bound up with it. And only love is important. In other words, the contractual relation between man and God is not altered by a change in the content of the contract, but ceases to exist entirely, and is supplanted by a relation of love. This is how Paul understood Christ's teaching, and Augustine, and Luther. Only that which comes from love has true value, and whatever springs from love cannot be judged by laws nor measured by a paragraph in a decree. No action matters unless it springs from a desire to do God's will. We all have duties toward the world, but no rights: no claims on it and no right to expect anything from it. Never before in Mediterranean culture had the principle of this fundamental dichotomy been stated so starkly, and it was expressed with great force: the soul and the will to do good on the one hand, the rest of the world and the totality of existing things on the other. Only the soul matters. In view of the approaching catastrophe, only a blind man would take comfort from his temporal achievements. The kingdom of heaven is a priceless pearl for which we must abandon all we possess, all our goods. "For what is a man profited, if he shall gain the whole world, and lose his own soul?"

The mission of Jesus Christ is to reveal the wretchedness of the temporal world. "Freely ye have received, freely give. Provide neither gold, nor silver, nor brass in your purses, Nor scrip for your journey, neither two coats, neither shoes, nor yet staves." All temporal bonds, all that links us to the physical world, is reduced to nothing before that single truly important bond: the bond with God. The rest is secondary – either indifferent or hostile. Jesus renounces his mother and brothers, saying that his disciples are his family; he demands that his followers abandon their fathers and mothers, wives and children, sisters and brothers, in his name. According to Luke he even demands that they hate their fathers, mothers, brothers, sisters, and children.

In the world Jesus reveals there is no gradation between good and evil. It is divided into the chosen and the cast out, the sheep and the goats, the heirs of life and the victims of eternal fire, the sons of the king-

Jesus Christ – Prophet and Reformer

dom and the sons of evil, good seeds and weeds. To him who has, will be given; from him who has not, even that which he has will be taken away. There is nothing in between. This division corresponds exactly to the division between the spirit of love and the spirit of lust. To be sure, Jesus speaks to everyone: he says that he has come to call sinners, not the righteous, to repentance; he asks that faults be forgiven up to seventy-seven times; he believes that the repentant heart will wash away sin. But at the same time he knows very well that he cannot break obdurate pride. He hates the proud, the powerful, the self-assured, the smug and self-satisfied with their privileges and power, the rich and the avaricious; to them he does not promise the kingdom. He embraces the despised and the wretched, prostitutes and tax collectors; they believe in him because they know that temporal life is misery and suffering, and this is what one must believe in order to accept and understand Jesus's teaching.

The dichotomy between the world and God's Kingdom is a radical one. It is also a complete reversal of all values: the despised are raised to glory, while the proud are cast out with contempt. This division is the second point which marks a crucial departure from the traditional Jewish view of the world. It is a universal division and uniquely important, unconnected to the division into the chosen people and the rest. Here, too, Jesus perhaps wanted to be only a renewer of the Judaic tradition, not its destroyer; here, too, he was building on foundations laid by the prophets. But in choosing its older and more radical form, he was opposing the tradition; by confronting his own teaching with classical Jewish law, he brought out the conflict between the two, and abolished the idea of the chosen people, introducing, in its place, a universal principle of division.

All these novelties were generalized, so to speak, by his disciples, above all by Paul. In his writings, law and faith are opposed; the principle of universalism is unequivocally formulated (for God "there is neither Jew nor Greek"); the wretchedness of temporal life becomes an injunction to asceticism. At the same time, however, and in the very same epistles, the new division became established as a dogma: condemnations of heretics began to appear. The death of Jesus cemented the reform and produced a separatist community: Christianity as a community was founded not on the disciples' belief in the truth of Jesus's teaching, but on their belief in his resurrection, and later in his divinity. And although in the later history of Christianity the deification of Christ – which is not confirmed in the Gospels – was sometimes questioned, even the doubters acknowledged that the only common dogma of Christianity as such, Christianity without further specification, was the belief that Jesus is Christ, that he was a historical figure, a man born in Galilee and crucified in Jerusalem, and that he is God's anointed. This dogma was constitutive of Christianity even in its "loosest" variants.

But Jesus remains alive in our culture not only for those who believe in his divinity or even just in his supra-natural mission. He is present in our culture not through the dogmas of this or that religious community but through the value of certain precepts which were genuinely new and which – crucially – remain vital not as abstract norms but as living principles, enduringly bound up with his name and his life as handed down by tradition and quite independently of that tradition's historical accuracy.

Jesus for Us

Let us summarize these new rules – rules which can stand independently of Jesus's apocalyptic prophecies and of the belief in the imminent end of the world, although we know that in his teaching they were a function of those prophesies. They may be summarized in five points:

1. *Abolishing law in favor of love*. Again, this must be stressed: *abolishing*, not supplementing. This idea entered European culture as the belief that *human* relations which are based on trust cancel or preclude contractual relations: if harmonious co-existence is based on mutual trust and love, there is no need for contractual claims and duties. When the God of the Pentateuch – a vengeful God, who demanded obedience, sometimes cruel obedience; a God who made the covenant with Abraham for the price of absolute submission, the readiness even to sacrifice one's only child – when this God was transformed into the God of mercy, a new way of viewing human relations was opened. The opposition between contractual relations and relations of love has remained alive in our culture in innumerable varieties, as something that, while genetically connected with Christian beliefs, is not organically bound to them. What is the opposition between "existential" and "pragmatic" communication in contemporary philosophy but a recreation of this distinction? For it was not only Christian philosophies that continued to recreate this opposition. It is recreated anew in the philosophy of Rousseau, of Kierkegaard, and of Jaspers. And when Marx contrasts the relations of interest that obtain in a society based on the exchange of goods with the relations of free association that obtain between people who are voluntarily bound by mutual solidarity, he, too, is recreating the same idea, taking it up, in turn, from the old socialists. It is an idea which is rooted in Jesus, but which in modern Christianity appears most often in heresies and most rarely in the Church. Even Nietzsche, when he says that whatever flows from love is beyond good and evil, is repeating,

unbeknownst to himself, the idea of the enemy. All utopias which want to abolish contractual and legal bonds in favor of voluntary and genuinely experienced solidarity, in short all utopias of universal brotherhood, flower from the same root, however indifferent they may be to their own remote origins.

2. *The hope of eliminating violence from human relations.* This is a hope that often seems to us to be particularly utopian and naive. Indeed, we can say with no hesitation that we have never seen a Christian who took his Christianity literally and really turned the other cheek. But this injunction is one thing when taken literally and something rather different in its restricted version, which demands the elimination of the sources of violence. No one expects Christians literally to fulfill the commandments of the Gospels; it is expected only that they take seriously the simple and elementary rules of tolerance laid out therein, and refrain from violence. But even this expectation is often considered wildly extravagant. People who like to pride themselves on their realism – as if this word meant anything, or as if any concrete directives could flow from its acceptance – consider the idea of abolishing violence a laughable one. But who is being naive here? Those who think, despite all the evidence of human history, that it is possible to diminish the part violence plays in human relations, that much has been already been achieved toward this end, and that more can be peacefully achieved? Or those who imagine that nothing can be accomplished without the use of force, and in particular conversely: that with it everything can be accomplished? No opponent of Christianity can deny that Christianity achieved without the use of force a position in which it could use force against others, and use the name of Jesus as an instrument of torture. It is also true that some forms of practical action based on the principle of applying pressure without violence (for instance, the strategy of Gandhi) have been quite successful. The principle of refraining from violence in international relations is verbally accepted almost universally. Yes, verbally, someone may say; so what? Well, plenty, I would reply. Those values which are verbally accepted and violated in practice are verbally accepted only because of the pressure of universal opinion, which forces agreement. There is no need to despair over hypocrisy; we should, rather, accept that hypocrisy is the testimony to the real social power of those values behind which it hides – the homage that vice pays to virtue, as La Rochefoucauld put it. Until quite recently heads of state did not hesitate openly to announce policies of expansion by war and conquest; but such announcements are now very rare; the idea of a world without violence has been accepted. This being so, the *hope* for a world without violence is not a ludicrous fancy. It is not those who believe that use of

force can decline, and who strive to bring about this decline, who are naive, but those who believe that force can resolve everything. This belief is like a kind of infantile fixation. The use of force toward children is unavoidable up to a certain age, but generally decreases with age; sometimes, however, parents extend the use of force for too long and beyond what is necessary. A person brought up in this way generally acquires the conviction that nothing except force can possibly regulate human relations. He builds an infantile view of the world from his own infantile experiences, promoting them to the status of a primitive philosophy of history, which he proudly calls "realistic," "without illusions," etc. In fact, the belief in the omnipotence of force is not only naive but also, in the long run, self-defeating: we know that collectivities which rely only on force and childishly believe in its universal effectiveness are doomed; they cannot survive, precisely because they cannot cope in situations where force is useless. On the other hand, people who are persistent and resolute often achieve their aims without the use of force, but rather by courage joined with intelligence. Renouncing force need not mean resigned passivity or cowed submission: Christ renounced force, but fought relentlessly for his own point of view; and in dying he broke the resistance of those who wielded power and were in a position to use force. The idea of life without force is neither stupid nor utopian. It calls only for courage – a virtue which is most lacking in those who worship force as a universal method, for they are prepared to fight only when they are in a position to use force against those who are weaker, never otherwise.

3. *Man shall not live by bread alone*. Christ quotes this sentence from Deuteronomy, a text he contradicts so often. But he gives it a broader sense: like the lilies and ravens, we should not worry about life and food. Is this, too, a product of pious naiveté? No. For centuries, people have battled for the recognition of values that are not reducible to physical needs and material satisfaction, for the acknowledgment that such values exist, and that they exist independently of all others; and these efforts persist throughout European culture. Such acknowledgment must seem trivial; it does not strike one with its originality. But after the passage of centuries, everything Jesus preached, if it has endured in our culture, comes to seem banal – and it is thanks to him that it has become so. What can be more banal than saying that man does not only clothe himself and eat? And yet the acceptance of this banality sometimes turned out to require a lengthy battle: for instance, a lot of persistent persuasion has gone into arguing that creative works of the human spirit cannot be assessed according to the dubious advantages they might bring to material production. Let us be grateful, then, to the man who

reminded us that we do not live by bread alone, while at the same time being aware that the injunction to live like the lilies and ravens cannot be taken literally.

4. *The abolition of the idea of a chosen people*. Jesus opened up God for everyone. Or perhaps he simply completed the opening process begun before him by the Jewish prophets. His God does not forbid his people to marry the daughters of unbelievers, nor does He require them to destroy other nations; he says that all the righteous are his people; he promises that many will come from east and west, from north and south, to be in God's Kingdom with Abraham, Isaac, and Jacob. Jesus's God was filled with love for the world; He so loved it, according to John the Apostle, that He gave His only begotten son for its salvation. There was neither Jew nor Greek for Him among His people. These, too, are banalities, of course, but they were not banalities when they first entered European culture: they were great causes; problems which, once posed, were irrevocable; values steeped in the blood of those who battled for their recognition. In the realm of theoretical reflection there is no proposal more modest and none that, when taken seriously, has provoked more dramatic conflicts, than the idea that there are no chosen nations, no people beloved above all others by God or by History and entitled thereby to impose its leadership over others in the name of any cause. It was thanks to the teaching of Jesus that this idea – the idea that fundamental human values are the common property of all, and that humanity is one people – became an inalienable part of our spiritual world.

5. *The essential wretchedness of the temporal world*. It does not matter, for these purposes, to what extent the image of the human world as incurably sick is "right." What matters is that this image became an invariable element in the spiritual development of Europe. It is a constantly recurring theme in every variety of philosophical reflection, by no means limited to Christian thought or to thought directly inspired by Christianity. Jesus told people that they were wretched and that they were concealing their wretchedness from themselves. Pascal, when he embraced this belief, made it central to spiritual life. It is true that this idea has sometimes served to check people's desire to improve their temporal lot, to justify a spirit of resignation to their fate, and to extort an acceptance of things as they were; that it was used to quash the protests of the deprived and oppressed when they rebelled against their exploitation; that it was interpreted in a way which made a virtue of discrediting the possibility of any real improvement in the world. It is also true that the chorus of the well-fed and well-satisfied sometimes clothed itself in the glorious robes of this idea in order to lecture the hungry and deprived about the worthlessness of earthly goods and the pointlessness

of worrying about their temporal lot. The history of Christianity so teems with these interpretations that we have almost ceased to notice how revolting they are.

But, despite all this, there is another interpretation; an interpretation that need not entail approval of the privileged and well-satisfied. The vileness of this approval was exposed a long time ago and Christianity, as we can see, is slowly renouncing it. The belief in the essential wretchedness of human existence does contain something that can be, and has been, a topic of philosophical reflection, quite independently of the base uses to which it has been put. It is something that has always been an important subject for philosophers; it can be reflected upon regardless of whether or not one believes in an afterlife; and it does not suggest the conclusion that, in view of the structural infirmity of our existence, all efforts to repair what can be repaired are vain and sterile. For one can try to change for the better all that can be changed in the conditions of human existence, one can battle for it relentlessly, while being aware that the absolute is unattainable, and that the essential frailty of human existence is irreparable, because it is a fundamental part of that existence, and arises from human finiteness itself. This topic will not cease to be of interest to philosophers.

Returning Jesus to Culture

This is the list – incomplete and selective, but not arbitrarily selective – of the values which, thanks to the teaching of Jesus, found an enduring place in the spiritual substance of Europe and of the world, in a way that was not essentially bound to Christian dogma. But the abstraction of these values, in their non-Christian form, from their personal roots, is a sort of cultural impoverishment. It is connected with the way Jesus has been monopolized by dogmatic Christian communities and with the decline of his presence as a person in other areas of the spiritual world. This poses the risk that all the symptoms of Christianity's decline will, unavoidably, also erode the historical meaning of the existence of Jesus. This is what we want to avoid.

It is true that many of the above-mentioned points could evoke the response, "we've heard all this all before"; it is not without justification that we look for similar themes in the religions of Asia. But in Mediterranean culture, the culture of our birth, these values are bound up with the teaching of Jesus and with his name; they are the spiritual fund which he introduced and to which he gave momentum. Hence any attempt to "invalidate Jesus," to eliminate him from our culture on the pretext that we do not believe in the God in whom he believed, is absurd and fruitless. Such attempts are made only by those primitive enough to imagine that crude atheism not only suffices as a view of the world, but can also justify trimming the cultural tradition as one sees fit, according to one's own doctrinal fancies, hacking away an essential part of it and depriving it of its most vital source.

Finally, if – as we uncertainly hope – the Christian world proves capable of real improvement and change, it will draw its reparative strength only from its own source (non-Christian critics can weaken Christianity, but they cannot repair it). Consequently, it can maintain its ability for self-repair only by constantly concentrating its attention on that spiritual fund which is bound to the name of Jesus.

Regardless of this hope, however, the person and the teaching of Jesus Christ cannot be invalidated or removed from our culture if that culture is to continue to exist and to create itself. The figure of this man, who for centuries was not just a teacher but the model of the highest human values, cannot fall into oblivion without a fundamental break in the continuity of spiritual life. For he incarnated, in his person, the ability to express one's own truth fully and loudly, to defend it to the end with no evasion, and to resist to the end the pressure of the established reality which rejected him. He taught how we can confront the world and ourselves without resorting to violence. He was a model of that radical authenticity in which, and only in which, every human being can give true life to his own values.

Leibniz and Job:

The Metaphysics of Evil and the Experience of Evil[1]

To review human reflection about evil is to review the entire history of theology, philosophy, religion and literature, from the Rig Veda to Plato to Dostoyevsky to Wittgenstein. And to consider the effective operations of evil in human life is to consider the whole history of mankind, from paleolithic tribes to twentieth-century man.

There are two ways – each of them with a number of variants – that philosophers, theologians, scholars, scientists, and ordinary people have tried, throughout the centuries, to cope with the so-called problem of evil. As with all important human issues, we can try either to solve the "problem" or to get rid of it altogether by declaring it invalid: by denying that the problem exists. Among those who have tried to tackle the problem we find adherents of two fundamentally opposed (or so it seems) metaphysics: Manichaeans and Christians. Among those who have denied the validity of the problem – though not all of them for the same reason – there are some mystics, some pantheists, all Marxists and communists, most other utopians, and most advocates of a naturalistic worldview, like Nietzscheans, Nazis, and philosophical Darwinists.

It is trivially true that the concept of evil as pure negativity is a simple deduction from the belief in a creator who is both unique and infinitely good so that whatever is, is good necessarily, and existence as such is good. This, to repeat, is a logical deduction, not a matter of experience. But it is mostly through such arguments that Christian theodicy has made its enormous, indeed heroic, efforts to respond to the most common experience of ordinary people – the experience of evil. When St.

---

1 This essay is the text of a lecture given at the 2002 Nexus Conference on Evil in Tilburg, June 2002. It was published in *The New Criterion* in December 2003. Used with the kind permission of the publisher.

Leibniz and Job: The Metaphysics of Evil and the Experience of Evil

Augustine says that the very presence of evil must be good because if it were not, God would not have allowed evil to appear, he is stating something that is obvious in Christian terms. This, again, is a logical deduction from the concept of God; it implies that God could, if He wanted, prevent evil from appearing, but for reasons best known to Himself preferred to let it stay.

Leibniz is more specific in explaining what those reasons may have been. He, too, does so by deduction. Having proved the necessary existence of God and, separately, His supreme goodness, Leibniz inferred from these that God must have created the best world that is logically conceivable, and that this is the world we inhabit; any other world would be worse.

Voltaire's famous derision of this idea is too easy. Leibniz was well aware of the horrors of life. Nevertheless, belief in the supreme goodness of creation is irresistible given such an idea of the divine being. And it implies that God, in His all-embracing wisdom, must have solved, as it were, an equation in an infinitely complex higher calculus in order to calculate which world would produce the maximum goodness. Christian tradition has always stressed, after Plato, the distinction between moral evil and suffering: moral evil – *malum culpae* – is the inevitable result of human (and angelic) free will, and Leibniz's creator reckoned that a universe populated by rational creatures endowed with free will, and thus capable of doing evil, would generate more good than a world whose dwellers would, in effect, be automata, programmed never to do evil (and presumably, though Leibniz does not say so explicitly, never to do good either, if by a good action we mean, as we commonly do, an action done out of choice, not from compulsion).

As for non-man-made suffering – *malum poenae* in the Christian idiom – there are two possible answers. One says that such suffering is the work of malevolent spirits whose work is permitted by God because it serves to punish, correct, or warn us. The other, in the Leibnizian spirit, says that it results from the workings of the laws of nature, and that God is not omnipotent in the sense of being able to combine everything with anything and impose on the physical universe an order where things would not move according to strict regularities, would stop interfering and colliding with each other. Those Christian thinkers who believed (like some fourteenth-century nominalists and, among contemporary thinkers, Shestov) that God is omnipotent in the absolute sense – i.e., that He can change the past and establish moral commandments and the laws of mathematics by *fiat* – left themselves more vulnerable to the traditional Epicurean criticism: if God could do these things, then – since there is evil in the world – He must be either evil or powerless. This criticism does not affect Leibnizian theodicy, where God cannot alter the rules of logic or mathematics. But His inability to do so is not a limitation of His omnipotence, for those rules, valid in themselves, are not imposed on Him from outside, like some alien law: they are identical with Him. Therefore we should not complain and ask God why He failed to make our universe a paradise without suffering. Besides, God never promised that He would suspend the laws of nature for our benefit and use miracles to prevent people from harming one another; He did not promise a world without wars, torture, Auschwitz, or Gulags.

All this is trivial and well known. Not surprisingly, however, many people have found that this theological structure fails to give them a satisfactory explanation of the evil they face, experience, and do. It is not convincing to the ordinary mind to be told that evil is pure privation, a purely negative phenomenon; that the devil is a good thing insofar as he exists; and that human suffering and pain are elements of the best arrangement God could have devised for the world. The ordinary mind is much more inclined to echo Voltaire's famous ironic question after the Lisbon earthquake: would the world be worse without it? It would seem that, according to this theological explanation, the world would be worse if there had been no Auschwitz and no Gulags, or, for that matter, if I had not broken my finger.

But here, again, Leibniz, or any other Christian theologian, would say that this is the wrong way of looking at the question. They do not claim, they would say, to be able to apply a divine algorithm and demonstrate that particular instances of suffering, however horrifying, turn out, on closer inspection, to be good – in the infinite global balance sheet, because each prevents a greater evil from occurring or makes a greater good possible. The balance sheet is known only to God; we cannot try to reproduce it, and it would be hopeless to try. Besides, we have no idea how to measure and quantitatively compare various evils and goods in their infinite variety. The proper attitude is to trust God's plan in advance, without calculation or complaint; to accept it, and with it to accept all human misery and the indifferent destructiveness of nature. The idea (present in St. Augustine and in Hegel) that evil is needed for aesthetic reasons – because it adorns the world by the contrasts and variety it creates – sounds even more preposterous.

It is understandable that in the face of so many tormenting riddles the human mind came up with another solution, which we usually, rightly or not, call Manichaean. It goes back to old Iranian mythology, and it seems convincing and in accordance with our everyday experience. It says that there are two powers, or twin gods, good and evil, which fight each other, and that the evil we know from experience – i.e., suffering – is simply the work of the evil god. In contrast to its Zoroastrian source, Manichaean theology, like its various gnostic relatives and unlike Christian doctrine, saw matter as the creation of the evil power. The Manichaean worldview has been a constant temptation for Christians, and for the European mind in general. The thought that Satanic powers, whatever their origin, are hard at work trying to upset God's benevolent blueprint, quite often successfully, seems more natural and in accordance with common sense than many other explanations of evil. Manichaeanism is absorbed by our minds, so to speak, with minimal resistance. Even Judaism, which has the reputation of being the one-God religion *par excellence*, the model of monotheistic thinking, is not free of this temptation. Gershom Sholem, one of the most distinguished scholars of the history of Kabbala and Jewish mysticism, tells us that the book of Zohar often presents evil as something real, or positive, not just as privation. God's powers make a good harmonious whole, His judgments are good, His right hand distributes love and mercy and His left hand is the organ of His wrath – but it is when the latter operates independently of the former that radical evil appears: the kingdom of Satan. We do not know whether Jacob Boehme was familiar with Kabbalistic writings, but his theosophy contains a similar idea: evil is the negative principle of divine wrath; it is independent of human will and is somehow embedded in the structure of the world.

Some ancient Platonists (e.g., Plutarch of Cheroneia or Numenius) also succumbed to this belief in two independent powers, good and evil. While for Plotinus evil is simply the absolutely inevitable bottom rung on the ladder of being; the absolute goodness of the One could not escape the natural descent of reality into matter. Nevertheless, we must still, of course, abhor the gnostic doctrine that the Creator of the world is himself evil.

Even in the dogmas of the Roman Church we find remnants of this "dualistic" theology. Matter itself cannot be evil, of course; and, conversely, the Church also condemned, in 1347, the theory of Nicholas Autrecourt, who wrote that the world is absolutely perfect, both as a whole and in each of its parts (*"universum est perfectissimum secundum se et secundum omnes partes suas"*) – presumably because such a daring statement seemed to suggest that there simply is no evil in the world: no sinful will of corrupted creatures, human or satanic. But the Catholic belief in the eternity of Hell and the irreversible fate of the fallen angels implies that some, indeed very large parts, of evil are indestructible, irredeemable, incurable; that the world will forever be split into two realms, morally opposed to each other. Not surprisingly, some of the Greek

Fathers, and some later theologians, were unable to stomach these dogmas or to reconcile them with the image of an absolutely good, loving, and merciful Creator.

Dogmatic pronouncements of the Church have often assured us that moral evil, while it is permitted by God, can never be caused by Him; that human misery and pain, if it cannot be attributed to the malicious will of other people, serves a good purpose – i.e., that it is not really evil. Priests and theologians may have tried to explain the suffering of individuals, particular calamities and atrocities, as parts of a shrewd divine plan, but the Church avoided official comments of this kind; it only advised us to be satisfied with global, unconditional trust.

In fact, we all know that pain and catastrophes are – on the face of it – distributed at random and cannot be interpreted in terms of merit and sin, reward and punishment. Job knew this as well. Job does not try to construct a theodicy. He has been a just man all his life and God knows that his misery is not retribution for his crimes. He suffers horribly for no reason, but he is able to say: "Though he slay me, yet will I trust in him" (Job 13:15). He accepts that God alone is the source of wisdom and that His ways are inscrutable. God Himself is angry at Job's advisers, theologians, presumably because they argue that Job's sufferings are the proper punishment for his sins. The whole of the book of Job seems to refute the theory of pain as just retribution.

This is what God said to Job and his wife many centuries later in Robert Frost's play "A Masque of Reason":

> I've had you on my mind a thousand years
> To thank you someday for the way you helped me
> Establish once for all the principle
> There's no connection man can reason out
> Between his just deserts and what he gets.
> Virtue may fail and wickedness succeed . . .
> Too long I've owed you this apology
> For the apparently unmeaning sorrow
> You were afflicted with in those old days.
> But it was of the essence of the trial
> You shouldn't understand it at the time.
> I had to seem unmeaning to have meaning . . .
> My thanks are to you for releasing me
> From moral bondage to the human race.
> The only free will there at first was man's,
> Who could do good or evil as he chose.
> I had no choice but I must follow him
> With forfeits and rewards he understood . . .

I had to prosper good and punish evil.
You changed all that. You set me free to reign.
You are the Emancipator of your God.

We see the horror of this: supreme goodness is incompatible with free will as we understand it. In every situation it has only one option: to maximize good. And Job's story changes that: it frees God. He can support the wicked and torment the just, according to His wish or whim. If so, no theodicy is possible or needed. Perhaps a consistent theodicy has never been written?

In various mythologies evil is explained in various ways; gods often share good and evil qualities, ambiguously. It is beyond the scope of this essay to plunge into the complexities of Hindu and Buddhist theories of evil. Nietzsche said that Buddhism is beyond good and evil. This might be true of some varieties of Buddhism, purified of later mythological imagery. To some Buddhist sages, and presumably to Gautama himself, the world we know from experience is nothing but misery and suffering; there is no liberation, no salvation except through abandoning it. This idea is in fact not alien to many European thinkers. We all remember the immortal words of the dying Socrates: "Crito, I owe a cock to Asclepius." This amounts to saying: here ends the sickness called life.

But this is not a universal belief. Some pantheists and some mystics live lives so immersed in the divine environment that evil is unnoticeable in their universe. The light of God penetrates everything; there is no reason to complain and no point in complaining, for the world is full of joy and "whatever is of God, is God," as Eckhart says. Or, in the words of the seventeenth-century French mystic Louis Chardon, "God in the sky is more my sky than the sky itself; in the sun He is more my light than the sun, in the air He is more the air than the air I breathe."

It may well not seem obvious why the same word should be used for both suffering and moral wickedness. Many thinkers, Christian and non-Christian, identified evil with moral evil. Epictetus says that there is no good or evil in things that do not depend on our will; that the blows of fate we cannot avoid cannot be evil; that we should seek Good and Evil in ourselves; and that a wise man can turn everything into good – illness, death, misery. The only thing in the world that is contrary to God is sin – so says the Cambridge Platonist Benjamin Cudworts – and sin is a nonentity: nothing. God Himself said to Catherine of Siena that no suffering can redeem our guilt, only repentance. And He added that the worst sin is the refusal or mistrust of divine mercy: the despair of Judas was a greater sin and a worse insult to God than his betrayal of Jesus.

All these considerations suggest that suffering in itself is morally indifferent: only our will, our intentions, our deeds can be morally assessed. It is evil to maliciously inflict pain on other people, but suffering pain is not an evil.

However, if I decide that the word "evil" can be used to describe my intentions but not my suffering, I am thereby suggesting that what other people do is of no interest to me. If they make me suffer, the evil done is not *my* evil, but an evil caused by them. Should I say that my problem is only my own saintliness and not the evil that exists in the world, or the problem of how to make the world better? This might be in keeping with Stoic moral doctrine, but not with common sense, which tells me to condemn not only my own evil but all evil, throughout the human world.

But in that case we might need another restriction. If we limit the word "evil" to what is caused by human will, then its meaning cannot be extended to encompass all suffering: suffering caused by natural forces, or even by human actions if their harmful or painful effects were not intended but happened by accident. And since the word "evil" in this sense clearly has a moral association, if we do apply it to earthquakes, plagues, or deaths from lightning, we seem to be implying that such events are intentionally produced: that nothing in nature happens simply as a result of the blind operation of natural laws, that everything happens by design. Such an interpretation is, of course, part of the religious view of the universe, and does not necessarily contradict the belief in the laws of nature. According to many theologians, God, in His omniscience, included natural events in the moral order of the cosmos: they happen by natural necessity, but at the same time they have a moral purpose; they are not miracles that break the chain of cause and effect. Such a view is, in fact, close to the Leibnizian position. And – as Malebranche said – even if natural events are caused directly by God, and the world is thus an infinite series of miracles, the regularity in the natural order of things remains undisturbed.

As for those who implicitly or explicitly invalidate the "question of evil" for religious reasons, they, of course, believe in good: they believe that good permeates the entire material and spiritual cosmos.

Then there are those who are at the opposite end of both the theological and the anti-theological spectrum, who believe that both "good" and "evil" are no more than mythical inventions. Pleasure and pain exist, of course, and can be explained within the natural order; but in themselves they have no moral qualities. Nothing is good or evil in itself; something can be pleasant or unpleasant, harmful or beneficial, to particular people – to you, to me, to him – and without this qualifier even the words "pleasant" and "unpleasant," not to speak of the words "good" and "evil," are meaningless. This is what Hobbes, Hume, and even Spinoza believed (although in the case of Spinoza things are more complicated). Nietzsche says that we do not need the word "evil," for

Leibniz and Job: The Metaphysics of Evil and the Experience of Evil

the world is "bad" enough as it is. But what is "bad"? Something that produces undesirable effects or does not fit the purposes we have in mind. The same idea is suggested by the very title of Konrad Lorenz's book on aggression, *Das sogenannte Böse*.

Within the naturalistic or materialistic view of reality the qualities of "good" and "evil" are inadmissible, or useless and misleading, for they suggest that something can possess these qualities in itself, unconditionally and independently of the circumstances, and this suggestion can be suspected of having a religious provenance.

This view is clearly visible in the Marxist or communist *Weltanschauung*. Let us take an example from literature.

A character in Solzhenitsyn's novel *The Cancer Ward* visits the zoo and sees an empty cage with a notice on it; the notice says that the monkey which used to live in that cage was blinded as a result of the mindless cruelty of a visitor: an *evil man* threw tobacco in its eyes.

Reading this notice is a tremendous shock for the visitor. How can it be? An evil man? Not an agent of American imperialism but simply an evil man? What sort of description is that?

The visitor's shock and amazement were genuine and quite understandable. The adjective "evil" (and no less so the noun) as the description of a moral quality was absent from the ideological jargon of the totalitarian Soviet world. There were, of course, criminals, monsters, traitors, foreign agents; but no one who was simply "evil." This was not only because the quality of being evil might easily have suggested the religious tradition. It also suggested an inherent, lasting property of a person or an act, independent of the political context. Whereas it is obvious to anyone who thinks dialectically that actions which are ostensibly the same kinds of actions can be right or wrong depending on the circumstances – or rather, on the cause in the name of which they are performed. Both Lenin and Trotsky were quite explicit on this point. Is there, for instance, something inherently wrong in slaughtering children? – No. It was right, Trotsky argues, to slaughter the children of the Russian czar because it was politically expedient. (Presumably it was not right to kill Trotsky's sons, however, because Stalin did not represent the historical interests of the proletariat; Trotsky, as far as I know, did not deal with this question directly, but such an answer would be perfectly in keeping with his fanatical mentality.) If we reject the principle that the end justifies the means, we can only appeal to higher, politically irrelevant moral criteria; and this, Trotsky says, amounts to believing in God.

This is not properly speaking a relativist doctrine. We normally reserve that label for the belief that an act can be good or evil depending on the circumstances; but this is not what the person who thinks dialectically says. The person who thinks dialectically says that when we talk about an action being right or wrong according to the circumstances, we are never talking about the same action; the similarity is only ostensible, merely superficial. In one case, by eliminating potential enemies of the proletariat, we are performing an act that is politically right; in the other, we are committing a crime against the mission of the proletariat. Similarly, an act that is an act of liberation of another country from capitalist oppression must not be called an "invasion"; Nazi concentration camps must not be compared with the educational system of a socialist state. And so on. We have scientific knowledge of the progress of history, and thus we know that once everything – including human beings – becomes state property, the way is open to universal rejoicing. And we know what is right and wrong, politically correct and incorrect; we have no need of superstitious descriptions like "evil." There is no point in dwelling on this primitive "dialectics" and mendacious language; it is well known.

What has happened to our question? Need we appeal to the idea of evil at all? May we not be satisfied with the distinction between "pleasant" and "unpleasant" (always relative to person, time and place)? But who would be bold and dogmatically rigid enough to claim that "good" and "evil" are not empirical qualities; that there is no perception of moral qualities, including the intuition of evil; that centuries of human experience, from the indescribable cruelties of ancient Rome to the monstrosities of the twentieth century, are irrelevant to the "question of evil" and may be dismissed as no more than a series of unpleasant impressions (and no one is denying that unpleasant things do happen to people)? I will end with a remark by a French Catholic theologian whose name escapes me; he said that he can understand people who do not believe in God, but the fact that there are people who do not believe in the devil is beyond his comprehension.

Concern about God in an Apparently Godless Age[1]

If we were asked, "What has happened to the `God question'?'" many of us would be inclined to respond spontaneously: Is there such a question? Perhaps there is no "God question"? This is what the thoroughgoing rationalists and scientists would maintain, claiming that the concept of God cannot be presented in any way as an understandable, non-contradictory intellectual construction. For before we ask the "question," we have to know what the question is about; we must therefore have at our disposal a clear conception of God before statements and questions like "God exists," or "God does not exist," or "Does God exist?" can be taken up as objects of reflection. This, however, is exactly what is impossible. Every statement about God is either contradictory or unintelligible as a matter of principle, because it can in no way be brought into contact with empirical reality. Because of this, the "question" is empty.

The "God question" also does not exist for believers – if there are such people – whose inherited faith remains rock-solid and unshakable. They know, without a doubt, that they live in a world steered by God. And for those chosen souls who have shared in the blessing of mystical experience, perhaps the word "faith" is inappropriate. For faith is only

---

1 Written in German ("Die Sorge um Gott in einem scheinbar gottlosen Zeitalter," *Der nahe und der ferne Gott: Nichttheologische Texte zur Gottesfrage im 20 Jahrhundert*, Mit einer Einleitung von Leszek Kolakowski, Ein Lesebuch, Severin und Siedler [Berlin, 1981]; reprinted in "Süddeutsche Zeitung" 203 [September 5–6, 1981]); translated into English by Frederic Fransen, and published in the June/July 2003 edition of *First Things* under the title "Visions of Eternity." This version has been revised by the author and Agnieszka Kolakowska.

active when a shadowy distance arouses the potential for uncertainty between the perceiver and the perceived. In mystical experience, all distance is lifted. These people, naturally, do not ask "God questions."

Nor does the "God question" exist for convinced atheists – if there are such people. For they know, without a doubt, that science has conclusively driven God out of the world, and that the concept of God merely expresses the remnants of old superstitions, ignorance, psychological defense mechanisms, or social conflicts.

But the world in which we live is not a world of people settled contentedly in stable lives of belief or unbelief. It is much more an era of the driven, of refugees and exiles, people floundering around, like the eternal "wandering Jew," in search of a lost spiritual or physical homeland. In this nomadic life nothing is certain, nothing guaranteed, nothing set permanently in stone, nothing – except wandering – unquestionably given.

The God who once confirmed a well-established order of values and social relations, rules of thought and of the physical cosmos, the God who was the dome encompassing this order, is no longer there, because no such order is there. So long as people could trust in the durability of this order, the godless also had their place in it (I have in mind here only European, Christian civilization), whether they were seen as mistaken, as crazy, or as messengers from Hell. If they were also persecuted, punished, or sentenced to death, they were at least, in a sense, fortunate, for they had not only certainty, but also freedom from spiritual worries: for them there was no God, and therefore also no Heaven and no Hell, and this was fine.

But even this is over. The self-assurance of unbelief, too, has been shaken, together with the self-assurance of belief. Unlike the old cozy world, protected by a well-intentioned, friendly Nature, the Nature of the atheistic Enlightenment, the godless world of today is perceived as an afflicted, endless chaos. It is robbed of all meaning, all direction, all road signs, and all structure. Thus spoke Zarathustra. Ever since Nietzsche announced the death of God, the cheerful atheist has been a rare sight. The world in which one had to rely on one's own powers, in which one declared oneself an unconstrained lawgiver, free to define good and evil, and in which, freed from the condition of a slave of God, one hoped to recapture one's lost dignity – this world has transformed itself into a place of never-ending worry. The absence of God became an open, festering wound in the European spirit, even as it slipped off into an oblivion induced by an artificial anaesthetic. It is enough to compare the godless world of Diderot, Helvetius, and Feuerbach with that of Kafka, Camus, and Sartre. The collapse of Christianity so eagerly awaited by the Enlightenment proved – to the extent that it did take place – to be almost simultaneous with the collapse of the Enlightenment. The new, shining order of anthropocentrism that was to be built in place of the fallen God never came. What happened? Why was the fate of atheism so strangely bound to that of Christianity, so that these two enemies accompanied one another in their misfortune and in their insecurity?

Certainly, the history of Christianity also left us great testimonials of spiritual restlessness from different periods: in the writings of the young St. Augustine, in Pascal, or in Kierkegaard. But restlessness as the quality of the human spirit *par excellence*, its *quidditas*, is a symptom of our century and our culture. It is a culture propelled forward in great leaps of breathtaking creativity; but at the same time we all feel that it is ailing, even if we cannot agree on a diagnosis of its sickness. Does its source lie in the fact that it has been abandoned by God? Was Kierkegaard right when he said that all our despair about the world is in fact – even if sometimes unbeknownst to us – despair about the Eternal? We cannot, naturally, prove this; we can only suspect it.

I am not talking here about the restlessness felt and expressed by intellectuals, philosophers, or poets, but about a restlessness that infects the European spirit as a whole, in its ordinary daily life. It is a restlessness that torments religious culture at both its poles – militant Christianity and militant godlessness; and it is also plainly visible behind the widespread indifference which today seems to be the main form of spiritual life. And even within apparent apathy, the disturbing void cannot be completely disguised. In the background of all our successes and experiences the apocalyptic warning sounds: "Because thou sayest, I am rich, and increased with goods, and have need of nothing; and knowest not that thou art wretched, and miserable, and poor, and blind, and naked" (Revelation 3:17).

Among the spiritual conditions that in modern times, and particularly in recent decades, have most contributed to the continuous growth of what we call secularization, two in particular are cited – both by those for whom secularization is a welcome liberation and by those who see it as a catastrophe. One is the progress of science, whose role has grown tremendously in every area of our lives, and in which God no longer has a place. The second is the inability of Christianity, particularly the Church of Rome, to cope with the great social problems that have come from the century's process of industrialization: Christianity, on this view, has proven itself unresponsive to new social conflicts and needs because its eyes are directed only toward Heaven and toward God; and the problems of the world which Christianity has forgotten must therefore take care of themselves – outside Christianity.

It may be worth explaining briefly why neither of these popular opinions seems credible to me.

What Is Wrong with God?

Concerning the first, it is certainly true that God is not an empirical hypothesis that can be put forward and scientifically tested. This is a permanent situation, not a question of the temporary insufficiency of our knowledge; there is no logically accessible way from empirical knowledge, however much it can be extended, to infinity – let alone to an intentionally active, personally conceived Providence. Ever since, in the seventeenth century, scientific research separated itself from theology and religion and codified its procedural rules, it was clear that its basis and methods were completely indifferent to the "God Question." The aim of this codification was to make scientific results into tools of prediction, and thereby to bring natural phenomena under human control.

It is not credible to claim that this is what drove God from the world, unless one confuses science with scientistic rationalism. The latter – broadly, the principle that truth-value is determined by the correct application of scientific rules – was conceived precisely in order to render religious belief worthless; it is an arbitrary epistemological doctrine, the arbitrary decree of philosophers. Scientism is neither a logical consequence of science nor – one may plausibly maintain – its social consequence; if the two have developed in parallel, this was not because science begat scientism. But of course their connection was not accidental. Scientistic rationalism is a normative principle, the expression of a certain hierarchy of values in which the goods whose production empirical science, as a social organ, is meant above all to serve, count as values *par excellence*. Naturally, God is excluded from the scientistic conception of the world, together with all that cannot be made to serve the human drive for domination over nature. But in accordance with this view, He would also have no role in a Christian worldview; for if He ruled the world in such a way that His powers were predictable, i.e., if miracles and other types of divine intervention were subject to permanent rules with predictable results, this would mean that the laws of the physical world had ceased to work. In fact, both Christian theology and its popular construction bear some responsibility for the confusion between rational knowledge and faith, in that both maintained that God's justice could be discovered in the world empirically, and that we could magically harness Him in our strivings and passions. This attitude – in my view a fundamentally anti-Christian one – is precisely what we call superstition. The superstition consists in conceiving of God as a machine which – through the application of the correct technique – will produce the desired effects, as if, for example, prayer were a technical operation that, if properly carried out, would infallibly bring about the expected results. To the degree that Christian teaching furthered such superstitious attitudes, it contributed to its own demise. The same is true of theologians who claim to practice "scientific theology." When faith competes with science and tries to apply its criteria, it is doomed to become a pseudo-science; its efforts will always be frustrated and its claims disproved. However, the more widespread the confusion between faith and profane knowledge became, the more educated people felt compelled to abandon faith along with superstition. The Christian worldview is a keen insight into human destiny. "Scientific theology," by contrast, is a superstition.

In a sense it can be said that scientistic rationalism had a healing effect on culture, in that it contributed to ridding Christianity of superstition and allowed it to regain its understanding of its identity and its aims. Atheism and scientism obviously strengthen one another. But neither of the two, I must repeat, counts as a true product of science. The origin of both is much better sought in our culture – for instance, in our inclination to scorn anything that seems useless to our drive for domination and possession. The present crisis of trust in science and technology in the face of its dangerous results may weaken the ideologies of scientific rationalism. This crisis, however, has nothing to do with the validity or invalidity of the norms of scientific knowledge.

Thus the reproach that Christianity is not "scientific" enough, and that this is why it has suffered such losses, seems to me astonishingly naive. The opposite is the case: whenever Christianity insists on its "scientific" value, it only invents a powerless pseudo-knowledge. It was precisely such claims, not its "unscientificness," that compromised it in its conflicts with science, and led to those conflicts in the first place. It was precisely Christianity's fearful reluctance to define itself in clear opposition to rationalism and to accept that it is what in fact it always was – the translation of the divine message into human language – that led to its fruitless attacks on science, and to the erosion of Christian faith. The very idea of a contradiction between science and faith presupposes a concept of faith as a kind of profane knowledge – and thus involves, in a real sense, a profanization.

Something similar can be said about the second reproach: that Christianity, because it concentrates exclusively on spiritual values, has neglected the real concerns of the world and neither sought nor found answers to the social problems of the modern age, and thereby brought about its own ruin. But here, too, it is rather the opposite that might be true. The error of the Church lies much more in that it bound its moral rules to a specific social doctrine, thereby exposing itself to the reproach that it had fused together its eternal values with contemporary developments – polluted the holy with the profane. There were some well-founded elements in the attacks that the socialists of the nineteenth century directed against the Church hierarchy; the Church's attitudes to social changes, to the poor and abused, were indeed open to criticism.

But every criticism, however justifiable, is travestied, indeed loses its meaning, if we express it by objecting that the Church "thought only about the other world," or that it was too busy with "religion" to pay attention to temporal life and suffering. One should, instead, say that it was too much a prisoner of existing social structures, and often gave the impression that these structures were firmly based upon enduring Christian values.

Christianity is still vulnerable to the same danger, in two opposing variations, both anchored in the same temptation. The danger does not consist in forgetting about the world, but rather in forgetting that the value of worldly things must always be relative; and it opens the way to godlessness in that it blurs the boundary between the holy and the profane. There is no profane matter – no social or intellectual end – that Christianity could defend better than the temporal powers who bear responsibility for such things; Christianity may want to engage in temporal politics and social conflicts, but it must, on pain of destroying itself, retain its view of all temporal things as relative. In our world, one cannot in good faith be apolitical; accordingly, the Church, insofar as it is an organ of culture, cannot completely renounce political responsibility or declare itself to be apolitical. But being politically active need not mean either identifying oneself with any existing political organization or movement, or maintaining political values and ends as ultimate ends. The Church's traditional connections with the established social orders of the nineteenth century were just as dangerous for the cause of Christianity as are modern attempts to connect the Christian idea with the political ideologies of revolutionary messianism. Neither tendency fulfills the hope of a new vitality of the Christian message; both are liable to succumb to the temptation to subordinate this message to temporal ends – that is, to transform God into a tool, a potential object of human manipulation. The (enfeebled but not yet dead) theocratic tendency – the disastrous and vain hope that humanity could be led to redemption by force – and the opposing tendency – the attempt to subordinate Christian values to this or that revolutionary ideology – both transform God into an instrument for the achievement of ends which, justified or not, may never be considered ultimate within a Christian perspective, because they carry with them the danger of turning the Christian community into a political party. Thus both represent an inner corrosion of Christianity. As always, the greatest threat comes from the enemy within.

Described so generally, the situation certainly does not appear new. The entire history of Christian teaching – however caught up in, and possibly even dependent on, social conflicts – can be considered an unending struggle about the boundary between the sacred and the profane. The strongest spiritual surges which appear as interruptions in this history, the upheavals and the moments of awakening, were usually attempts to stop the process of profanization, to return Christianity to its original calling and prevent its domination by temporal interests. Such upheavals never came without a price and were never completely successful. The danger could never be definitively set aside, because it lies in the nature of Christianity: in the eternal tension between its temporal and its sacral self-interpretation; for Christianity, while considering itself a repository of divine grace, at the same time remains an organism that exists in this world – culturally and historically determined, and forced to act with the temporal means at its disposal.

The Gospels bear witness to Christian solidarity with the poor, the oppressed, the miserable, and the defenseless; but no Gospel promises an earth without evil, suffering, or conflicts. The Gospels condemn those who, in their glorious comfort, remain deaf to the suffering and hunger of the disinherited; but no Gospel preaches social equality or inequality, or prescribes a recipe for a perfect social system, one that would fulfill all human drives and desires and banish all frustrations. The Gospels denounce tyrants and persecutors; but no Gospel prescribes a pact with one form of tyranny against another in the name of chiliastic dreams. A Christianity which stealthily accepts that God stands ready to serve us, to protect any kind of cause, doctrine, ideology, or political party, is disguised godlessness.

In this sense one can say that both the inherited theocratic tendency and Christian "progressivism" have furthered de-christianization; and indeed each suspected the other of secularizing Christian values. What people seek in religion is – *mirabile dictu* – God, not the justification of political values or "scientific" explanations of nature. A Christianity that bows before intellectual and political fashions in the search for transient success participates in its own destruction. It can never match or surpass science in the application of scientific criteria when it tries to use them to bolster Christian teaching. It can never match or surpass the promise of earthly happiness offered by political ideologies, and when it tries to do so it unavoidably shows its powerlessness and seems useless and irrelevant. Christianity sees human fate in light of the Gospels and the Book of Job, not in the categories that theocratic, technocratic, or revolutionary utopias have formulated.

Perhaps – but this is only speculation – dechristianization, to the extent that it has accompanied the decline of the temporal power of the Church, will prove favorable, even salutary, for the cause of Christianity. If we take this cause seriously, we have no reason to be horrified by the demise of a Christianity that was accustomed to being identified with power politics and diplomatic intrigue on the one hand, and with fanaticism and raw clericalism on the other. From the painful but beneficial purgatory of a ruthless and profane history, perhaps a Christianity will emerge that is truer to its spirit. Perhaps.

It is rightly said that Christianity must alter the language of its teaching and adapt to cultural change. It has done so more than once, not without huge difficulty. But in this process of adaptation there is always the danger that in the search for new forms the content will be forgotten. It seems true that, as many have pointed out, the modern European is mostly deaf to the conventional language of theology. The immense importance of Thomism in cultural history is indisputable, but it has proved unsatisfactory as a conceptual net in which to capture the cosmos today. The problem is not that traditional teaching is "incomprehensible" for people in the modern world, as is sometimes claimed; there are no grounds for thinking that we have suddenly become stupid, so something that was understandable for the people of the Middle Ages has become inaccessible to us. The main problem is simply the distance between the experience of our everyday life and the inherited theological idiom. Each search for meaning in the world must not only take account of the order or disorder of civilization at the time, including all of its components, and take this as its point of departure; it must also be alert to how the permanent presence of evil in human destiny is revealed in that civilization's particular disturbances, sufferings, and concerns. Of course, this is easy to say in such a general way. Attempts to create a new language for Christian teaching will certainly take much longer, and it is not clear how successful they will prove to be.

We urgently prayed to God, asking Him to leave the world. This He has done, at our request. A gaping hole remains. We still pray to this hole – to nothing. No one answers. We are angry or disappointed. Is this proof of the non-existence of God?

What is new in our experience? Evil? But evil has always been with us; it came from us. Is it really much greater than before? We sometimes ask, Where was God in Auschwitz? In Kolyma? In genocide, torture, and war? Why did He remain idle? But this is a bad question. Firstly because the atrocities that humans perpetrate on each other have been perpetrated in all periods of history; genocide, bloodbaths, and torture have always occurred; evil – the evil in us – never ceases its work. And secondly because this question contains an assumption we have smuggled in: the idea that God has a constant duty, through miracles, to protect humans against their own evil and ensure their happiness despite their self-inflicted wounds. But such a God – a God who acts as a magical power in the service of our needs – was never the God of Christian faith, or of any other great religion (despite the frequency of this image of God in folk religion). If He had been, one would have expected the early

Christian martyrs to have lost their faith very quickly, seeing that He offered them no miraculous aid to deliver them from their executioners. Belief in miracles was, of course, always part of the Christian faith, but so was the warning that we must never rely on them.

No, Auschwitz and Kolyma are not the cause of godlessness. On the contrary. And just because such monstrosities were the work of godless people, some people think they should be used in defending the cause of God. But this temptation is dangerous because history also contains much cruelty at the hands of the pious. When people observe evil today, it does not move them to unbelief. The way they perceive evil is already determined by their unbelief, so that their perception of evil and their unbelief bolster each other. The same holds true for believers. They perceive evil in light of their faith, and thus, when they see evil, their faith is not weakened, but rather affirmed. It is not credible that evil in our time causes us to doubt the presence of God; there is no compelling logical or psychological connection.

The same is true for science. Pascal was terrified at the "eternal silence" of Cartesian infinite space, but both silence and the language of God are in the ear of the listener. His presence or absence is in faith or lack of faith, and each of the two, once acquired, will necessarily be confirmed by all observations. The historical meaning of the godless Enlightenment is still not entirely clear, because the collapse of traditional belief and the collapse of the Enlightenment – before our eyes and in our souls – happened simultaneously. Do we live in a time of "transition"? It would be almost tautological to affirm this, for history is nothing other than a series of transitional periods. But where we are transiting to – this we cannot know. One might plausibly claim that the Enlightenment, together with its godlessness, was the condition of all the intellectual and technical achievements of modernity. And yet our discomfort with the Enlightenment is becoming ever more palpable. Was Jung right when he said that in mythological archetypes, God's death always precedes His resurrection? Do we live in the terrible two days between Friday and Sunday, during which the Redeemer, already dead and not yet resurrected, visits Hell? This, too, we cannot know. We are only sure of our own insecurity.

Finally, as an example, a history lesson in which a few important and less important facts are listed:

– in 490 b.c., the Persian army, as was naturally expected, annihilated the much weaker Athenians at Marathon;

– in 44 b.c., the fifty-six-year-old Julius Caesar followed the advice of the seer Spurinna and did not go to the Senate;

– in 33 a.d., in response to Pontius Pilate's question about who should be released, the mob in Jerusalem cried: Jesus!;

What Is Wrong with God?

– on the 22nd of December 1849, a young Russian, Fyodor Mikhailovich Dostoyevsky, was shot to death for his revolutionary acts in St. Petersburg;

– in 1836, the eighty-year-old Wolfgang Amadeus Mozart died in Vienna;

– on the 30th of August 1918, Fania Kaplan shot Vladimir Ilyich Lenin to death;

– in August 1920, Jozef Pilsudski made a small mistake. The Red Army occupied Warsaw; then Poland; then Germany;

– in 1938, Adolph Hitler died of a heart attack;

– in 1963, Joseph Stalin died.

What would our world look like today, after these events?

Only God knows. Or does that mean that no one knows? And what does all this have to do with God?

People, at least all those who do not want to be blind, have long known that the cloth of history is woven out of tiny accidents. If there is a plan and reason in history, it can only be God's plan and God's reason. No one knows what they are; we can only believe in them.

Is all this banal? Certainly. The cause of belief, along with that of unbelief, is banal, because it is ubiquitous.

The unbeliever thinks that concern about God is disguised concern about the world. For the believer exactly the opposite is the case; he thinks that our concern for the world is, unbeknownst to us, disguised concern about God. This dispute has to do with the ultimate sense of our destiny, and consequently can never be decided by means that are recognized by both sides as reliable. For both, however, the restlessness of a world abandoned by God is tangible.

This restlessness also reveals that the victory of the godless and self-confident Enlightenment cannot be secure. In its victory it showed itself so ambiguous and contradictory, and its successes have brought so many new uncertainties, that our era can only be described as apparently godless: apparently, because it is too intensely aware of the absence of God. For this reason, the "return of the sacred" has become an important theme, as godlessness desperately attempts to replace the lost God with something else. Enlightened humanism proposes a religion of humanity, but Nietzsche already exposed the fruitlessness of such *ersatz* replacements. The followers of Comte and Feuerbach in our century – such as Erich Fromm or Julian Huxley – sound, of all the godless, the least convincing. Naturally, one can condemn God as morally dangerous, dismiss Him as inaccessible to reason, reject Him as the enemy of humanity, or excommunicate Him as the source of enslavement. But only if the Absolute were forgotten could it be replaced with something unabsolute and finite; and if this were possible, we would have no need of a replacement. Thus the task could only be completed if it were no longer necessary. But of course the Absolute can never be forgotten. God's unforgettableness means that He is present even in rejection.

Crime and Punishment[1]

I recognize that the title of this essay is not strikingly original; nor is the topic. I should say at the outset, therefore, that this is not an essay about Dostoyevsky, or even about legal theory – an area about which I am largely ignorant. It is rather about the traditional question of whether punishment can be justified, if at all, on other than practical grounds – and whether the practical, or instrumental, justification suffices.

Familiar justifications for punishment include the idea that the punishment is a deterrent for others; that it is a *preventive means* that makes the criminal physically incapable, temporarily or permanently, of committing further crimes; that it is an instrument of reeducation; and that it is an act of retribution. One also finds some combination of the above. In the first three cases, the justification for punishment is practical; only in the case of retribution is it moral.

None of the practical reasons offered for punishment seem to require the notion of responsibility, at least if this notion implies freedom of choice. One may always argue, like Spinoza, that such a notion is irrelevant: do we not kill poisonous snakes without asking whether they enjoy *liberum arbitrium*, or even if we are certain that they do not? Do we not remove a stone from the road when it impairs our movement? On this view, punishing criminals does not differ from these sorts of practical measures.

The obvious trouble with this simple explanation is that we normally believe that people *do* differ significantly from snakes and stones. We believe that people are able to make choices, that there is a distinction between instinctive reflexes or mechanical movements and specifically human behavior mediated by reflection, and that our thinking about

1 Reprinted from *The New Criterion* (November 1991). Reprinted with the kind permission of the publisher.

crime and punishment naturally involves the ideas of justice, responsibility, and duty.

Of course, a consistent behaviorist can easily dismiss such doubts. Maintaining that the concepts of justice, responsibility, and duty are no more than philosophical fancies or remnants of religious superstitions, the behaviorist holds that we would be much better off scrapping such concepts altogether (though it is not clear how he knows that we would be better off). According to him, our behavior – whether or not it is mediated by reflection – consists of events determined entirely by prior conditions (again, it is not clear how the behaviorist knows this). Consequently, he regards punishment merely as a technique for modifying human conduct: for him, punishment needs no other support. Whether it does or doesn't need additional support is the question I wish to address.

That no human society could survive without deterring its members from what it considers anti-social behavior is obvious. At least in our time, whenever legal restrictions become for any reason unenforceable, the result almost invariably is mass looting and vandalism. And this is true not only in Somalia or Liberia but in New York as well, as we saw after the sudden blackout there a few years ago. Not everyone goes wild on such occasions, to be sure, but an anarchic minority suffices to break society apart and make life impossible. If my heart is rather on the side of anarchy, my reason is not, and I have to admit that anarchy is (alas) a childish dream. No doubt there are encouraging counter-examples. Alexander Solzhenitsyn tells a story about a Soviet concentration camp in which the inmates overpowered the guards and seized control for about three days. On that occasion, miraculously, the camp remained in order: there was no violence and no rape, even though the population consisted mainly of hardened criminals. The suddenly regained feeling of freedom created a kind of fraternity. But such examples cannot, unfortunately, be extrapolated into a general principle. We have to admit that no human community, unless it wants to disintegrate, can dispense with the institutions that deter would-be criminals with the prospect of suffering.

But the idea of deterrence is not above criticism. It has often been observed that there is something wrong with inflicting suffering on some people in order to terrify others. Doesn't it run counter to the Kantian principle which demands that we treat every human being as an end in himself, never as a means? What right do we have to employ people as instruments of deterrence? Moreover, the very idea of deterrence suggests that its validity is to be measured by its effectiveness. The simplest example: in all debates about capital punishment, its opponents argue that it is useless because it does not deter terrorists or murderers; it is said that statistics do not reveal any clear correlation between the abolition or re-imposition of the death penalty and increase or decline in the number of relevant crimes. Perhaps. But surely the death penalty would work as a deterrent if it were applied swiftly and infallibly – preferably amid horrid tortures in a public square – to people who ride city buses without a ticket or fail to fasten their seat belts when driving a car.

A silly joke? Not necessarily, if we wish to measure the validity of punishment solely by its efficacy as a deterrent. Everybody would say, of course, that my suggestion involves a glaring disproportion between the offense and the punishment. But how do we know what is or is not proportionate in such matters? In various historical periods, people were hanged for stealing a few shillings, buried alive for adultery, and burned for not believing in the Holy Trinity. The present penal system in Western civilization is of relatively recent origin and has by no means acquired universal recognition or approval. What penalty is proper for what wrongdoing is a matter of changing conventions, feelings, and sensitivities – as is, for that matter, the scope of acts that are penalized. In those countries where no strict penal code is in existence, we still observe a wild discrepancy between penalties meted out for the same crime, depending upon the opinion of a judge. There is no *a priori* and no empirical foundation, no transcendental wisdom and no religious tradition, on which we could rely in establishing the right proportions between various criminal acts and various ways in which they are punished. In those matters, justice is always arbitrary and there is usually no way by which the crime and penalty could be reduced to the same currency.

The idea of punishment as a preventive is not liable to the objection that it views individuals merely as a means to instill dread into other people. It seems to justify the ultimate prevention – the death penalty – even better. And in cases in which there is practically no probability that the criminal might commit the same crime again – and such cases are frequent – it suggests that there is no need for punishment at all. As to the question of proportion between punishable acts and the punishment, the idea of prevention does not seem to provide any better clues than does the idea of punishment as deterrence: here, too, the matter is bound to be decided by historically relative consensus.

The concept of re-education as a theoretical foundation of the penal system provokes other doubts. Whether and how punishment educates criminals is a matter of empirical inquiry, and I am not competent to venture into this area; it is enough to say that, according to the considered opinion of many knowledgeable people, prisons are more likely to provide an education for crime than for decency; and if this is the case, the idea of re-education as a justification for punishment is simply pointless.

Setting this empirical question aside, however, we should ask what is meant by re-education. If it consists in instilling fear, in altering a person's conditional reflexes so as to dispose him to change his conduct in the future, it does not seem to differ fundamentally from deterrence, in that it acts on the criminal himself, rather than on other people. And if moral education in the proper sense is meant, then it would seem that punishment is altogether dispensable if other means – for instance, ordering people to attend classes in moral philosophy instead of sending them to prison – prove more efficient (unless, of course, attending such classes is in itself a penalty heavy enough).

But even if we grant the uncontestable assumption that it is impossible to dispense with the instruments of deterrence lest the whole fabric of society fall apart, there is still another question: can the idea of deterrence and, in general, practical justifications of punishment, suffice to ensure a level of community without which life becomes intolerable? In other words, do we need the idea of retribution?

The concept of retribution seems close enough to that of revenge to provoke understandable suspicion. But the two concepts can be separated. Revenge is neither punishment in the legal sense nor retribution in the sense of natural law. It is an emotionally motivated act with the exclusive aim of doing harm to people who, in our opinion, did harm to us directly or indirectly; the intensity of the thirst for revenge has little to do with the extent of the harm caused by the person involved, as we can see from many cases of people killing each other for ridiculously slight reasons. The desire for revenge is perhaps natural and unavoidable, but a widespread moral intuition recommends that we forbear from actually taking revenge, even in cases of obvious and serious wrongdoing, since taking revenge would make us at the same time plaintiff, judge, prosecutor, and executioner in the conflict – a state of affairs that runs counter to the very concept of law. It is true that vengeful feelings often make up the background of public pressure exerted on penal legislation. Indeed, we all know of crimes so hideous, so abominable, that the demand for the death penalty is understandable. In countries where the death penalty has been abolished, this generally came about through a legislative decision against the opinion of the majority of the population. The same can be said of the abolition of witch-hunting.

While we can, and probably should, dismiss the idea that vengeance is a compelling justification of any penal system, we may still wish to retain the idea of retribution and argue that it is important to keep it. Retribution is not revenge, nor is it necessary as a concept of positive law. It is not revenge because it does not imply an emotional urge to hurt the wrongdoer; it is not part of positive law because it cannot be properly defined in legal terms. The idea of retribution could retain its validity even if it were proved – and this is an empirical issue – that punishment is inefficient as a deterrent, as a preventive measure, or as an educational device. It is a moral – as opposed to practical – justification of punishment. To be sure, it is no more able than practical reasons to define the proportion between the character of a crime and the extent of the penalty. One may say nonetheless that, without it, human communal life would be devoid of substance and would probably collapse.

The idea of retribution has, I believe, mythological origins. We cannot *prove* its validity empirically or give it *a priori* grounds. Yet there seems to be a widespread mythological belief – perhaps more often implied than explicitly stated – that there is a kind of moral mechanism of equilibrium at work in the arrangement of the cosmos whereby evil must be repaid, or canceled, by suffering; and that therefore suffering has redemptive power, and restores the order of Being which is continually disturbed by our evil acts. Suffering thus has a meaning that cannot be reduced to its hypothetical functions in legal machinery: it has a place in our lives, since we are participants in the cosmic order of things, and it has a place in mankind's moral order – an order that was not arbitrarily invented by us but was found ready-made, sacred, compellingly imposed on human communities.

In the legal order, crime is what is defined as such by penal law. The scope of what is considered criminal may change one way or the other; some items are decriminalized, others are added to the list of punishable actions. Legal punishment is for transgressions of the law, but retribution is for sin, and sin is part of the moral order of the universe. The ideas of sin, of evil, of guilt, of repentance, are beyond the scope of the legal system; the law can function well without them. But can we? In terms of secular constitutions, our only duty is not to violate the laws set by the state. Duty in the moral sense has little to do with positive legislation. We have duties that no positive law can prescribe; we may even, on some occasions, have a duty to defy or violate the existing laws.

In secular states within a nominally Christian civilization, the areas of sin as defined by church doctrine and of crime as defined by the law overlap. Some criminal acts, such as murder, rape, and stealing, are sinful in a religious sense, while others may be considered *adiaphora*, or indifferent, by religious rules. Conversely, some sins are not crimes according to the law. Lying, for instance, is a crime only in special circumstances, as in the case of perjury; but Christian doctrine teaches that all lies are sinful. Certainly, any Christian Church is in an ambiguous position: it is supposed to convey to the faithful the divine commandments, but it is a legally ordered institution as well, and it would be impossible to claim that everything in canon law or in the commandments of the Catholic Church is *de iure divino*. Therefore the area of what is defined as sinful is not immutable. One no longer needs to confess to a priest the sin of eating meat on Friday, and even though a married priest is still a sinner, exceptions are permissible and nobody maintains that the celibacy of priests is *de iure divino*. The use of contraceptives is in principle still a sin but probably so few Catholics bother about it nowadays that it is practically, albeit grudgingly, tolerated, like premarital sex.

But although sin cannot be defined in formal terms, i.e., in terms of currently binding ecclesiastical rules, and the Church as a legal order – as distinct from the Church as *corpus mysticum* – cannot be considered infallible on the question of what sin is, we may still believe that evil is real. That is, we may still believe that evil is a real characteristic of life and that we carry in us a kind of moral intuition that enables us to recognize it as such. We intuitively know, or at least we are capable of knowing, when we do evil and when our fellow men do it, whether or not this evil is defined as a crime in penal legislation.

The question of the *desirable* relationship between sin and crime has been the crucial area of conflict between theocracy and liberalism in modern civilization. The theocratic tendency in its strongest form – which is hardly noticeable in the history of the Christian West – consists in the demand for direct rule of the state by the Church and the clergy. A weaker version, while accepting the distinction between secular and spiritual powers, wants everything that is sinful according to the Church's moral doctrine to be punishable by secular law – as was often the case in medieval civilization and later – apart from sins for which the punishment would, for technical reasons, simply be unenforceable (for instance, mental sins). If this tendency prevailed, such sins as adultery and homosexuality would be illegal, not to speak of atheism and heresy. It took a very long time before such sins were decriminalized; homosexuality was punished in Britain until quite recently, and it is still illegal in some American states, regardless of the extent to which such laws are enforced (and this in Western civilization; in Islamic states the theocratic tendency has always been much stronger). Orthodox Jews would like to impose Old Testament law on the state of Israel, including the interdiction of the sale of forbidden food, the interdiction of travel on the Sabbath, etc.

The liberal tendency refuses to abide by religious doctrine in defining the limits of the forbidden and the permissible, and defends the principle of the separation of church and state. But it must still answer the question: what are the sources of law in such matters, once the validity of religious tradition has been done away with? To say that it is the voice of the people, or public opinion, is not always convenient, because public opinion often opposes liberal legislators; as I have mentioned, a number of important decisions have been made by legislative bodies against the views of the majority. Whatever the mechanisms of making law, liberal doctrines cannot accept that their spokesmen in legislative bodies should merely follow the current voice of the majority without correction. Liberal ideology *is* an ideology, and it is bound to fight for its principles, whatever the majority might think. Liberal doctrine on this point can perhaps be summed up in the principle that only those acts may be declared illegal which, if permitted, would make life in this society intolerable and cause the peaceful order to collapse or to deteriorate significantly. Murder, obviously, belongs to this category, but homosexuality, for example, does not. Some cases are debatable – the use of drugs, for instance – but it is supposed that arguments for or against a given activity can be based on empirical evidence.

This principle seems to be reasonable and to conform to current perceptions about the law. Liberal legislation has been gaining ground since the sixteenth century in Western civilization, and the vestiges of the theocratic tradition, though still discernible, are now of little significance. Islamic countries will probably move in the same direction, although we cannot know how long it will take. But accepting this principle, with all the problems and ambiguities it must create, does not help us answer the question with which I am concerned. If all we have at our disposal is penal law, more liberal or less, based on practical considerations alone, and no living moral beliefs that give validity to the ideas of evil, guilt, sin, freedom of action, and retribution, can human communities survive at all? Penal law, supported solely by practical considerations, acts by fear of punishment alone. Can fear suffice? Fear may restrain the natural human impulses of greed, aggressiveness, and lust for power. But can we assume that such a morally emptied Hobbesian society, in which fear is the only binding force, would be viable?

Or, to put it differently: can we live without feeling that the law is to be respected, not only feared?

This distinction between respect for and fear of the law is, of course, crucial in Kantian moral philosophy. Respect, in Kant's view, is not supposed to be an emotion (emotional motivations are morally worthless) but a phenomenon *sui generis*, neither fear nor love. But can we respect positive law for no better reason than that it is law? And why should we? Most of us know only a tiny part of the immense body of legal regulations that proliferate endlessly, from one month to another. And these regulations are frequently changed, for good or bad reasons. What could produce in me a quasi-religious feeling of awe in the face of this *mysterium numinosum valde deridiculum*, this ridiculous deity, that consists of paper mountains which I would never be able to wade through? And I leave aside cases of oppressive codes in totalitarian or tyrannical regimes, where obeying some of the laws would be morally repugnant and defying and violating them is strongly recommended.

No, we can neither expect nor demand respect for the law just because it has been promulgated, regardless of its content. What matters is not respect for this or that (often accidental) decision of the majority in a parliament or of a judge. Rather, what matters is respect for the moral law, which may or may not coincide with the positive law and which involves the legally irrelevant distinction between good and evil.

Kant, when he talked about respect for law, had in mind moral law as he understood it; but I do not think that this part of his doctrine is entirely acceptable. To be sure, the Kantian distinction between obeying a law for prudential reasons and obeying it for moral reasons is obvious and valid. We may not normally steal packets of butter at the grocery store, but this does not mean that we are honest people; we do not do it simply because it would be silly to do so, as the gain is minimal and to be caught would result in unpleasant consequences. This is admittedly a very simple example. But even when we do something apparently honest, without calculation and without any risk of punishment if we fail to do it, this by no means proves that we are up to Kantian standards. When I do something apparently good – help other people, save them, even sacrifice myself – if I do so out of compassion, that is, if I am moved by an emotion, my act is morally worthless in Kantian terms, since only those acts are moral which are motivated by the pure will to fulfill the law and nothing else. Kant admits, first, that such acts are rather unusual and rare. He admits, second, that when such an act does occur it is impossible to be certain that it really has occurred, since we have no means of establishing the real content of other peoples' minds. He admits, third, that the agent himself is, practically speaking, incapable of stating firmly that his action is as pure and as devoid of emotional admixture as the moral imperatives demand. Self-deception is easy, and we often attribute to ourselves nobler motivations than we actually possess.

Moreover, it is plausible to argue that when Kant speaks of acts that externally conform to the law but are performed for the wrong reasons, he uses a concept that is invalid on his own premises. For in order to conform to the law, our actions should be precisely what the formal imperatives say they should be: that is, they should be motivated by a "maxim" that the agent is prepared to make universal. It seems, therefore, that there is simply no such thing as "external" compliance with the moral law: compliance must involve the proper motivation. And, since evil is defined as disobedience of the law, we may even suspect that in Kant's terms – although he does not say this in so many words – when I do something out of compassion and love, my act is not just morally worthless but positively evil, which sounds outrageous to our normal moral intuition.

Kant's moral doctrine seems very poorly designed as an educational device, more poorly even than the Augustinian-Calvinist theology of grace that it partially resembles. It suggests that as long as I am not perfect and holy I am simply evil in whatever I do, and to suggest this is the best recipe for nihilistic indifference – for we know, and Kant knew, that nobody is perfect. In other words, in practice we do not need to bother much about our conduct, since we are certain in advance that holiness is beyond our reach.

But however impracticable Kantian philosophy may be as a tool of moral education in the real world, it was the boldest attempt the Enlightenment ever made to establish moral principles as a separate realm of reason, logically independent from the legacy of a revealed religion and irreducible to empirical grounds or to hedonistic justifications. The idea that no empirical evidence can be miraculously transmuted into moral rules was one that Kant shared with Hume, but he did not conclude that therefore no such rules can be rationally constructed.

I am not, of course, concerned with the validity or soundness of Kantian ethics as a whole. But Kant was right, I believe, when he said that if we deny the validity of the distinction between right and wrong, good and evil, we are denying the very possibility of morality in the normal sense of the word; and if we deny this, there is no longer any way that respect for the moral law can be distinguished from fear of legal punishment. To accept this does not entail that one is logically compelled to embrace Kantian formalism, with its subsequent elimination of compassion and love from the catalogue of worthy motivations for morally good acts. Yet if the distinction between respect and fear is real, it seems to imply the validity of the concepts of sin, guilt, responsibility, and retribution. It implies, consequently, the idea of freedom of choice as well. And if freedom is empirically unprovable, this may be for other reasons than those adduced by Kant. Indeed, it might be precisely because freedom is a perfectly simple and very elementary experience which, being so simple and so elementary, is not analyzable any further – like the idea of the self. It is one of the building blocks of our world of experience, but is not itself validly deducible from any empirical evidence that would be admissible in scientific procedures.

The same may be said about the distinction between good and evil, between moral duty and legal duty, between legal punishment and retribution. To believe that those distinctions are valid is to believe that there is a kind of natural law that binds us, that does not depend on arbitrary conventions or decrees, and that is accessible to us through moral intuition. Throughout history many people have believed, and indeed still believe, in such an order of things, no matter how this insight is phrased and how it is connected with – or disconnected from – its religious background. Are we still capable of sharing this belief? Certainly not if we surrender to the dogmas either of empiricism or of historicism. But why should we surrender? That there is anything compelling in these dogmas has not been persuasively demonstrated.

In addition to making philosophical arguments for or against natural law, we may reflect on the likely outcome of a process whereby the notions of good and evil, of sin and retribution, would simply disappear from human minds. They have not disappeared yet, but they have been severely eroded in our civilization. Many people still believe that they should do something simply because it is right, or forbear from doing it simply because it is wrong, not because they are terrified by the specter of the police, judges, prison, and execution. My naive question is: could mankind survive without such people? And my answer is no. Mankind as we know it would not survive if the only instrument to prevent us from following our desires and indulging our passions was the fear of legally inflicted suffering. This seems to me to be common sense, based on the distinction between the human race and rats. It is also based on a strong disbelief in the doctrine according to which human behavior is entirely reducible to a system of inherited instincts and conditional reflexes.

Because there is evil in us, we do, of course, need penal machinery: laws, threats, and fear. But if there were nothing but evil in us, the very concepts of good and evil – as distinct from the concepts of pleasure and pain, profit and harm – would be so redundant, so utterly useless, that it would be hard to see why mankind should have concocted them at all. And the same may be said about the pair sin/retribution, as distinct from crime/punishment. Because we are not entirely and irredeemably evil, it is good for us occasionally to think that we deserve retribution or that retribution may restore the order of the world we have disturbed by our sins. To dismiss this belief as a myth is easy, but it leaves unanswered these questions: Why has mankind, throughout its history, required a mythological order of the universe in addition to a technical one? And what might happen should this order evaporate altogether?

On Natural Law[1]

My topic is not constitutional. It is, to put it somewhat pretentiously, the metaphysical, perhaps even theological riddle that may emerge from reflecting on constitutions as such, that is to say, reflecting on natural law.

Natural law is supposed to be law that is not invented by us, but found ready-made, independently of our conventions, customs and regulations. It provides us with supreme normative rules; and it is to those rules that our constitutions and codes have to conform if they deserve to be called *just*.

The concept of natural law has been criticized for centuries, in a variety of theoretical idioms, and it is much easier to repeat these criticisms than to articulate the principles of natural law. The critic asks: where is this supposed natural law to be found? One cannot infer it – as Locke suggested that we could – from what is common to all legislative systems, or even from any tacitly assumed principles underlying their foundation. There is no universal core for all legal codes; not even rules that might seem to us intuitively self-evident – such as the principle that only people who have committed a crime should be punished, and not others – are universally accepted. (According to an old Polish anecdote, a locksmith once committed a crime for which the penalty was capital punishment; but there was only one locksmith in the village whereas there were several blacksmiths, and so it was decided that a blacksmith should be hanged instead.) Under Hammurabi's Law it was legitimate in some cases to kill people who had not contributed at all to the crime: if John had killed Martin's son, Martin had the right to kill John's son, who was not guilty of any crime. In Stalin's criminal code, there were some political crimes that demanded punishment not only for the criminal, and not

1 A shortened version was published in *Critical Review* 15, Nos. 1–2 (2003).

only for all those who had known about the crime and failed to inform the authorities, but also for members of the criminal's family or even of his household – people who knew nothing about the case. (Thus innumerable thousands of women, known by the acronym "Zhir" – wives of traitors to the Fatherland – lived out their lives and died in Soviet concentration camps. This was according to the letter of the law, but the practice was far worse.) Nor is there any universal acceptance of the (no less intuitively self-evident) rule that it is our duty to keep our promises (a principle that may perhaps be considered the supreme principle of civil law); or of the rule that law cannot be valid retrospectively. And there is no need to point out that equality before the law, religious freedom, freedom of speech, and so on, are relatively new, and were absent even from many modern constitutions.

A more skeptical critic could go further: even if we discovered norms common to all known constitutions and codes, past and present, such a discovery would be just an empirical fact. We could not infer from it that such norms are inherently just, right, or true. Universal agreement, a *consensus omnium*, is not a criterion of scientific truth, so why should it be the criterion of the validity of a norm? When philosophers asked about the content and the grounds of natural law, what they wanted to know was not when and where particular legal norms have been accepted, or even whether there are any moral or legal norms that are accepted always and everywhere, but which norms are really legitimate and how we might go about establishing their validity.

Let us suppose that one day a sensational archeological discovery is made: archaeologists find the Ark of the Covenant and in it the stone tablets on which Moses carved out the Ten Commandments. We would still be unable to prove that this was really a text dictated by God and thus absolutely valid.

Should we then, in the face of this criticism, reconcile ourselves to the view – expressed countless times by so many: by some of the Sophists in Plato's dialogues, by Hobbes, and by many more recent authors – that what is just is what has been laid down as law by the legislator, and that there is no other valid law apart from this? This view can of course be expressed with varying degrees of consistency. The radical version says that whatever a sovereign or ruling power has established is indeed just: Hitler's Nürnberg laws, and Stalin's codes, and the American Constitution – all are equally just. But this compels us to accept the inconvenient conclusion that norms which contradict each other may be equally legitimate and equally just. Advocates of this view, therefore, usually try to circumvent the problem by arguing that the value-laden concept of justice has no discernible meaning if it is taken to suggest a supreme paradigm according to which we can measure and assess existing legislation; if, on the other hand, "justice" means nothing except positive law, i.e., what is established in existing legislation, it is a misleading and useless concept.

A critic who scorns the idea of natural law as a myth, a fabrication with no basis in reality, can still try to rebut the objection that in his view both the Nürnberg laws and the American Constitution must be equally good – not in the sense of "just," but in the sense of "valid," because they were established as the law of the land. He might protest that nothing imposes this conclusion on him; he might say, "Of course I don't believe that it is all right for me to express opinions that contradict each other. Accepting such a conclusion would be evidence of my intellectual feebleness. No," he will say; "these opinions would be contradictory only on the assumption that the quality of being 'good' or 'just' applied *in fact*, independently of my or anyone's judgments. But there is no contradiction if what we mean when we say that some laws are good and others not is that we approve of them; we are simply expressing our moral feelings, feelings that we share, to be sure, with many other people." Thus the critic will maintain that when he says, for example, that the Nürnberg laws are evil and the American Constitution is good (or vice versa), he is not making a statement about those laws or this constitution, but about himself, and about those who share the same opinion.

Does this conclusion, which must seem difficult to stomach for many people, actually follow from the rejection of the idea of natural law? It seems to. Critics of such a conclusion might argue, for instance, that the American Constitution, which says in the Preamble that it serves justice, peace, human welfare, and freedom, and goes on, in the text proper, to set down the details of the representative system and, in the Amendments, to establish religious freedom, freedom of speech, and the illegality of slavery – one might argue that it is a good thing, because it is impossible to deny that peace is better than war, freedom better than slavery, etc. But the critic would reply, "Not at all. For centuries slavery was considered part of the natural order of things, also by the United States, under this very Constitution, up to Amendment 13 of 1865. War, too, has been exalted, and for centuries seen as part of the natural order of things. And religious freedom in the Christian world is a very recent phenomenon, a novelty by no means everywhere accepted, even today. All such things are conventions; they are accepted in some historical eras but not in others. And there is no proof that these conventions – which we may accept if we wish – reflect any normative order of the universe, any order that is embedded in the nature of things and which we can discover ready-made."

Thus, according to this critic, if someone refuses to recognize that freedom is better than slavery or peace better than war, or that torturing people is evil, or that people are equal in a fundamental sense (i.e., in their dignity), there is no way of convincing him otherwise. One cannot, for instance, reproach the rulers of Communist China because they repudiate the idea of human rights as a bourgeois or specifically European doctrine. According to this view, to say that certain norms are valid is meaningless without explaining, "valid for whom?" They may be valid for a specific historical period, for a civilization, for a well-defined social milieu; to say this is to say that they are accepted in that period, or in that civilization, or in that milieu, and that, of course, is just an empirical statement, without any normative content. But to say that a norm is valid in itself is a fantasy, born of myth.

Those who believe in natural law have frequently been accused (for example, by John Stuart Mill) of committing what analytical philosophers call the naturalistic fallacy: that is, of attempting to deduce normative propositions from empirical ones (an impossible feat), or confusing the two. According to this cricicism, believing in natural law amounts to failing to distinguish between law as a regularity in nature, such as Newton's laws, for instance, and law in the sense of a norm established within a legal order. This charge can be justified in some cases of natural-law theory, but not in others. Aquinas believed that all things in the world participate in the eternal, God-created order, but human creatures, being endowed with reason, participate in it by conscious obedience: the rules of natural law, including the distinction between good and evil, were inscribed by God in our minds, and so everyone, including pagans, participates in this knowledge.

Clearly, however, "participation" in the physical and moral order is not the same. All things in the world, including human beings, are subject to the law of gravity, which no one can invalidate or violate. If, however, we "participate" in the Ten Commandments, it is in the sense that those commandments bind us. In this sense of participation, we also cannot invalidate the laws in which we participate, but we *can* violate them. The failure to distinguish between these two kinds of "participation" may justify the accusation of naturalistic fallacy.

But the accusation need not apply to the theory according to which the divinely established distinction between good and evil is legitimate, i.e., that when we say that something is good or evil we are saying that this is *really* the case (even though, being endowed with free will, we may act in a way that ignores this distinction). On this view the laws concerning good and evil are as valid as the laws of chemistry, because they are founded on divine decree; and for God, who is absolute unity, there is no distinction between a truth that describes a natural regularity and one that expresses what God has decreed about good and evil. Both kinds of laws are true and of equal status, despite the different ways in which we "participate" in the laws of nature on the one hand and moral laws on the other. And both are of divine origin. But they do not result from an arbitrary decree which would have been as valid had it been different: they are rooted in God's infinite wisdom. Thus it is wrong to say that the content of the divine commandments is the result of the Creator's whim, and equally wrong to say that the Creator is subject to external laws, ready-made rules that exist independently of Him which it is not in His power to invalidate. The first would question God's infinite wisdom, the second His omnipotence – His position as the unique and ultimate source of all creative energy. From the Thomist standpoint it is utterly wrong to say (as did some later Nominalists and some modern thinkers, including Descartes) that all truths – both mathematical and moral – are freely decreed by God and could have been different, so that, if God had so wished, He could have decided, for instance, that two and two is seven, or that two propositions which directly contradict each other can both be true, or that it is a virtuous deed to murder one's parents. Those who held this view claimed that to doubt this would be to question God's omnipotence. This is wrong in Thomist terms because in God there is no distinction between intellect and will; one may not attribute to Him the distinctions that appear in human beings. And although we cannot truly inderstand the divine mode of existence, we can know *a priori* what must be true of God – or, rather, what cannot be true of Him.

For the Thomist it is obvious that natural law presupposes the existence of God. But is this a necessary, logical implication? Is it not logically possible to believe in natural law without believing in God? Modern theorists of natural law, such as Grotius and Pufendorf, say that it is, and affirm the logical independence of the two. Grotius allows that some of God's commandments would be unknowable without Revelation; we could not discover them with our own reason. Divine legislation *makes* some acts virtuous or forbidden. But apart from these laws there are the commandments of Reason, whereby we can discern good and evil in all human actions according to their conformity, or lack of it, with human nature. Such laws, says Grotius, do not depend on divine decrees, and God Himself could not alter them any more than He could invalidate the rules of arithmetic. Natural law operates in human life only; the concept of justice does not apply to animals. But it is not a man-made convention. Nor is it a decree freely made by the Creator. It is a set of rules which are, as it were, embedded (Grotius does not use this exact expression) in the ontic condition of humanity – in human dignity; without knowledge of these rules, we would not be human.

According to this view, then, natural law is present in the world, but it does not logically presuppose a legislating personal God. It does, however, imply a certain metaphysical faith: the faith (which goes back to the

Stoics) that there is a Reason which rules the universe, a Reason whose nature we can recognize and which enables us to distinguish truth from falsity as well as good from evil. It was a widespread (though not universal) view in the Christian Middle Ages that knowledge of natural law is accessible to us apart from Revelation because the Creator endowed us with the intellectual faculties necessary and sufficient for this purpose. In this respect our natural knowledge of the world does not differ from the natural recognition of moral principles. Cicero observed, in a number of his writings, that the rules which command that we help each other, do no harm, display gratitude for other people's kindness, and so forth, were created not by man but by nature, and that they are eternal; despite the evil things we do and despite our corruption, which often stamps out in us the power of Reason, we do know what is good or evil.

Belief in natural law was popular among the writers of the Enlightenment, too, although it was variously expressed (as becomes apparent if we compare, for example, Montesquieu and Kant). Kant argued that our duty is to do good because it is good and not because God orders it; if we do something because it is a commandment, we are not truly free and rational agents. He also thought that we are capable of discovering which fundamental moral rules are obligatory, because we participate in a universal Reason that was not created by divine decree but is simply there, indestructible and eternal.

Many thinkers, Christian and otherwise, have believed that natural law provides us with a paradigm according to which we can judge positive law. Many of them thought that we have no obligation to obey laws that are incompatible with natural law; we may, even should, reject and violate such laws.

Here, then, is my main question: mindful of the skeptical challenges I have reviewed above, can we still believe in natural law? My reply is yes. Not only may we believe in natural law, but by denying it we deny our humanity. We may believe that good and evil, instead of being projections of our likes and dislikes, emotions, or decisions, are *real qualities* of human life – of our actions, thoughts, desires, our conflicts and our friendships. And if someone were to say, "We can determine the speed of light and the chemical composition of ethyl alcohol, and we can prove that heat causes gases to expand, but we cannot prove, in the same sense, that torturing people is evil and helping the homeless is good," we may reply, "No, such moral judgments cannot be *proved* in the same sense as the laws of chemistry and physics, but need we accept the kind of proofs required in experimental science as the only model for all our truth-judgments?" Nothing compels us to embrace the view of proponents of logical empiricism that only propositions which are empirically verifiable (or perhaps falsifiable), in the same way as propositions in the sciences, are meaningful. The principles of empiricism, as many have pointed out, are not themselves empirical propositions. They are norms, commandments, and we may ask about their justification; they are by no means self-evident. Empiricism is not an empirical theory. Similarly, large areas of our knowledge have their indispensable foundation in intuition, the intuition of experience, and we do not for this reason dismiss them as figments of the imagination. Why, then, should we dimiss our intuition about moral experience? There is a moral intuition by which moral truths can be recognized, just as there is the intuition of sense experience and that of mathematical and logical truths. These three kinds of intuition are not reducible to each other; they work separately. Moral intuition is also a kind of experience, different from sense perception – and neither of them is infallible.

Our belief in natural law is not impaired by the fact that the results of this intuition are not necessarily identical in everyone's mind, always and everywhere, nor by the fact that centuries were needed before people recognized the good and evil of their various actions and institutions – before they admitted, for example, that torture is evil and equality before the law good. This has also been the case with many discoveries in empirical science: it took centuries before people realized that their ordinary intuitions were wrong: that the sun does not revolve around the earth, or that a force is not necessary to cause movement, or that events are never absolutely simultaneous. All these erroneous beliefs were natural and understandable. So why should we not accept that the principles and norms of natural law reveal themselves to us gradually: that we must go through a process of growth before we understand certain moral truths and laws and recognize them as such? (Although it should be said that since antiquity there have been people who preached those principles and norms with full conviction – without, however, gaining universal approval.)

There is no reason to accept the nihilistic doctrine that because various contradictory norms have been accepted and applied at various times and in various places, they are all, in terms of Reason, equally justified, which is to say equally groundless. While belief in natural law does not – I repeat – require belief in the existence of God as a necessary premise, it *does* require the belief in something that one might call the moral (in addition to the physical) constitution of Being – a constitution that converges with the rule of Reason in the universe. All the evils of the human world, its endless stupidity and suffering, cannot impair our belief in natural law in this sense. Two other realms of intuition – perception and mathematics – also require suppositions that cannot be proved but are indispensable for the knowledge we acquire by those intuitions. Our life as rational creatures occurs in a realm that is constructed with the aid of various non-empirical but fundamental courts of appeal, among them truth and goodness. Nor need our belief in natural law be impaired by the fact that it is not universally observed. This fact was well known to Seneca and Cicero, to Gratian and Suarez, to Grotius and Kant, but it did not weaken their conviction that the rules of natural law are valid, no matter how often they are violated.

Natural law does not, of course, allow us to infer from it the details of any constitution or civil or penal code. It does not allow us to infer, for instance, whether or not capital punishment or voluntary euthanasia is permissible, whether a proportional or a majority voting system is better, whether or not monarchy can be a good thing, whether property rights should have priority over other rights in case of conflict, whether censorship can be recommended on moral grounds, and so on. Nevertheless, natural law erects barriers that limit positive legislation and do not allow it to legalize attempts to infringe the indestructible dignity that is proper to every human being. Natural law is built around human dignity. Thus it invalidates legislation that, for instance, admits slavery, torture, political censorship, inequality before the law, compulsory religious worship or the prohibition of worship, or the duty to inform the authorities about the non-conformity of people's political views. Within these limits various constitutions and various codes are possible; natural law does not dictate their details.

The barriers mentioned above are usually accepted today in the legislation of civilized countries, but we must keep in mind that they are relatively recent; that they are not recognized everywhere; and that in many places where they are present in constitutions they remain mere words on paper. Natural law should be like an uncompromising demon breathing down the neck of all the legislators of the world.

Who Are We?

On Collective Identity[1]

It is not collective identity in the Leibnizian sense that will concern us here. For Leibniz the concept of identity was mainly a logical device, and was applicable only to entities such that every proposition which is true of them at one point in time is true of them at all times; it was not applicable to single entities (material or not) with a continuous existence in real time. It did have a metaphysical sense, insofar as it entailed two assumptions important for Leibniz's metaphysics – a system where all relations that obtain between monads must have their equivalents in each monad's immanent properties. It entailed a universal (but only phenomenal) interdependence between all the elements of the universe; and it entailed the identity of indiscernibles: that there cannot be two objects (monads) which differ from each other only numerically. Leibniz thought that if two objects are identical in all respects (indiscernible), they must also be numerically identical – i.e., they must be one and the same object. But Leibniz's metaphysics is irrelevant to our present purposes. The question I want to consider here is how a monad or a set of monads can retain its identity over time, regardless of the changes it undergoes.

When we consider the question of the identity of human collective bodies (keeping in mind the obvious *caveat* that all definitions of non-mathematical objects will inevitably be shaky and imprecise), we observe that it is analogous to the time-hallowed problem of personal identity discussed by Locke, Hume, and many contemporary philosophers. Conversely, certain aspects of personal identity have their equiv-

---

1 This essay began life as a lecture given at Castel Gandolfo in 1994, at a session organized by the Institut für die Wissenschaften vom Menschen. Published in *Partisan Review* (Winter 2003).

alents in collective identity. In short, it is impossible to talk of one without considering the other.

Of the aspects common to both personal and collective identity, the first is substance, or soul – the non-material aspect of personality – and the problem of its connection with the body. This connection has been defined in a variety of ways, depending on the metaphysical doctrine one chose to adopt – Platonic, Thomist, Augustinian, or Cartesian. For as long as the concept of substance (whether considered to be a separate entity or, as in Aquinas, a composite of body and its form, i.e., the soul) retained its unquestioned legitimacy in philosophical discourse and was accepted as the immutable seat of mental life, the thing that preserves its *ipseitas* through all changes, personal identity was easily defined by reference to it. But once empiricist critique had undermined and dethroned it, pointing out that its presence could not be established, either directly or indirectly, substance was demoted from the status of empirical fact to that of metaphysical presupposition. Of course, the dogmas of empiricism are themselves far from immune from criticism, in particular from the (frequently made) charge of being arbitrary. However, even if we abandon the idea of substance, we are still left with the problem of how to define the experience of self – the "I" at the root of personal identity.

The followers of Hume and Mach insisted that the word "I" had no referent, and claimed that the idea of the ego was no more than an artificial construct; but such a claim is even shakier than the arguments for rejecting the idea of substance. For one might reasonably argue that "I" am the object of my own experience, and hence that the issue is an empirical one after all. To this critics might object that the word "I" is used here as if it corresponded to some reality: that it presupposes a referent, and that it is, in fact, exactly the same thing as "substance," and therefore liable to the same charge. But such an objection would be groundless; there seems to be no compelling reason to extend the scope of this charge. To be sure, the content of whatever the word "I" refers to is accessible only to me, but then it is equally true that in general my perceptions are uniquely my own and no one else's. I am the referent of the word "I." There is always something awkward about using this pronoun as if it were an ordinary noun (or replacing it by other artificial constructs such as "the self" or "the ego"), but this philosophical parlance cannot be avoided, even if it makes our speech sound odd. When I say, "I had dinner last night," I assume (and so does everyone else) that I am the same person I was last night, and I assume this without appealing to any metaphysical idea of substance. Indeed, it is hard to say what exactly is wrong with this ordinary way of speaking – particularly since dismissing the continuity of the "I" entails, among other things, abandoning the idea of personal responsibility, without which life in a human community would be impossible. The referent of the word "I" is established in experience, and no one, with the exception of a few Buddhists at a very advanced stage on their path to enlightenment and an even smaller number of philosophers, can cast any real doubt on the validity of this experience.

However, the experience of the continuous "I" also presupposes memory. *Memory* is the second element inherent in the idea of personal identity, and it is an essential one. There would be no continuity of identity if the entire memory of a person were erased; there can be no personal identity without the memory which makes it conscious, without, in other words, the consciousness of one's history. Christian theologians maintain that God is both a person and a timeless being. Such a statement may be meaningfully uttered, but we lack both the conceptual and the empirical tools to understand such a being or gain any insight into its existence.

In discussing the question of personality, Freud introduced a distinction between two kinds of growth: between things which change like cities, with new buildings and streets growing up around the old center but leaving it untouched, and others which do not grow by accretion but change like living organisms, their structure remaining unaltered as they grow. Freud thought that the growth of personality is more like the former, preserving what was there at the beginning: he thought that the minds we had as children are still there in us, are a part of what makes up our adult identity, as if our entire stock of memory, whether conscious or unconscious, were indestructible. Whichever of these metaphors is the more accurate, there is no doubt that memory is an essential part of identity.

Personal identity requires not only the consciousness of one's past but also, and in equal measure, an attitude with regard to the future: a conscious anticipation, usually tinged with a variety of emotions like hope, fear, uncertainty, joy, or despair. *Anticipation* is a feature of human existence which a variety of philosophers, usually those of an "existentialist" bent, have attempted to describe, and it is the third element of identity.

The fourth element is *body*. The body is an essential part of the very idea of personality, but this claim does not settle the question of whether disembodied human life is possible, and is logically independent from it. We have no reliable empirical access to disembodied persons.

Bodily identity has been a subject of controversy at least since the paradox of Theseus's ship: if we gradually replace every part of a ship by a new one until all its parts have been replaced, is it still (given that neither its structure nor its appearance has changed) the same ship? The problem with the human body seems similar, but there are important differences. First, the human body is a conscious thing, and we cannot consider its identity over time without considering the contribution of memory to that identity. I remember my body as being my own: it is always the same body, *my* body, no matter how much it has changed since I was born and regardless of the constant changes taking place in its constituent parts. Second, we each of us have, as we now know, a unique and constant genetic make-up which defines the identity of our body, not only during our lifetime but even after death. The fact that we are conscious of only a fraction of the processes which take place in our bodies does not alter the status of the (conscious) body as an essential part of identity: however large or small that fraction might be, we still experience the continuity of the organism to which we belong (or which belongs to us, if it seems more appropriate to put it that way – either way will do). The fact that personal identity is only partly remembered in no way affects the continuity of personal identity through memory.

The fifth element in personal identity is the consciousness of an *identifiable beginning*. We do not, and perhaps cannot, remember the first event of our lives – our own birth – but we know that it took place. This knowledge is so basic and so patently indisputable that it might seem unnecessary to mention it at all, but it is indispensable, for it is what allows me to utter with conviction the apparent tautology "I am I." If at some point I simply discovered myself as a conscious and thinking being and had a Cartesian uncertainty about where I came from, the feeling that "I am I" would probably be impossible. I imagine that people who are uncertain about their origins in the weak, not the Cartesian, sense – i.e., people who, although they know they must have been born somewhere, sometime, do not know who their parents were or where and when they were born – must have a seriously damaged sense of identity.

Substance, memory, anticipation, body, and an identifiable beginning – these are the five elements (four if we set aside the first as empirically inaccessible) which together make up personal identity.

But personality is of course a cultural as well as an "existential" phenomenon. My belonging to various collective entities is also part of what makes me a person (although this does not entail that I am no more than a part of these collective entities, nor that I am literally nothing if I do not belong to them). And human collectivities have identities of their own, which can be described in similar terms and categories.

Collective identity is, even more than personal identity, a matter of degree. This is evident as soon as we begin to think about it, from the fact that we need a number of independent criteria to describe it. The concept of collective identity is a legitimate one; its legitimacy is not undermined by the fact that both personal and collective beings are only "more or less" self-identical. Their identity is no more suspect in this regard than that of physical objects. This becomes clear when we look at examples of collective entities such as ethnic communities and nations.

It is an obvious truth that no nation can survive without a national consciousness. How strong that consciousness is depends on a variety of historical circumstances. When we speak of nations, we usually have in mind historically well-established ethnic communities, most often European ones, and we are reluctant to use the term more widely: to apply it, for example, to African or Asian tribes or even to remote outposts of European civilization in North or South America or in Australia. States which lack ethnic homogeneity naturally have their own interests, and some of them may one day establish themselves as nations on the basis of the common aspirations of their people, if these prove stronger than ethnic divisions. But when we consider peoples whose status as nations is not in doubt, as in the case of nearly all European states, we see that their collective identity is made up of the same five elements discussed above.

The closest thing in collective identity to the metaphysical idea of substance is the vague idea of "national spirit" or "*Volksgeist*," which finds its expression in cultural life and collective behavior, especially at times of crisis. The Volksgeist is supposed to be something that underlies cultural phenomena but is not identical with them; unlike them, it is not an object of historical experience or a collection of facts, but a metaphysical entity (discovered by Hegel and the Romantics) with explanatory powers similar to those of a *res cogitans*. Like the *res cogitans*, it is a substance which is not reducible to the sum of its thought-acts, but is an essential condition of their occurrence.

While the idea of the *Volksgeist*, like the idea of substance, is not empirical, and easily disposed of by empiricist philosophers, the other elements of collective identity are less problematic.

No long proofs are needed to establish the obvious fact that national identity requires *historical memory*. It does not matter, for this purpose, how much of the content of that memory is true and how much half-true or altogether legendary. What matters is the consciousness of a past: no nation can survive without the awareness that its present existence is the continuation of a past one – and the further awareness that the older those (real or imaginary) memories, the deeper they reach back into the past, the more firmly its national identity is established. The past is preserved not only in historical knowledge but also in such things as symbols, idioms, and other particularities of the language, old buildings, temples, tombs, and so on.

These observations are all platitudes, so obvious that they hardly need saying. It is worth adding that what decides whether a nation is the same nation now as it was at any point in its past is that nation's present collective consciousness. If contemporary Greeks, Italians, Indians, Copts, or Chinese genuinely "feel" that they belong to the same, continuous ethnic community as their ancient forbears, then one cannot convince them otherwise or argue that they are mistaken. Some emerging nations – a number of cases come to mind – have simply invented a past for themselves, *ad hoc* and without any genuine or verifiable historical continuity. Such inventions are tolerated because they are necessary.

National cultures change imperceptibly; we cannot pinpoint the moment of their metamorphosis. They evolve like languages and, like languages, at some point they do evolve into what is clearly a different entity. We have no doubt, for instance, that the language of Montaigne is the same language as modern French, despite all the changes which have occurred in the meantime, and we also know that Latin is not: it is a different language. But a nation can lose its language without losing the consciousness of its identity (Ireland might be an example of this sad fate).

Anticipation is as essential to national as it is to personal identity. A nation, like an individual, looks to the future and thinks in terms of its future interests; it worries about what might happen, tries to assure its survival and takes measures to protect itself against possible adversity. There is, however, one important difference: a nation, unlike an individual, does not usually anticipate its own demise.

The fourth aspect of the collective national "personality" is body: the nation's territory, the natural particularities of its landscape and the physical artifacts which have reshaped it. A counter-example which immediately springs to mind is the case of the Jews, who survived for so long without a land of their own. But they had their substitute for body: their religious identity. This was what ensured their distinctness throughout all the centuries of life in the diaspora. In the past, the Jewish religious and ethnic identities were virtually indistinguishable, and the Jews would surely not have survived as a distinct ethnic community without their religious identity, their laws and their rituals, to support and distinguish them.

The fifth element essential to national identity is a nation's awareness of its origins – of an *identifiable beginning* at some point in time. Every nation has myths which testify to this: legends about founding events or ancestral figures to which the origins of the nation can be traced. Sometimes these events and figures cannot be precisely located in time, but this does not matter: it is enough that they represent an *exordium temporis* – a beginning of the nation's historical time.

These five elements, through which the collective "person" can identify itself as a distinct entity with a continuous identity in time, are also clearly visible in the way in which religious bodies define themselves.

In no religious body is continuous identity so firmly established as in the Catholic Church; and the same five elements which make up its identity are also present in its constitution. This is partly because of its high degree of institutionalization, unequaled by any other religious community.

In the case of the Catholic Church, the idea which most closely corresponds to that of *substance* is the idea of the Church as a *corpus mysticum* – as the bride of Christ. Just as the idea of substance is not an empirical one, so this, too, is unverifiable: it is a question of faith. But it is essential to the preservation of the idea of the Church, the *Ecclesia*, as a charismatic body established by God and deriving its legitimacy directly from divine intervention in human history – an intervention more momentous than any except the act of Creation itself. And the Church as a mystical body owes its unblemished purity and sanctity not to the impeccable moral conduct of its members, but to its divine origin and mission. This is why, for example, St. Augustine's battle against the Donatist heresy was so important: if the validity of the sacraments depended on the moral qualities of priests, or the perfection of the Church on the perfection of the faithful (as the Pelagians thought), the identity of the Church body would soon have been destroyed. The Church's substance, the *corpus mysticum*, cannot be damaged or polluted by human sins or offenses.

The collective *memory* of the Church is preserved not only in its sacred books, in historical records of its vicissitudes, in the lives of the saints and in material monuments of faith such as temples and works of art; it is also embodied in the long tradition of Church dogmas, considered (along with Scripture) as a source of doctrinal truth, and not merely as the product of the exegetical labors of theologians, popes, Council fathers, or the Holy Office. This tradition (when articulated in the official pronouncements of authorized bodies) is of course considered to be the true interpretation of Scripture, not the product of human thought: it is divine truth, not human opinion. It extends our understanding of the meaning of Revelation, but that meaning, although hidden, must already have been there if the dogmas are to be valid: it is discovered, not created.

Here we touch upon the delicate question of the "evolution of dogmas" – an idea developed in the modernist heresy, condemned by the Church and revived by Bultmannist theologians. How far the matter really affects the Church's sense of identity depends on how one interprets this "evolution." It is obviously important for the continuous identity of the Church body that the basic tenets of faith be preserved forever as they are, untouchable, like the Apostolic symbols; it is equally obvious, however, that there is hardly a word in them that has not been the subject of theological and philosophical examination, questioning, argument, and dispute – beginning with the adjective "omnipotent" (apparently stronger and implying more than the Greek "*pantokrator*"). Both the scholastics and modern philosophers like Descartes and Leibniz have struggled with the perplexing questions to which this word gave rise: can God reverse time and change the past? Do the truths of logic and mathematics depend on His will? And so on. The Church, understandably, has always insisted on the absolute validity of the *credo*, regardless of all the hermeneutics and debates, and this insistence is one of the forms in which it asserts its doctrinal identity. Whether the (tacit or explicit) consensus of the community of the faithful as to the meaning of this and countless other words has changed over the centuries is a matter for historians to investigate; but it seems reasonable to suppose that there is a core of basic beliefs (and thus a basic collective memory) which has withstood the efforts of theologians and philosophers to erode it. On some points of detail we may doubt the perfect consistency of the proclamations issued by the Holy Office at various times over the centuries, but the majority of the faithful is not much concerned with subtle theological distinctions, and the basic foundations are strong enough to allay the suspicion that they are "evolving" (in the sense in which this verb is used in the modernist heresy). Interpretations may change, and do, as do the liturgy and canon law, and forms of organization, and Church policy on various matters; but dogma, strictly speaking, does not, and nor do the basic divine moral commandments. For a truth cannot cease to be a truth – a statement to which not only Catholics, but also many rationalists, would assent.

The third element of the Church's identity, corresponding to *anticipation*, is its *orientation toward the future*. This, of course, remains as it has always been: the Church is the guide which will lead humanity to the harbor of salvation. But in the case of the Church there is an additional sense to this element which is absent from, or at least not always present in, other kinds of collective identity: it is not just anticipation of the future and future interests, but the consciousness of having an active mission. The idea of a mission can – but need not – be part of both a nation's and an individual's perception of themselves: nations, and their ideologues, can, in addition to proclaiming the superiority of their culture, believe that they have a duty to propagate it, or that they have a special role to fulfill in world history; individuals can believe that God's will or destiny has entrusted them with a special mission, or they may believe that their calling in life is to serve others. But for the Church its mission is an essential part, indeed the basic core, of its meaning; it is built into its very constitution.

The fourth component of the Church's continuous identity, corresponding to *body*, is the *Apostolic Succession*: the perfectly traceable and uninterrupted continuity in the handing down, over the centuries, from one generation of priests to another, of the gifts originally bestowed upon the Apostles. Individuals are born and die, but the body of the Church, in the form of this succession, retains its identity as the treasury of redemption. It is the Apostolic Succession that lends the Church a bodily identity which is stronger and clearer in its continuity than that of other collective organisms, such as states, political parties, corporations, or universities. These may claim continuity over generations, as new members take over from those who have left or died, but there will always be an element of doubt (similar to the doubts about Theseus's ship), whereas the Apostolic Succession provides the Church with clear criteria for the legitimacy of each new generation: it is always clear who may take his place in the collective body as the rightful successor of the Apostles, on what conditions and on what grounds. In this very particular sense it is not a collection of physical persons that makes up the body of the Church but the "spiritual body" which these persons together represent.

The fifth and last element of the Church's identity is its *identifiable beginning*. This, of course, is the birth and baptism of Christ, as well as the miracles he performed, his teaching, his transfiguration, his passion, and his resurrection. In this context it need not be established when precisely, in historical terms, the ultimate separation of the Christian community from the Jewish temple took place; the question is irrelevant here, and it is not one I am competent to discuss. What matters is the beginning as perceived and accepted by the Church for centuries.

For all these reasons the Catholic Church retains, in spite of all the changes it has undergone, a clearer, stronger, and better-attested continuous identity than any other collective body. The fact that all the elements of its identity are strengthened by or dependent upon the power of faith is immaterial; self-perception is an essential element of continuous identity, just as in the case of personal identity. I will not go into the question of how and to what extent these criteria apply to other religious bodies, Christian and non-Christian; none has such a well-grounded identity. The position of Christian communities which broke away from the Church of Rome in the sixteenth century or later is shakier with regard to their apostolic legitimacy. Although their history from the moment of the split is well known, they have often been accused of breaking the continuity which is essential to the Catholic Church, for they abolished the sacrament of the priesthood and denied the validity of tradition as a separate source of doctrinal authority. The Jewish religious identity does not meet all five of the criteria discussed above, but this is compensated for by an insistence on the immutability of divine law, which in Jewish religious communities is handed down uninterruptedly from generation to generation. The great Oriental religions have their sacred books, of course, but none of them has a well-defined body of scripture endowed with the status of divine revelation, as in the case of Christianity, Judaism, and Islam. Here, too, identity is a matter of degree.

It is worth noting that the Church's recent expansion of ecumenical spirit and increasing openness toward other traditions is perceived by many as an erosion of its identity. And it is true that this trend to openness (of which the Church's decision to stop condemning heresies is also part), however laudable, might blur the borderline which makes the Catholic Church distinct from other churches. But acceptance of tolerance and religious freedom can coexist with the Church's persistent will to assert its distinctness and its unique place in the world.

Since the Devil, as theologians used to teach, is the ape of God, there is nothing astonishing in the fact that some more recent, secular ideological bodies also appeal to similar criteria of identity. The communist movement had an analogous attitude to its sacred texts (*memory*), which could be reinterpreted and applied in new conditions without in any way undermining the eternal validity of the originals. The movement was supposed to be embedded in the great plan of History, and its aim was to further the realization of this plan; thus it acquired both its universal meaning (*substance*) and its mission (future-directedness, i.e., *anticipation*). It had a hierarchy and a supreme authority, whose members were empowered to pass judgment on the validity of its particular elements (*body*). It considered itself appointed by History as the carrier of truth and the leader of mankind on its march to ultimate salvation, but it could also point to a well-defined origin in time (*an identifiable beginning*), namely the birth of the collective Messiah. Similarly with the orthodox Freudian movement, where we can observe a fairly exact parallel with the Apostolic Succession: the healing art may be practiced only by those who have been anointed by another who has been similarly anointed, and so on down to the initial, self-anointed Founder (the only one who could, and did, apply the liberating therapy of psychoanalysis to himself; no one after him was able to repeat this feat).

Both ideological movements and religious bodies consider themselves to be the bearers of truth; the *claim to truth* is inscribed into the very meaning of their existence. Such a claim is not among the criteria of identity which can be applied to other continuous entities, nations or individuals; but such entities do make a claim which may be considered roughly analogous, namely a claim to *legitimacy*. Both persons and nations claim legitimacy by the very fact of their existence: they are there, so they are there legitimately, just because they are there. Moreover, they are there necessarily, not contingently: both persons and nations, in their act of self-assertion, assert the *necessity* of their existence, for they cannot conceive of a world from which they are absent. Their being there not only entails that they are entitled to be there but belongs, as it were, to the very constitution of the world. This claim of legitimacy and necessity is similar to the truth claims of religious and ideological bodies.

There is one more thing that should be mentioned. The assertion of self-identity, whether by an individual, an ethnic group, or a religious body, always involves a danger: the danger of aggression or of a desire to dominate others. In defending his legitimacy, an individual may easily come to feel that he must affirm it by expanding his power; a nation will protect its identity by hostility to other nations, by conquest and domination; a religious body, as the bearer of truth *par excellence*, is easily tempted to believe that it is its right and its duty to destroy the enemies of truth, i.e., other religious communities and forms of faith. Even if we admit that the desire to assert one's identity by hostile expansion is by no means always and everywhere inevitable, the truth remains (however Nietzschean it may sound) that it is ultimately the stuff of which most of the world's history is made.

The Demise of Historical Man[1]

Homo historicus in the sense I have in mind here is a modern invention. More specifically, he is an internal reaction against the modern world.

It has often been claimed that to be human is to be historical; that mankind robbed of historical consciousness is a monstrosity, even a contradiction in terms; and that collective memory, crystallized in historical knowledge, is not only a necessary condition but the very foundation of our self-identification as beings that live in a community – that is, as humans. This commonplace is hardly controversial. But the fact of our being historically oriented in this obvious way does not make us historical beings in the modern sense. Of course people have always been interested in their collective past; of course they have always needed – as a tribe, as a nation, or as a religious community – a mythological foundation for their existence that told them about the origins of their world and allowed them to grasp its sense.

History as knowledge of origins played the role of myth, irrespective of the varying proportions in which it combined truth and poetry. Its function was to provide a self-grounding: to give the community a sense of the legitimacy of its existence, to ground it in its ancient origins. History-as-myth provided more than just interesting information about a community's genealogy; it also provided a principle of legitimacy, and thus gave meaning to the community's continuing existence – a meaning defined and situated, so to speak, at the source of being. A "grounding"

1 Originally a lecture delivered in Stuttgart in 1989 upon the invitation of the Bosch-Stiftung. The German original ("Ist der 'historische Mensch' gestorben und sollen wir sein Ableben betrauern?") appeared in a special pamphlet published by the Bosch-Stiftung. An English translation was published in *Partisan Review* 3 (1991). This translation is a version revised by Agnieszka Kolakowska.

fact was more than just a fact, a chance event that could just as well not have happened; it contained within it its own necessity, and in this sense it seemed timeless, outside the temporality of facts.

This awareness of origins and grounding in history, the sense of an existence rooted in an absolute beginning which, petrified in a timeless moment of the ancient past, endowed it with meaning and legitimacy, was indispensable for societies whose distinctive feature was what Edward Shils calls "primordiality": the bond created by a common ancestry, the self-definition of a tribe by "blood," its rootedness in a common, more or less legendary, past in which all individual genealogies converge. A similar, although not identical, phenomenon can be observed in religious communities, which also define themselves through participation in a common past. This is also true of the so-called universal religions, where ethnic bonds play no role; belonging to a religious community is defined by spiritual, not biological kinship. And spiritual kinship is defined historically: through participation in the same holy history which goes back to the beginning of things, when God – or gods, or a messenger of God – called this spiritual tribe to life, endowed it with certain privileges, and imposed certain duties, giving it access to the truth which brings salvation and entrusting it with a mission.

In both cases of kinship – spiritual kinship and kinship defined by blood ties – history is the binding force whereby a tribe identifies itself by opposition to the rest of the world. People are historical beings in the sense that they are sole owners of the past in which their world, their tribe, or their religion were grounded and shaped; and they naturally need this past in order to give meaning to their lives and to the universe as a whole.

This "historicity" which binds all communities has not been utterly extinguished; it still exists both in national consciousness and in religious bonds. But it is a vestigial existence. The victorious march of Enlightenment rationalism, and the transition from tribal life to civil society, have radically enfeebled it, and driven it out almost entirely.

The connection has often been remarked between the rationalist view of the world, which evolved upon the ruins of religious tradition, and civil society (in the Rousseauian, not the Hegelian, sense), which replaced tribal kinship. In civil society the individual acquires his belonging to the social "whole" not through blood ties or the bonds of a common genealogy, but through his participation in an abstract legal order; historical considerations are not needed to determine or establish this belonging. What makes us a society is the power of the law: a law which extends over a certain limited area and before which all individuals are equal. (It took a long time, of course, for the belief in equality before the law to become entrenched; as long as legally defined estates and aristocratic privileges were upheld, historical criteria continued to function, albeit more and more feebly.) In short, history is no longer needed to establish the legitimacy of a social order and the place of the individual in it.

Rationalism in the modern sense of the term – that is, the rationalism we associate chiefly with the Cartesian heritage – emerged as, roughly speaking, the belief that the criteria of validity in the intellectual realm are the same as those applied in scientific procedures. Rationalism and civil society (regardless of which came first or was prior in the order of causality) converge in their common indifference to history. They share the belief that *history cannot confer validity*; it cannot establish, justify or explain the validity of anything. It is naive superstition to imagine that the truth of a proposition can be established by the fact that it has been believed for a long time, that our ancestors believed it, that it was revealed as God's word by some prophet, etc. In order to establish the truth of any opinion, we must apply the clear and absolutely binding mathematical and empirical criteria elaborated by science. Religious truths, too, are valid only to the extent that they can be rationally – i.e., "geometrically" or empirically – verified. Nor is the history of science relevant to the understanding of science: we want to know the truth, so what use is there in studying a series of absurd blunders? Similarly with issues concerning laws and government; these must be decided by considering what form of government would best preserve the peace, ensure social order, and serve people's interests, not by appealing to tradition. In such matters the theory of social contract and enlightened egoism provides sufficient guidance: everyone attends to his own affairs, and from these countless egoisms the "invisible hand" of the market forges a functioning whole. Scientistic rationalism, the development of civil society based on equality before the law, the theory of enlightened egoism and social contract, the spread of the market, economic theory – these things together are a tightly woven whole, and all its components give rise to indifference or disdain for history, which is rejected as a source of legitimacy both in the intellectual realm and in social affairs.

The view of the world I have sketched here, in a rough and simplified form, determined the ideological framework of modernity, and exerted a tremendous influence on eighteenth- and nineteenth-century European thought. Not, of course, without encountering a good deal of resistance: the strength of ethnic bonds and the vitality of religious tradition were still such that rationalist attacks could not defeat them entirely. The doctrine according to which the interplay of colliding egoisms in a society based on greed ultimately brings universal happiness proved highly dubious in light of the effects of the Industrial Revolution

– a fact to which representatives of early socialist thought did not fail to draw the attention of the European public. And once rationalist and skeptical attacks had deposed first divine authority, and then also natural law (which had been treated as a sort of watered-down form of divinity, or a more modest substitute for God), the simple question of how good could be distinguished from evil seemed unanswerable. The reply that the question was meaningless or wrongly put could not really make people happy.

To be sure, Kant tried to prove that the question could be answered within the framework of a rationalist worldview, without appealing to history; he argued that the foundations of moral judgment could be established by transcendental rationality, in which we all participate. However, very few Enlightenment skeptics were convinced by this.

The Romantic movement seemed to be an attempt to return to the old historicity: to the belief in the legitimizing power of the national bonds established in an ever-present past. The Catholic temptation in this movement is entirely understandable, for the Church of Rome could boast of the uninterrupted continuity of its existence and lay claim to being the guardian of the original treasure of Christianity.

Both liberals and socialists have ignored the reality of nations; most of them saw nations as the remnant of a past era, doomed to extinction by the all-unifying force of modernity and the development of communication and of the global economy. Their predictions were based on sound arguments; they would surely be astonished if they could witness the rebirth of nationalism in our time. And yet the socialist movement was nourished and given its impetus by the same instinct that nourished Romanticism: not in the sense that the socialists extolled the values of national tradition (although in fact some did) or the beauty of an idealized medieval spiritual unity, but in the sense that they deplored the domination of egoisms and the loss, in the market economy, of natural human solidarity; they dreamed of a society in which every individual would spontaneously and disinterestedly identify with humanity, thus ensuring everlasting harmony. But if remnants of the old historicity – the belief in the happiness of primitive, classless tribes – have survived here and there in socialist ideologies, it is no longer as a validating principle of present society, but rather as an abstract, ahistorical image of a Golden Age; a model, not a source of energy as in the past. Thus this belief was not properly an instance of the old historicity. And the most powerful theoretical expression of the socialist idea, the Marxist doctrine, evolved from an entirely different kind of historicism, associated, of course, with the name of Hegel.

The issue here is not to interpret the Hegelian idea or to ask whether and how this idea – a reaction to the antihistoricism of the

Enlightenment – was itself unambiguous and coherent. The point is that two mutually incompatible varieties of a new historicity seem to have grown – whether legitimately or not does not matter here – out of the Hegelian legacy; and the *homo historicus* I have in mind here was shaped by one or both of them.

It was also Hegel who taught us – directly or indirectly – that we live in history and contribute to its shape; that history includes what occurs here and now. The widespread feeling that we shape history is probably Hegelian in origin (though it was anticipated by Vico). It irrupted into our language and ensconced itself in it so comfortably, with its aura of pathos, that we do not think to question it. History used to be either simply a chronicle of past events or – on the Augustinian approach – a succession of divine interventions in human affairs. But today it is no longer either of these things. I eat breakfast, lecture at the university, talk with friends, go to an art exhibition, and doing all these things I am not only surrounded by "history" as a kind of invisible natural environment, but contributing to its progress. We either internalize history as our way of life or we interact with it in an intimate, quasi-erotic way, as if history were a lady one could seduce. In doing something, I am not simply doing this or that, eating breakfast or visiting an exhibition; in everything I do, I am making history.

What use do people have, or what use did they have, for this curious and unnatural feeling invented by philosophers? The Enlightenment, having pronounced the death sentence on divine providence and then on God himself, rejecting Him as the source of meaning and as the tribunal that could be entrusted with matters of good and evil, soon went on to kill Nature – a substitute for God that provided both moral rules and principles of rationality. History became a substitute for the substitute – a newly discovered infallible foundation on which meaning could be built, and the binding power that could reconstruct a meaningful whole from disconnected pieces and define our place in it.

Historical man need have no historical knowledge or interest in real history; he knows history simply as a reliable and trustworthy legislator. And he believes that history is *real*: not simply something that once was, but a living being. History "marches on," like an army; it will "decide if we were right," like a judge; it will "be the judge of events," like a scholar. And so on.

This, then, was an attempt to make history the carrier and guardian of all human values, the divine authority that could issue verdicts about good and evil and provide access to the sources of higher reason and meaning. But – as the later career of this idea shows – it was doomed from the outset by a fatal ambiguity, as a result of which the authority of history not only broke apart into two irreconcilable tendencies but was also brought, ineluctably, to its own destruction, dashing all hopes of rebuilding meaning.

Both God and Nature were immutable; and their judgments about human duties and human dignity, the meaning of life, justice and injustice, truth and falsity, were supposed to be immutably valid. History is by definition incapable of issuing such judgments, for it is mutability itself; change, and nothing other, is precisely what history consists of. How, then, can we trust it and profit from its wisdom?

One of the Hegelian answers is that the actual historical process is the only authority that can produce reason and truth; only it can confer absolute validity. Abstract moral judgments about the historical process are empty and fruitless. From this assumption some Hegelians concluded that this process *in toto*, with all its cruelties and atrocities, must simply be accepted as rational and therefore good. But history so conceived can no longer be a source of wisdom or rules of behavior; it cannot be our teacher and guide in life. Like a tyrant, it demands to be worshipped as it is, for what it is. At best, all we can say is that what is good and rational today was absurd and wrong yesterday, and may also be wrong tomorrow. This relativist and ultimately nihilist interpretation of Hegel was certainly a great simplification, but it was not entirely wrong; and "historicism" in this sense could recognize some of its ideas in the Hegelian construction. But this form of historical relativism was, of course, much older than Hegel; it had been present in European thought since Montaigne: "Diabolical today, holy yesterday," "Just on one side of the Pyrenees, unjust on the other," etc. This simple skepticism cannot be attributed to Hegel without restrictions, but then – as Hegel himself pointed out – we do not read philosophers the way they would like to be read, but the way our era dictates that we should read them. And on this reading, history is self-sufficient and self-supporting; it has no ontological background except itself; and everything – every truth, every validity, every kind of Reason – is immanent in it.

So conceived, the so-called historicism inevitably turned against itself. For to say that truth is historically relative, that something is true only "for a certain era," is tantamount to saying that there is no truth in the normal sense. Thus we no longer need history or historicist philosophy; the question of truth has simply been abolished. Nietzsche knew this; he also knew that he had drawn all the conclusions from God's death, and wanted to make us face the world as it is – without God, and thus without meaning, without good and evil, without truth. For the next hundred years the European spirit was to live in the shadow of his nihilism. Nihilism is still with us, and it does not need to express itself in so-called historicist categories; universal relativism and nihilism are plentiful enough.

WHO ARE WE?

But there was another side to the Hegelian heritage: belief in progress and in the fulfillment of history. The idea of progress, however defined, necessarily implies that we have at our disposal certain non-historical criteria, criteria that are not entirely dependent on the actual course of events, which allow us to say that truth – truth *tout court*, not truth for some historical era – increases, or evolves, or manifests itself increasingly, in history; or that the essence of humanity develops and matures in time. And the idea of fulfillment suggests that there will come a point in the historical process at which an absolute state will have been achieved – not just in the sense that history will tire of going on, or exhaust itself, and just decide not to progress any further, but also in the sense that it will attain its plenitude, its perfect form.

Hegel, despite his intransigent anti-utopianism, did believe in an ultimate stage of the evolution of mankind. His anti-utopia was directed against all the arbitrarily constructed visions of the perfect society that people have thought they could deduce from moral principles alone, without taking into account the actual historical process; there was no conflict between this criticism and his belief in the fulfillment of history.

The tension between the belief that all truths and ideas are historically limited and the anticipation of mankind's ultimate fulfillment was inherited by the most successful form of historicism in our century – Marxist philosophy. According to Marxist doctrine, there are no eternal ideas; every product of culture is a disguised expression of the real interests of various social classes. According to this same doctrine, however, we also know what the essence of being human is and what is required for its actualization; only on this assumption can we use words like "alienation," "liberation of mankind," "the end of alienation," etc. Thus on the one hand everything is historically determined, but, on the other, the ultimate state of humanity, which may shortly be expected, will – though it is called the "beginning" rather than the "end" of genuine history – be the fulfillment of mankind. So it seems that not everything is historically determined after all.

But the Marxist utopia can hardly be described as historicism in the proper sense. It certainly included the belief in "laws of history" that would unfailingly, and within a very short time, elevate us to the heights of perfection and bring about an ideal world. But the past was irrelevant; the anticipated future would consign it to oblivion. The meaning of the past can be grasped only from the vantage point of the expected ultimate fulfillment; it is the future – something that is not empirically given – that defines the meaning of both present and past. History in itself is unproductive; it can give us no guidance and no access to truth, or only in a perverse way, in that it acquires its meaning from the future – i.e., from something that does not exist.

And thus history, the last rampart from which the Enlightenment hoped to defend itself against nihilism – its own creation – and rediscover the source of meaning, collapsed under its own weight, unable to go on performing its task. "Historical man" split into two figures, and for both history gradually became less and less significant.

For those who drew their utopian dreams from Marxist ideology, history was no more than a pretext for believing in a quasi-natural inevitability that would soon transform their fantasies into reality. Messianic hopes justified all means, all forms of violence, which might bring millenarian happiness closer. Nothing in the present, and thus all the more emphatically nothing in the past, was of any significance; only the future mattered. The reality that did not yet exist had much more importance – indeed, much more existence – than the real, palpable world. "Historical man" abolished history.

The variety of historicism which saw history as an all-encompassing, all-exhaustive, self-grounding absolute was also forced, in the end, to deny history. The logic of this peculiar self-devastation seems simple enough. People were aware that different periods and different civilizations gave rise to different beliefs; historicism was the generalized theoretical expression of this ancient discovery. Consistent historicism entailed the belief that something could be valid only for a given era, for a given *Zeitgeist*, within the context of a given culture, etc. And this meant that nothing is valid in itself. To say that something is valid for a given historical epoch, a *Zeitgeist*, a culture or civilization is tantamount to saying that it was considered valid, or true, or obvious, or uncontroversial, in that era or for that culture; apart from this context the adjective "valid" has no meaning. Thus universal relativism no longer has any need of history. And the path from historicism in this sense to simple, all-embracing, and all-engulfing relativism was a straight one. The next stage – the structuralist ideology – was to proclaim that knowledge of history in the traditional sense (which included knowledge of conscious human intentions) is neither possible nor useful; following swiftly upon it was the further discovery that all meaning we imagined ourselves to have found in the past is our own meaning, imposed by us. For instance, no text has any meaning in itself (presumably with the exception of texts by those who make this very claim). A convenient theory, one may note in passing, in that it frees us from the need to read, since whatever we read, we are in fact reading nothing.

Thus "historical man" committed suicide and was resurrected – as nihilistic man.

Where do we stand now, at the century's close, with our uncertainty about history, and at the same time our unease in it and our longing for it? Will relativism and nihilism (which Husserl warned us against at the start of the century), first historically grounded, then ahistorical, be definitively, irrevocably victorious?

The utopian mentality, after so many great disillusionments, seems to be in decline. Fewer and fewer people seem to believe that there is a technique that will lead us infallibly to a paradise where all human needs have been satisfied and all conflicts reconciled. There is no doubt, on the other hand, that more and more effort, toil, and money will be needed to repair the damages we ourselves have wrought, to ward off ecological catastrophes and to solve demographic problems. It would be naive to hope that in some indefinite future we will all have more and more of everything. The utopian faith in the benevolent designs of history seems to be waning.

But relativism, freed from its "historicist" origins, seems to be enjoying continuing good health. In its popular and most widespread form, it tells us that we have no absolute criteria whereby we might evaluate and compare different civilizations, belief systems, or norms, and that all elements of all civilizations are therefore equally legitimate. In short, slavery is as good as freedom, or at any rate neither is "better" in any real sense. A pragmatic variety of relativism, with a more developed theoretical framework, is based on the idea of consensus: it claims that everything will be fine, we won't have to worry about a thing, if only we can reach a consensus.

Since this relativism is associated particularly with the American mentality, it is perhaps not out of place here to remark on the difference between the American and the German approach. The American approach is to say, for instance, "No one here defends slavery; it would be very hard to find someone who believed there was nothing wrong with slavery and expressed regret that it had been abolished. Thus we can say, without a shadow of a doubt, that there is a consensus about slavery, and nothing more is needed." The German spirit, however, is not satisfied with this solution. The German approach is to say, rather, "Consensus is never enough. I want to know whether slavery is in fact evil, not just what people think about it. Otherwise, if someone says that slavery is evil, he can be taken to mean only that most people in a given society consider it to be evil. But that is not what he means: such a reduction is contrary to people's real intentions; this is not the meaning people assign to their words when they make such a statement. When I say that slavery is evil, I mean that slavery is in fact evil – that it is evil in itself, not that other people, or even most people, believe it to be evil. Moreover, this reduction implies that while slavery might be evil today, it was not evil in the past, when it was considered quite normal. But those who fought against slavery did so because they believed that it was evil and contrary to human dignity, irrespective of any consensus in the matter. If they had not believed this, slavery would never have been abolished. And if the words 'good' and 'evil' have no meaning except in this sense, then, if slavery were re-established and again considered quite normal, it would become good *in fact*." Thus the German spirit wants to know what is good or evil, real or unreal, true or false. It found its expression in the Kantian and Husserlian tradition; it even invaded the Frankfurt School, which never abandoned the hope that a *logos* free from all contingency might be discovered that would provide us with genuinely valid rules, both for thinking and for issuing value judgments.

Historical man may be in decline, he may even have died, but his offspring, the carrier of generalized relativism, lives on and flourishes. A number of features peculiar to our time may be put forward to explain his resilience. One of them is the all-pervading spirit of popular scientism, which rejects everything that cannot be assessed in terms of visible goods; on these criteria, the distinction between good and evil, and that between true and false in any but a pragmatic sense, is meaningless. Another reason is the aversion to ideological fanaticism, whether religious or secular, whose inhuman consequences we have had so much occasion to observe in our century. However, this admirable rejection of fanaticism often seems no more than a disguise for quite a different attitude. For relativism is convenient; it is convenient because it sanctions our *indifference*. And we would like to ennoble this indifference, to give it a good name – as if there were no difference between fanaticism and the search for truth, or between tolerance and indifference to truth; as if nihilism were a defense against fanaticism.

So we can find reasons why "historical man" was born and why he died – though not without progeny. Faced with the progressive waning of religious belief, with the loss, too, of faith in the wisdom and immutability of nature, our culture set up history as the tribunal in which we can put our trust if we are not to be engulfed by the desert wastes of nihilism. But this contrivance proved weaker than the cultural forces against which it was meant to defend us. Historicism was transformed into relativist indifference, leaving us in the same spiritual wasteland, with the same void it had promised to fill.

This wasteland is comfortable, but also hard to bear. People need, and have always needed, to believe that the world can be not only dominated but also understood; this need is surely part of what it means to be human. This is why we have seen, in our brutal century, various attempts to find a way back to the meaning we have lost. It seems unlikely that traditional historicism will find this way for us: unlikely that we could ever again be persuaded to put our faith in history as it actually is. If anything, we seem, rather, to be witnessing a new longing for the old historicity. In defiance of all rational expectations, the need to establish one's identity through tribal membership, to define oneself through the values of a national culture, is not fading; it is getting stronger. (And we know the dangers to which this quite understandable need gives rise when it degenerates into militant chauvinism.) Above all, and again in defiance of rational expectations, there is a renewed longing for self-identification through religion. In all the chaos and uncertainty of our times, our religious heritage seems to provide a more reliable source of support than anything else.

Of course, it is hard to make predictions on such precarious ground. But it seems safe to say that we have seen the demise of secular history as the grounding for existence and the source of meaning, and that the third Christian millennium, which is almost upon us, will have to rediscover our old religious roots – so that we can survive.

On Our Relative Relativism[1]

According to Heraclitus, in the eyes of God everything is beautiful, good, and just. It is not so in our eyes, of course. But Heraclitus's assertion does not imply a "relativistic" melancholy (God sees things one way, human creatures another); we must assume that God knows better and thus that everything really is beautiful, good, and just, and our impression is not just different, but plain wrong. It is conceivable – at any rate not logically inconsistent – that we know that this is God's view of the world and that it is correct (for instance, because God Himself has told us so), but are incapable of sharing it (except perhaps in the case of mystics who momentarily participate in the divine vision; but they have no means of conveying that vision to others).

If we fail to perceive the beauty, justice, and goodness of the world, and instead see vast swathes of ugliness and injustice, does it matter that we know, or pretend to know, that the world is indeed beautiful, just, and good? I believe it does. It does not change the content of our perceptions, nor does it make us more efficient in what we do; but it may affect our attitude toward the world. People who strongly believe – on the basis of divine revelation, or because of some non-transmittable experience, or (like Leibniz, for example) as a result of *a priori* reasoning – that there is a good moral order in the universe and that ultimately everything is for the best, are not protected against ugliness, injustice, and suffering. But they are better able to absorb the adversities of their existence, even though their image of things cannot be formulated as an empirical hypothesis in accordance with the rules of scientific procedure.

---

1 Published by the Institute of Philosophy and Sociology of the Polish Academy of Sciences in *Debating the State of Philosophy: Habermas, Rorty and Kolakowski*, ed. Jozef Niznik and John T. Sanders (Westport, Conn.: Praeger Publishers, 1996). This is a slightly revised version.

This difference is worth pondering when the question of truth is discussed. It is hard to refute the traditional arguments against both relativist and absolutist claims about human knowledge. The gist of the antirelativist argument is as follows: the relativist denies any eternal and absolute standard of rationality. In his view, if we say that something is true to the best of our knowledge, we must assume, implicitly or explicitly, that it is true for a particular civilization, or in particular historical conditions, or by virtue of our biological structure, or within a linguistic game. But in this way, critics argue, the relativist is entangled in his own snare: he cannot escape the antinomy of the liar, for his general statement about the relativity of all knowledge falls victim to its own verdict and is as relative as any other; albeit conceivably true, it is, as it were, unutterable. The relativist could try to get around this difficulty by transforming his epistemological proposition into a normative rule; but this would be a spurious solution, even if it removed the problem of self-reference, for such a prescription would be either arbitrary and therefore unjustified, or justified by the very proposition that has just been rejected.

The same applies, for that matter, to another kind of relativism, expressed in one of the most celebrated sentences of contemporary philosophy: Paul Feyerabend's "anything goes." If everything is permissible, then all restrictive cognitive rules are equally permissible; in other words, the rule, "It is not the case that anything goes," also goes. Thus we may say that if anything goes then it is not the case that anything goes. This reckless permissiveness does not seem a very promising foundation for a theory of knowledge (to tolerate everything means to tolerate intolerance).

The Popperian variety of relativism may succeed in avoiding the self-reference paradox because it deals with empirical hypotheses and does not pretend, if I understand it properly, to be one itself; but it entails other unfortunate consequences. If we assume that, even after a perfectly thorough process of elimination, there will always be a number of mutually incompatible explanations for the same empirical phenomena, then it seems conceivable that our knowledge, accumulated in empirical hypotheses and laws, consists entirely of false statements, and moreover that this will always be so. The distinction between truth and falsity is not abolished, but it is of little use; falsity can be established, but truth cannot. No doubt, one can formulate rules of acceptability or admissibility, but not criteria for establishing the distinction between what is merely acceptable and what is true.

In all three variants of relativism the concept of truth in the everyday sense of the word has been discarded. But to reject any of those variants on logical or other grounds is not to reassert the concept of truth. On the contrary; the ancient skeptics' traditional argument about the infinite regress that inevitably arises in the quest for criteria of truth still seems cogent.

The outcome of these well-known arguments is equally well known. There is no zero-point in the search for knowledge, no uncontaminated source from which certainty – real, unconditional, unimpeachable certainty – springs. Husserl's unflagging pleas for Truth – with a capital T – in the face of the relativist corruption of European civilization went largely unheeded. This was not because his arguments were necessarily flawed but rather because the prevailing cultural trend was in another direction, gradually eroding belief in eternally valid intellectual standards, in the regulative ideal of *episteme*, and finally in the very usefulness of the concept of Truth. This trend has reached its climax in our time, but we can trace it back, with the benefit of hindsight, to the very beginning of the Enlightenment (in the broadest sense of this loose term).

Modern skepticism, one may suppose, resulted from contact with other civilizations and concerned, as we see in Montaigne, not only moral rules and customs, but all kinds of truth. This was, to be sure, before modern science emerged in the beginning of the seventeenth century, soon to be codified in a set of distinct abstract procedures. But the great thinker, the reputed pillar of modernity, who contributed to this codification and whose work could initially be seen as a philosophical response to Galileo's physics, was to become, unwillingly, a part of the skeptical conspiracy. Descartes's attempt to restore certainty and his approach to the reality of our world of experience has of course been endlessly analyzed and commented upon. But few have accepted it as a reliable method for establishing trust in our cognitive prowess; it was Descartes's skeptical questioning that most strongly influenced his readers, and was repeatedly denounced as the main source of modern idealism.

It was the Enlightenment proper which, from various directions, cast more and more doubt on our proficiency in the search for truth as it had been traditionally defined. Hume, of course, became one of the main culprits when he ultimately reduced knowledge, tautologies apart, to the content of particular perceptions, immobilized in their particularity, and everything beyond that to pragmatic values. So did Kant, at least in the popular perception of his work. Schopenhauer even argued that the Kantian distinction between phenomena and the thing-in-itself, and his insistence that objects were co-created by transcendental forms of consciousness, led to the conclusion that our world of experience is a realm of dreams (we should suppose, therefore, that once Kant had been awakened from his dogmatic slumbers by Hume, he realized that he had been, and still was, living in a dream and that the world of experience is Maya, as Vedic wisdom taught).

This might seem a somewhat exaggerated interpretation, and Kant himself did not say this in so many words, but when we look at great philosophers as cultural facts, what counts is less their genuine intentions than the way their thought influenced and was perceived by the general educated audience. When Kant said that his place was the "fertile depth of experience," he meant it, and his writings, sometimes opaque, were not designed to instill in his readers a feeling of tragic renunciation or a terror of the great Unknown. But his simplified message was that the world as it really is, is beyond our reach: God's existence is unprovable, and morality is severed from its religious roots. This was supposed to be "the withdrawal from immaturity, [an immaturity] for which we ourselves are to blame," that is to say, the Enlightenment. To be sure, one school of Kantians altogether rejected the thing-in-itself as a fictitious construct and made Kant the herald of the absolute sovereignty of Thought, but another school reduced his transcendental forms to psychological, species-related conditions of knowledge, thus reinforcing the relativistic side of his legacy.

Hegel also took part in the conspiracy; again, less perhaps through his notoriously ambiguous intentions than through the way he was read. And it was fairly easy to perceive him as a historicist for whom all products of human thought, including philosophy, metaphysics, and religion, must be seen as temporary instruments of the great impersonal spirit in search of itself, and truth as time-bound and culture-related. His philosophy was frequently misread as Reason's approval for all historical contingency.

A further vigorous stimulus to relativist thinking came from the philosophical elaboration of Darwinism. From a theory implying that all development of life is guided by a single factor – the mechanical elimination of the worse adapted – it was possible to conclude that the specifically human Reason we boast of, including its power of abstraction, is merely an effective instrument in the adaptation of the species to the changing environment, and that no other meaning can be attributed to it; in other words, that the proper measure of knowledge is the ability to predict and efficiently control events in order to counteract the hostile contingency of nature. The ideas of Reason and Truth in the Platonic, Aristotelian, and even Cartesian sense became empty and irrelevant to this task. This was what the empiricists of the late nineteenth century explicitly and consistently argued.

Does the reduction of knowledge to a self-defense mechanism of the species fall prey to the antinomy of the liar? Not necessarily: not if it is transformed into a prescription which can be applied to itself. It may be argued that in some interpretations the discovery of the theory of evolution is itself an instrument for improving the survival chances of the species that contrived it. For example, one could argue that it would be good for humanity as a whole to slaughter its ill-adapted members; certain English lovers of mankind like H.G. Wells and George Bernard Shaw even suggested as much at one point.

But philosophical Darwinians usually do not bother about this issue. The Darwinian theory is accepted as a scientific discovery, and the assumption that it is true (in the normal sense of the word) is stealthily smuggled into arguments which deny the meaning of truth on the basis of this same theory.

Nietzsche, of course, was the loudest voice of the cultural mutation of relativism, for all his contradictions. Quite often we glimpse a hidden despair looming up from behind his triumphal war cry over the dead bodies of God, Truth, Reason, and a well-ordered universe. But the crucial, poignant message was unmistakable: nothing but pathetic wreckage remains of the lofty Platonic mirage of wisdom. We are no longer pilgrims doggedly and tirelessly striving toward this great treasure; the treasure does not exist – it is a figment of our hollow craving for the impossible. We live in an aimless chaos and try to assert our individual or collective will to expansion. Our philosophy, our religious search, often even our art, are illusions, veils behind which we enclose ourselves in order to face the world as it "truly" is (never mind that there is no Truth).

But civilizations cannot survive in despair, not for long at any rate. So an effective medicine was found: an optimistic interpretation for what many people might have seen as a disaster. It goes as follows: There is nothing disastrous in our reasonable renunciation of the chimeras of Truth and Reason. These were merely specters which had been haunting our civilization for millennia, and to some extent continue to haunt it. Why should we despair because we have stopped trying to stalk an animal from a fairy tale? Our knowledge has proved efficient and provides us with predictive power. What else do we need? If parts of it prove inefficient or even counter-effective, they are cut off like dead twigs; we accept what remains as healthy, and science has devised good criteria of acceptability. People have debated, for instance, about "the existence of the world." But even assuming that we could define and grasp the meaning of such a bizarre question, it is a futile and empty one. Whatever we decide concerning the existence or non-existence of the world, nothing changes in our life, our perceptions, our practical business, or our science. We must discard such nonsensical problems, which possibly originated in sick minds.

Similarly with most traditional problems of metaphysics and epistemology, except those that are of an empirical nature and belong to psychological or linguistic analysis rather than to epistemology proper in the Husserlian sense. Neither ordinary people nor scientists are tormented by the distinction between the coherence and correspondence theories of truth; they discriminate between the true and the false on the basis of common criteria of acceptability, which in turn depends on the answer to the question, "What can we do with this truth?"

Even physicists, who tell us that some descriptions of the phenomena they examine depend on the observer or the measuring devices used, and cannot be made without including them, have contributed to the belief that our pursuit of Truth can never be entirely independent from the fact that we are engaged in this pursuit; and perhaps to the belief that the very idea of Truth is unintelligible. Einstein might have been dismayed by this perspective, but most scientists are not.

Replacing criteria of truth with standards of acceptability thus conceived belongs to the program of moderate pragmatism, which invalidates metaphysics but does not affect science, which can continue to function according to rigorous standards without bothering about truth, except in the sense of acceptability. Immoderate, or extravagant, pragmatism, which instead employs criteria of usefulness or even "happiness," may be left aside. Not because it is false – this is an arbitrary prescription anyway – but because it is impracticable: it is impossible to specify how such criteria should be applied. No one can say how, for what, or for whom they should work, or in what time scale something should be judged useful or productive of more happiness, or how "happiness" is to be defined. (Drugs produce happiness for a while, but misery in the long run. And who is wise enough to calculate the global amount of happiness, given how unpredictable are the effects of so many human endeavors?)

Needless to say, extravagant pragmatism may not appear a compelling conclusion to be drawn from the moderate variety. But the cultural impact of ideas does not operate according to logical rules. "Efficiency" and "usefulness" do not mean the same thing, but in cultural and psychological terms the path from one to the other is short. The claim that there is no truth in the Husserlian or Platonic sense does not, of course, logically entail that "anything goes," but the road from one to the other is as easy (albeit longer) as, for example, the route from the demand for freedom to anarchy. It goes without saying that I am for freedom and against anarchy, but one can follow the changes, sometimes unnoticeable, in the prevailing use of concepts, whereby concepts eventually take on a meaning far removed from or even opposite to their original sense. And, of course, it is not just wordplay that causes such displacements but cultural processes that occur in other areas of life – in the hierarchy of values, in customs, in science, in technology, in social stratification, in religious beliefs, in information systems – all of them acting independently. For this reason isolating the precise impact of any one of those forces is usually a matter of speculation.

The path from the austere, ascetic, and lucid thought of David Hume to the contemporary philosophy of hippies and flower children, often called postmodernity, is convoluted and twisting, but it can be traced. Nevertheless, it is not one step that causes the next one but external energies, often hard to identify.

Despite the massive assault on universal, intellectual, and other standards, there are, fortunately, areas where standards still apply – notably in the sciences and especially in the so-called hard sciences, which do not seem to have been affected by the irresponsible philosophy of butterflies. They can do without the idea of Husserlian Truth; they have no need explicitly to assert the eternal criteria of rationality; but they have elaborated some fairly precise rules of acceptability that work, all doubts and disputes notwithstanding. Things are worse in the humanities, to be sure. But it would be an exaggeration to say that standards in historical studies have already been killed off by postmodernist propaganda, which manifests itself more in programmatic appeals than in the actual practice of science. But signs of the invasion can already be detected. The "anything goes" creed has clearly won in the arts and made fairly strong inroads into moral beliefs.

If we are to single out a particularly powerful cultural factor that has contributed to the progressing collapse of standards, we are tempted to point to the enormous increase in mobility, both spatial and social. The virtual extinction of village life in the developed areas of the world has destroyed the spiritual organization of space as a guarantor of stability and eroded trust in tradition, which formerly provided people with a number of basic moral norms and the belief in an order of things that bestowed meaning on life. This is not a new observation. Many people have seen uprootedness as a distinctive mark of our times; this widespread feeling of insecurity, of the absence of spiritual shelter, naturally found ideological or philosophical expression. We shed our archaic "irrational" habits of mind not in order to enter the glorious kingdom of rationality but, on the contrary, to adopt new habits which disregard the idea of rationality altogether.

There is no way back to the old unsullied order; no amount of nostalgia will reverse the course of change nor undo its alarming, perhaps calamitous, effects. But the need for certainty and Truth, to know the world as it really is, is not limited to philosophers, nor invented by them; it is simply human, and it is most unlikely that it will ever be extirpated.

Who Are We?

Various plagues of our civilization may be traced back to the loss of spiritual security. They include the widespread use of drugs, which give people an illusory and short-lived feeling of reconciliation with life; they also include the growth in violent criminality, a symptom of the refusal to find oneself a place in an order which is experienced as no longer being an order. Religious fanaticism and the search for pathetic satisfaction under the guidance of grotesque prophets also belong here. For any unprejudiced mind, as Hegel says, Truth will always remain the great word that makes the heart beat more strongly.

Quine, whose thinking may be seen as an expression of moderate pragmatism, says that both objects and God are cultural artifacts, but the former are superior in that they are more efficient for predicting events. Even if Quine is right, the fact remains that the fictitiousness of the objects which science deals with is not something many people are bothered or saddened by, whereas once God is declared an artifact and people accept this judgment, their world is really changed, both intellectually and emotionally; the absence of God is really experienced.

Science is usually trusted because it works. But it, too, has contributed, in a different way, to this same feeling of insecurity, because it is unintelligible to most nonscientists, and parts of it, especially quantum mechanics and cosmology, have become increasingly counterintuitive.

Even if we assume that truth is prepositional – and this is a discretionary decree – rationalism remains another discretionary decree. Its criteria of acceptability are based on the extent to which the truths thus discovered allow us to predict and control phenomena; this is to say, truth is conceived in terms of moderate pragmatism. This is culturally and historically explicable, but if it is understood unrestrictedly, it dismisses the idea of Logos as an unattainable mirage, a capricious fancy. Critics who attacked this scientific, or rather "scientistic," instrumental reason – for example, the Frankfurt School – and tried to safeguard the supremacy of Logos, were unable with precision to define its scope of domination or the criteria it was supposed to use in its discoveries. Consequently, their philosophy could be accused of being no more than a yearning after the lost Platonic or Hegelian paradise.

And then we are back at the beginning: since no compelling logical argument can be provided either for adopting so-called instrumental reason or for embracing the Logos of its critics, the ultimate justification of both lies within the realm of human needs. And no one can say, "Your needs are not genuine; I know best what you really need." The quest for the kind of knowledge that would satisfy our need for an all-embracing meaning of life and for valid, "true," moral rules, can, of course, easily be discarded as having nothing to do with truth. But so can those needs which stir or steer our curiosity when the point is to control our environment. If there is no unmediated truth, that is, no truth in which the knower and the thing known coincide, if our words are tools rather than a mirror or the carbon paper on which the universe leaves its direct mark, there seems no escape from the rules of moderate pragmatism – unless we accept that another route of knowledge lies open to us, one where words cannot be so deftly manipulated but rather suggest or draw us near a reality that is not empirical in the sense of ordinary perception. Let us repeat: to concede a monopoly to the rules of scientism would be an arbitrary verdict. Does the refusal to do so amount to groping blindly for a lost treasure in the darkness? Perhaps. As Epicharmos said, everything precious is usually found at night.

We survive uneasily in a perplexing chaos, having forfeited our belief in infallible guidelines for thought. Ours is a post-Enlightenment world in that it is Enlightenment turned against itself – the loss of Reason as a result of Reason's triumphant victory over the Unreason of the old mentality. And better not to venture into "futurology," since the future by definition does not exist. Strong beliefs easily breed fanaticism; skepticism, or the lack of beliefs, easily breeds mental and moral paralysis.

What Are Universities For?[1]

Since every sphere of human life is now said to be in a state of "crisis" it is no wonder that from time to time we hear about the "crisis of the University." I do not think, however, that this expression is really justified. It is not the case that research and teaching in institutions of higher learning is essentially badly done and requires fundamental reform; nor is it that no one knows what universities are for; nor that universities fail to prepare young people for the demands of contemporary life, etc. In this sense there is, in my opinion, no crisis. But there are many problems for which there are no easy or immediate solutions.

Let us list ten problems that are most often discussed in the context of the crisis of the university.

1. The relationship between the teaching and research roles of the university.

2. The relationship between the university as the seat of theoretical knowledge that develops in accordance with its own immanent principles and the university as a set of vocational schools.

3. To what degree is it desirable that the university should comply with so-called social demand or even with direct and detailed orders from the government or industrial corporations?

4. To what degree is it desirable that the university be exposed to the influence of the cities and towns in which it is located, and to make

---

1 Originally a lecture delivered at a conference on "Dilemmas of Higher Education," in Warsaw, June 1993, sponsored by the Viennese Institut für die Wissenschaften vom Menschen. Published in Polish as "Po Co Uniwersytet?" in a booklet printed by the city of Radom, "Honorowy Radomianin," 1994, in honor of the author. Published in English, in a translation by O. A. Wojtasiewicz, in *Poznan Studies in the Philosophy of the Sciences and the Humanities* 50 (1997), pp. 27–33. This version revised by A. Kolakowska.

efforts to coexist in harmony with them? (The issue of "town and gown," as one says in Britain.)

5. How can one oppose the division, certainly detrimental but probably largely inevitable, into "two cultures" – the humanistic and the scientific – among both the students and the academic staff? What are, in this connection, the advantages and disadvantages of the two-tiered education system?

6. Is it true that the immense growth of colleges and universities in Europe and in North America in recent decades has resulted in the deterioration of general standards?

7. What does the "politicization" of the university mean? How far is it admissible and how far is it destructive of the university's functioning?

8. Is it desirable that schools of fine arts and performing arts, such as theater, painting, and music, be incorporated into universities?

9. To what degree is it desirable that students participate in the decisions made by universities?

10. What kind of contact between teachers and students is best from the point of view of the task of the university?

These are only a few of the most important questions, each of which has been discussed in many debates. Many can easily be answered in general terms. But it is difficult to make the questions specific enough to enable the answers to become foundations for detailed decisions. One can easily eliminate extreme solutions within the life of academia; but even if we accept partial solutions, the range of possibilities is considerable. It is, of course, not my intention to consider all these issues in this brief summary. Instead, I would like to offer some quasi-philosophical remarks about the life of the university in the "ecological" situation of mankind.

Scientists told us long ago that the human species differs from all others in that human beings have, throughout their lives, the ability to explore their surroundings disinterestedly, regardless of current needs or dangers. The university is, so to speak, the institutionalized form of that specifically human biological trait – curiosity as an independent urge, the desire to know the world for the sake of knowledge itself. But the university is also, obviously, a specific organism that conveys and improves all the technical skills on which civilization depends, including medicine, engineering, law, the economy, and agriculture. It is the place where knowledge which is ancillary to such skills is acquired. It does not make sense to ask which of these two functions is "more important," but it is legitimate to say that a university deprived of all applied sciences would be greatly impoverished, and might lose its social credibility and validity. On the other hand, the university totally reduced to a set of vocational schools would cease to be a university and would lose the very function by which it is historically and, as I have suggested, biologically, defined.

It is an obvious and well-known truth that some extremely important technical achievements are the result of research that was not guided by any prospect of application but by purely cognitive considerations. This includes the discovery of electricity, X-rays, and antibiotics. Several very abstract fields of mathematics, born of the theoretical curiosity of several eminent minds, have unexpectedly proved extremely useful. This includes non-Euclidean geometries, Boolean algebra, and even number theory. But these are exceptional cases. It is also common knowledge that an immense number of perfectly good scholarly dissertations disappear, so to speak, into nothingness: they result in no further work and arouse no interest. But there is nothing one can do about that.

As a result of the extraordinary specialization in present-day academia, thousands of scholars must publish to obtain tenure and promotions. An enormous number of colleges and universities publish books and periodicals; specialists exchange papers within their respective circles, without any contribution to the general culture. Some of those specialties wither away with the passage of time. We must be resigned to the fact that some of the work that meets the accepted standards will remain useless. And it is impossible to assess its usefulness in advance, on the basis of the subject matter alone; we know that there are excellent and important works whose subjects seem totally exotic. Everything depends on the talent of the researcher and his passion. Scholarly works produced solely in order to obtain a degree or a promotion, works not inspired by passion, usually have little chance of surviving as a contribution to culture.

The university is most obviously both an organ of the current life of society and an organ of the universal drive for knowledge of the world. These two functions restrict one another and may give rise to conflicts. On the one hand, there is a tendency in Europe (perhaps less so in America, where most of the best universities are private) to demand that the university, financed by the state, should demonstrate its usefulness, or even earn its existence by carrying out various orders. This trend might be summed up thus: "Anyone may, if he wants to, study the Hittite language, black holes, the differences between St. Cyprian and St. Augustine in the interpretation of baptism, and Japanese Zen gardens, but why should the taxpayer pay for this? And what benefits accrue to the taxpayer from the study of such things?"

Should such a tendency prevail it would mean the destruction of the university, and, more generally, the ruin of our civilization. The above questions are dangerous, but also ill-formulated. It is, in fact, impossible that every taxpayer derive visible and tangible advantages from the fact that someone knows Hittite or the designs of Japanese gardens. The question can be formulated in a more general way: why should we have a culture that does not serve technological progress or increase material well being? The only answer to that question is: in order to let mankind be what it has always been. If culture means luxury, then this is perhaps because mankind itself is a luxury of Nature.

To demand that the sciences should justify their existence by producing immediate benefits was, as we know, characteristic of the communist system, with its obligatory state ideology which claimed omniscience. In accordance with that ideology, the humanities and social sciences were supposed to be instruments of political propaganda. After the Stalinist era that principle was not observed rigorously even in the Soviet Union, and less so in Poland, owing to increasing loss of faith in the official doctrine. Those employed by the Academy of Sciences under the communist regime remember that when they regularly submitted their research plans to the Academy authorities, they had to explain their significance for the national economy. For instance, I used to work in the Institute of the Polish Academy of Sciences and Letters, where I was concerned with research on Socinian theology during the second half of the sixteenth century. We used to invent absurd answers to absurd questions about our research. But it must be said that practically no one was interested in our answers and did not take these absurdities seriously. Hence it was possible to pursue such research projects without ideological obstacles, provided that political issues were not involved.

Nevertheless, the trivial truth should be repeated that the university is an institution of public life and must report its results. If it were perceived as a place for esoterica its justification would be questionable. And this was in fact the case in the past. The present prestige of universities is not age-old; in the sixteenth and seventeenth centuries universities did not play a visibly significant role in culture, and the social prestige of their professors was mediocre; they were often treated with contempt and ridiculed – some not without reason (it suffices to mention Rabelais and Molière). The great products of intellectual labor usually emerged outside universities. The famous sigh of Faust, who after graduating said, *"und bin so klug als wie zuvor"* (*and I am as wise as before*) was still not exceptional in Goethe's time, as we can see from this case of a bachelor who complained of his wasted years of study and the incompetence of his teachers, who lied to their students. Nevertheless, the seventeenth century saw a sustained struggle to free universities from under the control of the Church and its theologians in Europe (this was less marked in American universities, still very young at the time). Had the universities not won, they would have become insignificant and disregarded appendages, and spiritual culture would have shifted elsewhere. But in present conditions there is little place for *Privatgelehrten* (private scholars). We have no slaves, we are not supported by the Church, and we have no hereditary real estate; we are hired laborers, and for all the autonomy of the universities we are paid for discharging our duties. What is expected of us is, of course, in the first place teaching; research comes second. This is as it should be. It would not be a good thing if we treated teaching as an onerous addition to research work proper, because teaching is the reason for our existence in the universities.

In the United States there are colleges that are oriented solely toward teaching; they do not require from their professors achievements in scholarship but demand good teaching work. Some of them, it is said, are very good and highly valued. There is nothing discreditable in such an approach. It is worth noting that in Kant's time the pedagogical duties of academic teachers were much greater, and far more comprehensive; the load could be even four times heavier than in our case. Ours are, one might say, moderate, but there are reasons to argue that at continental universities, including universities in Poland, they should be either increased or modified. On the one hand, it is often pointed out that general courses – *les cours magistraux*, as the French call them – are now superfluous and could be successfully replaced by textbooks, while teaching proper could take the form of seminars and discussions, where it would be most useful, and would benefit both students and lecturers. On the other hand, the British and American practice, where students are expected to write essays which are then evaluated and graded, is very successful; it requires a thorough knowledge of the assigned texts and improves both writing and logical skills. But this obviously involves a considerable burden for the teaching staff. In the ancient British universities this task is performed mainly by tutors, and in America, in the case of courses attended by large numbers of students, by teaching assistants, who are usually postgraduate students. It involves a considerable burden for the students, too, but in the humanities and social sciences there is no better form of teaching. Without this emphasis on writing students could glide their way through their entire course of studies, up to their dissertations, almost without writing anything at all (this was the case in my time, in Poland, a quarter of a century ago). But an institution intended to train the intellectual elite of the country must resort to a rigorous system if it is to carry out its task successfully. Life should not be made easy either for students or for teachers if our civilization is to survive.

In every country there are better and worse universities. But if the secondary education is bad, so are the universities. And if education in

What Are Universities For?

the family is careless or nonexistent, the schools are bad, too. There are no infallible institutional measures, but the worst way of coping with the existing situation is to lower standards with the noble intention of not making people unhappy.

All the dilemmas mentioned above are real and require compromise solutions, but they still do not amount to a crisis. The greatest danger for the university is neither the increasing pressure to adopt a more professional orientation, nor the loss of public confidence owing to excessive concentration on trivial or esoteric research. Nor does it come from the large number of students, or even from the laziness of students and teachers.

The greatest danger, most clearly observable in the United States, is the invasion of an intellectual fashion which wants to abolish cognitive criteria of knowledge and truth itself, as a value established in our culture. The humanities and social sciences have always succumbed to various fashions, and this seems inevitable. But this is probably the first time that we are dealing with a fashion, or rather fashions, according to which there are no generally valid intellectual criteria and all meanings are freely generated. At the same time these fashions want to impose on others their own, purely ideological criteria, for instance feminist or racial (in accordance with black racism, but not *vice versa*). Should the "ideologization" of universities in that spirit prevail, we might find ourselves longing for the good old days of universities ruled by the obligatory Marxist ideology, with its formal rules of historical correctness and truth. Even though these rules were systematically violated, it was at least possible to force the ideologues to explain things in accordance with them, and this resulted in a weakening of ideological pressure.

If one claims that there are no universal criteria of cognition, then the only possible way of establishing scientific validity is by recourse to terror. If universities were to become so corrupted, they would soon lose their social prestige to such an extent that they would be relegated to the margins of the life of society. Culture would shift elsewhere because no society can survive for long without producing its own elites.

Anthropologists tell us that there used to be tribes in which intellectually outstanding individuals were quickly killed off. But those tribes did not survive for long; they were inevitably exterminated by other tribes which were free from such forms of egalitarianism. Because a return to such barbarism is hardly probable, the universities destroyed by the new ideologies would be turned into state-owned charitable institutions, and then new ones would emerge, training students in accordance with permanent "non-particular" rules of cognition.

In recent years several important books have appeared on the state of education in the United States. Their authors accuse American universities – even the best ones – of intellectual corruption and of gradually replacing scientific and educational standards by so-called "political correctness" – strikingly reminiscent of Stalinist jargon. These are, indeed, alarming fashions. In the name of what is proclaimed to be "pluralism" and "multiculturalism," academic teachers – as a rule third-rate scholars – are trying to impose upon others the idea of casting off academic rigor (which is also moral rigor). In accordance with their specific interpretation, pluralism and toleration means that certain privileged segments of academic communities no longer need to justify or substantiate what they preach. Nor do they need to observe logical rules, because criteria of scholarly validity were invented by "white heterosexual males," and those who do not belong to this segment of the population need not comply with their criteria. In practice, everyone is free from complying with them.

The university has always been weak and vulnerable. Its only source of strength and vitality is the obstinate adherence to universal rules of Reason and making proper use of the intellect. Those rules, both logical and empirical, are the same in the natural sciences and in the humanities, and their abandonment would mean the suicide of the university and a return to barbarism. Fortunately, the intellectual virtues are preserved in the natural and mathematical sciences, and their presence, as well as their effectiveness, make a laughing stock of the "post-modernist" ideologues who want to make themselves comfortable by "freeing" themselves from logic and facts.

The university, however, is responsible for the continuation and transmission of culture. Hence its existence presupposes a belief in that culture, and a belief that it is worth preserving. If that belief is gone, there is really no point to the existence of the university.

The weakening of this belief, of this confidence in our own culture, coincides with an immense growth in academic teaching and the student population. At one point the curve of this growth was such that it was possible to extrapolate it to the moment when there would be more professors and students than human beings on the globe. This growth had to be stopped, but the number of colleges and universities is still immense. In the United States alone they exceed 3,000. Like everything in the world, this growth has its advantages and disadvantages. No one would question that it is better to have more educated people. And even if some of those universities and colleges are poor, and must devote some of their work to compensating for the defects of secondary education, it is not the case that the students there do not learn anything. Poor education is better than none – on the assumption that university departments are not centers of ideological indoctrination. On the other hand, in developed and moderately developed countries the population cannot absorb such huge numbers of people with university degrees and offer them jobs corresponding to their education. Unemployment among graduates is high everywhere, not only in "soft" fields where the courses of study are comparatively easy, but also in the "hard" disciplines. This results in immense frustration. Unfortunately, at present there are no good solutions in sight.

Neutrality and Academic Values[1]

Let us try to define neutrality in a way that does not commit us to considering neutral behavior either as necessarily virtuous or as necessarily reprehensible. Let us assume, in accordance with common sense and the ordinary meaning of the word, that neutrality may be possible or impossible, recommended or condemned, depending on the circumstances.

Neutrality presupposes a conflict; and it presupposes that the neutral person is not a party to it. Neutrality cannot therefore be conceived as a trait of character or an aspect of the personality; I can be neutral only with respect to a particular situation of conflict. *I am neutral with respect to a conflict when I consciously behave in such a way as not to influence its outcome.*

This definition seems to accord with ordinary usage. It implies the following things:

1. That neutrality is always intentional. I am not neutral with respect to a conflict if I am unaware of it. Nor can I be said to be neutral if I am merely indifferent to it. Non-involvement through indifference, lack of interest, or lack of knowledge precludes neutrality. I can be neutral only if the conflict somehow falls within the field of my interest.

2. That I am not, or do not consider myself, a party to the conflict. If I do consider myself a party to it, I can (at best) be impartial, but I cannot be neutral. Considering oneself a party in a conflict implies making an effort to influence its outcome.

3. That neutrality and impartiality are mutually exclusive in the same situation. I am (or try to be) impartial if I assess the conflict and the

---

1 Published in *Neutrality and Impartiality: The University and Political Commitment*, Alan Montefiore ed. (Cambridge: Cambridge University Press, 1975). This version has been revised by Agnieszka Kolakowska.

rights and wrongs of both sides according to more general rules which I accept *independently of this particular case*, i.e., without allowing my personal preferences or biases to influence my judgment; but I am not neutral, since "to be impartial" in a conflict implies intervening in it and attempting to influence its outcome. The general rules I should be guided by will be rules that are considered valid irrespective of the case under consideration. They may be a civil code (the impartiality of a judge in a civil case), or logical rules (the impartiality of a scholar), or moral norms (the impartiality of a witness with respect to standards of veracity), etc. It is quite compatible with impartiality to help one side in a conflict against another or to consider both sides as partly in the wrong. When I consider myself impartial, I see myself, as it were, as a bearer of impersonal rules that are applicable to the case in question. I may also justify my neutrality by appealing to general rules, but if I am neutral, I will avoid any intervention in the course of events, and thus I cannot be impartial.

4. That neutrality is a formal characteristic of behavior and that no material values are involved in its concept. The concept itself implies nothing about whether and in what conditions neutrality may deserve approval or blame.

Alan Montefiore defines neutrality as an attitude of equal goodwill or hostility toward all parties to a conflict; the avoidance of any manifestations of goodwill or hostility would be the limiting case of this attitude.[2] This definition is not entirely satisfactory, because it appears to allow the same term to be used for a whole range of attitudes with respect to a particular conflict – attitudes which may be not only different but indeed opposed to each other, *both in their expression and in their motivations*. A state can sell arms to each of two states at war with each other; it may do so because it is not interested in the outcome of the war, but only in selling arms; or it may do so because it is interested in the prolongation of the war and in weakening both parties. It may also refuse to sell arms to either party for – curiously – pacifist reasons, or because of other circumstances that make peace at this moment more beneficial to it, and so on. It seems to me that treating all these cases equally as instances of neutrality leads to unfortunate results. To sell arms to each side in a war *is* to be actively involved in the conflict, regardless of the reasons for one's involvement and regardless of whether the aid provided is equal in absolute terms or proportional to the relative strengths of the conflicting parties and intended to bring them into balance. In particular, if neutrality is limited to those cases where I attempt to create an equilibrium of strength, it emerges, on this

2 *Ibid.*, pp. 1–46.

definition, that I am neutral only when giving unilateral aid to the weaker side. Neither of these conceptions of neutrality – as manifesting goodwill or hostility to both sides equally, or as aiming for an equal balance of strength in the conflict – can be reconciled with the ordinary meaning of the word.

Let us now consider the abstract problem of whether neutrality as I have defined it above is possible in practice and, if so, what might be its moral justification.

Political radicals often like to claim that neutrality is impossible simply because to refrain from influencing the outcome of a conflict is, in effect, to support the stronger side. This argument is usually based on a simplistic interpretation of existentialism or Marxism. But there is an obvious distinction to be made between the idea that certain neutral acts can be morally assessed and the idea that such acts are in principle impossible. It is undeniably true that if I refrain from involvement in a conflict the outcome of which has a moral dimension, my non-involvement can (unless it is due simply to some physical or mental incapacity) be morally assessed – though it need not be judged wrong. In this sense neutrality is a choice that is not morally indifferent if the conflict itself is not morally indifferent and if the neutral agent could have intervened had he chosen to do so. But this does not mean that neutrality is impossible. One cannot reasonably claim that a state would be doing exactly the same thing in offering large-scale military aid to one side in an armed conflict and in waiting passively for the outcome. There are many cases where my involvement in an already existing conflict does not depend on my decision; but there are others where the option of remaining neutral remains open to me.

But the claim that neutrality is impossible is often an awkward way of formulating another idea, namely that neutrality is always wrong. This claim, however absurd, contains a hidden meaning which deserves attention. I want to argue that neutrality, whether justified or not, is always the result of weakness, although this weakness is not always something to be condemned, nor need it always be attributed to the neutral agent; it can sometimes be attributed to certain peculiarities of our culture.

The simplest example is of neutrality that results from intellectual weakness. I may be interested in the outcome of a scientific debate but still remain neutral toward it because I am not competent to intervene; my participation in such a debate would conflict with a value that I consider important, namely the requirement that scientific controversies should be decided according to the rules of scientific procedure. Thus to choose neutrality in this case is to declare allegiance to certain intellectual values which I recognize. My choice is justified, and my lack of competence to intervene in accordance with the rules of science should not be condemned: I cannot, after all, be blamed for not being omniscient.

In cases where moral or psychological considerations are involved, it is much harder, if not impossible, to formulate general, universally applicable criteria for assessing the rights and wrongs of neutrality. It is, of course, very easy to find examples where neutrality is morally unacceptable (for example, if a rape is taking place in my presence). But we are not justified in concluding, by multiplying such examples, that neutrality is always wrong. If I considered it my duty to intervene in every personal conflict between other people, I would be an importunate meddler rather than a heroic anti-neutralist; which of us would want other people to intervene in all our conflicts without being asked? If examples of unacceptable neutrality and unacceptable non-neutrality are easily found, any attempt to establish a general criterion to distinguish between them seems doomed to failure.

More important, however, are those cases where we have reason to believe that our choice to intervene or to remain neutral involves certain (significant) values, and that choosing neutrality might destroy them – either because they are incompatible with the values that would be served by our involvement, or because of other causal connections in the world. Our decision can be wrong intellectually, in the sense that we have wrongly predicted its results, or it can be wrong morally; but this is not always the case. The French who in 1939 refused to "die for Gdansk," or the American socialists who opposed the active involvement of the United States in World War II, were certainly wrong in both senses. But only a blind faith in the perfection of history could justify us in condemning a small nation that preferred to remain neutral in a conflict between great powers for the simple reason that taking sides, whichever side it took, would entail a measurable risk of its annihilation. One might argue that such a state should try to defuse the conflict rather than take sides in it; in this case it would not be neutral (because it would be seeking to influence the outcome). But this excellent advice is not, alas, applicable in all cases. In many situations the only possible way to influence the outcome of a conflict is to take a side in it. This is to be attributed to the nature of the human world and not necessarily to our mistakes. The weakness of the neutral agent in such a case comes from the fact that it would rather continue to exist than contribute to the resolution of a world conflict.

A situation of conflict may arise in which any choice will involve the risk of destroying something that we have a moral duty to defend. If the values involved are extremely important, we are faced with a case of genuine tragedy: a conflict in which evil must win, in a moral as well as a material sense. The anti-neutralist who maintains that there are right moral choices in every conflict is in fact claiming that tragedies are not possible in our world – a view that seems as convenient as it is optimistic.

Where, among all these distinctions, is the problem of the so-called political neutrality of the university located?

The postulate of political neutrality for universities requires that the university as an institution – which does not of course mean the individuals (teachers, students, administrators) who together constitute it – refrain from taking positions on controversial political issues of the day. The arguments usually put forward against this requirement are as follows:

1. Universities in democratic countries (not to speak of totalitarian ones) are politically involved in any case: they contribute to military research, they sometimes apply political criteria in selecting their members, and their teaching, at least in the social sciences and humanities, is often politically biased and reflects the political preferences of the teachers.

2. The neutrality of the university is in any case impossible, since universities are necessarily organs of society. They serve society; in divided societies they are generally at the service of the ruling class; and so on.

In order to consider the validity of these standard objections, we must introduce some further distinctions and explain certain confusions from which such objections arise. Let us first try to summarize the classical liberal idea of the university. According to this idea, the university has four main functions in society. These are:

(a) To provide higher professional training in a limited sense. (By "limited sense" I mean that while the university, especially in the social sciences and humanities, does not provide specific professional qualifications, it does provide its students with the theoretical, factual, and logical knowledge and skills that allow them to master a certain area of culture and can later be applied in various professions, which normally require additional training.)

(b) To ensure the continued transmission of culture.

(c) To enrich our knowledge of the world – this knowledge being defined not only by its content, but also, and above all, by the specific procedures which justify its validity.

(d) To inculcate and propagate certain values, applicable not only in science, but in all areas of social life, including politics; these values include impartiality of judgment, tolerance, the spirit of critical inquiry, and observance of the rules of logic.

Clearly (as far as I know, this claim has never been seriously questioned), there are some values which reflect the essence of the university. According to the liberal idea, the very functioning of the university implies certain value judgments, which – like other value judgments – are historically conditioned rather than transcendentally valid. It is equally undeniable that the university has always been an organ of society and has always been aware that its activity has social consequences. For this reason the slogans commonly trotted out against the political neutrality of the university – that "the university is not an island," or that "teaching has an impact on society," or that "teachers must be aware of the social consequences of their teaching and assume responsibility for them," and so on – are worthless platitudes.

Contrary to the typical claims of revolutionary rhetoric, the difference between the liberal and the political (or simply totalitarian) idea of the university does not lie simply in the acceptance or rejection of a few banalities about the university's social responsibility or the social meaning of its activity. It lies in defining just what it is that the university is responsible for. According to the totalitarian idea, there are no human values that transcend the particular interests of conflicting political groups. This principle obviously entails that anything in culture that cannot be used as a tool for the pursuit of "our" political goals is necessarily a tool for "our" enemies. Hence the conclusion that if the teaching and research carried on in universities are of no political value for "our" victory, they must be at the service of the shady interests of some particular group or groups (such as, for example, the Jewish plutocracy in Nazi Germany, or world imperialism in communist thinking) and should therefore be destroyed.

The liberal or – as it may be preferable to call it, in order to avoid any misleading associations that may go with the word "liberal" – "open" idea implies, on the contrary, that a continuity of culture exists in many domains and that there are some values that are not confined to the particular interests of given political groups, social classes, or ethnic, national, or racial communities. This belief does not necessarily entail the assumption that certain values are of divine origin or valid in a Platonic sense; it is perfectly compatible with the acceptance of the historical origin of all values. It implies only that in some important areas of culture there is a continuity in time, and that some values are universal in the sense of being independent of social and ethnic divisions. This modest philosophy is a latent and necessary condition of the open idea of the university; but it is also a sufficient condition for it. This means that the totalitarian idea cannot, if it is to be consistent, accept the universality, in the double sense above, of certain areas of cultural values.

This conflict is not, fortunately, based on arbitrary choice alone. The idea of the universality of certain values can be subjected to historical analysis; it can be shown that the essential constituents of some values have persisted unchanged through a variety of historical circumstances and ethnic and social conditions. The belief in the historical continuity and universality of culture (in short, the belief in the basic unity of the human species) is not just an arbitrary choice, neither more nor less justified than the opposite belief – that all values are necessarily bound to the interests of some particular social, political, or ethnic group. The person who claims that Einstein's theory of relativity is based on certain rules of thought whose validity is not limited to Einstein's time, social milieu, or ethnic origin, is in a different cognitive position from the person who claims that the theory of relativity is a product of the degenerate Jewish mind (an opinion that now seems to have been abandoned) or a capitalist ploy invented to deceive the working class (an opinion that also seems to have been abandoned today).

The reason I think the totalitarian idea of the university cannot accept the idea of cultural continuity is simply that the latter seems to provide a sufficient basis for the view that institutionalized forms of this continuity are possible, justified, and indispensable for society.

Totalitarian doctrines are not entirely unjustified in their claims, although the real justification is quite different from the arguments which totalitarianism explicitly invokes. For totalitarian movements by their very existence *produce* a situation similar to that which they claim is "natural" for all societies. In denying that cultural values can transcend the particular interests which they supposedly represent, a totalitarian movement *brings about* a state of affairs in which every institution based on the belief in such values becomes, by its existence alone, a social entity that undermines the particular interests of that movement. It follows that the university, precisely because it is founded upon the belief in the universality of certain values, is anti-totalitarian: that is, it is not neutral in the conflict between those who aspire to totalitarianism and their opponents.

This does not mean that the university is compelled to participate directly in the struggle between political parties. But it does mean that, since it believes itself to embody certain non-particular values, all those who in the course of their education have been imbued with the spirit of the university and continue to take it seriously will reject totalitarian demands. Involvement in this kind of non-neutrality is not the university's decision. If someone suddenly hits me on the head, I am already a party in the conflict, even if I do nothing to resist my aggressor or to strike him back; the very fact of having been struck involves me in a conflict. The university is in exactly the same situation. Only in this sense can it be said not to be neutral in a situation created by a totalitarian movement. And this kind of non-neutrality has nothing to do with the idea that the university must necessarily be at the service of the particular interests of certain classes, nationalities, races, or parties.

In other words, human societies are and probably always will be politically divided. The university, in defending the values that lie at its foundation, is inevitably entangled in these divisions whenever those values are at risk. It is not neutral in the conflict between the idea of intellectual impartiality and the belief that such impartiality is impossible because we can only think in accordance with the interests of our race or class; nor is it neutral in the conflict between those who believe that tolerance is better than police control of teaching and those who believe the contrary.

It follows that the idea of the university cannot be violated when the university is engaged in activities that accord with its own basic principles; and that it is the university's duty to react whenever such issues as freedom of teaching, of research, and of discussion, refusal to submit to compulsory indoctrination, etc., become the object of political conflict. When the university is faced with a political conflict of this kind and defends these values, as it must, it cannot be blamed for abandoning neutrality – as long as it maintains a clear distinction between its support for a social order that would best protect them and its support for the particular political group which represents that order at any given moment. To be sure, this distinction is sometimes blurred, especially at times of violent conflict; nonetheless, it is a real distinction, not just a piece of casuistry invented in order to justify the violation of neutrality. For example, there is an important difference between supporting or opposing a legislative proposal related to the values the university is supposed to defend and supporting or opposing a political party which happens to be engaged in the same cause.

It may be argued that since the university must, and should, be involved in conflicts about its fundamental values, there is no good reason why it should avoid involvement in other political conflicts, provided only that it does not take a stand that could jeopardize its existence as an open university. In other words, if we agree that the values which the university is committed to upholding are not confined to its own particular interests, why should it abstain from involvement in political conflicts that are not directly connected, or indeed in any way connected, with its fundamental tasks? The answer is that the neutrality of the university – unlike impartiality in research and in teaching – is not one of the fundamental values which the university must uphold on pain of self-destruction; it is a necessity imposed upon it by its inevitable vulnerability. The university is and always has been vulnerable in the sense that it has almost no means apart from its own intellectual dignity to defend itself against political pressures which, while trying to destroy its neutrality, at the same time attack its impartiality and other fundamental values. Although in any single conflict neutrality and impartiality are, as I have argued above, mutually exclusive, the converse does not follow: one can be both non-neutral and non-impartial with respect to the same conflict. In the ideal case, I can imagine remaining impartial in a conflict to which I am a party; such a situation is not logically impossible where social conflicts and great institutions are concerned, though it is clearly impossible for psychological and social reasons. Those who seek to destroy the neutrality of the university always seek something more: to destroy its impartiality in teaching and in research and harness its entire activity to the service of their own interests. If political neutrality is required from the university, it is not because non-neutrality is logically incompatible with the fulfillment of its tasks, but because social conditions make it incompatible in practice. The observation that the university is vulnerable and easily corrupted is an empirical one: we have seen – in Nazi Germany, in communist countries, in McCarthy's America – how political pressure can be exerted on universities, and how their fundamental values can be destroyed by destroying their neutrality. The university's only weapon, its only means of defending itself against intimidation and pressure, is to proclaim its political neutrality – not as a goal in itself, but as a means. A university that deliberately violates its own neutrality loses all right to resist pressures which aim to transform it into the tool of whatever political group happens to be in power.

The sense in which the university can become a "political tool" needs no explanation. The university violates not just its neutrality but its own most fundamental values when it yields to pressure to provide selective information according to particular political interests, when it uses political criteria in appointments and admissions, or when it restricts free discussion in the name of those interests. The standard argument advanced by partisans of the totalitarian university is that this is precisely what happens at all universities. But this argument cannot be used in good faith to demonstrate the alleged necessity of the university's political involvement in the sense indicated. One probably cannot claim that the highest requirements of impartiality have been met absolutely at all universities; it is also true that no university, even under the worst conditions, was ever so utterly corrupted as to leave no element of its teaching or research free from political bias. But to infer from this that the difference between the open and totalitarian university is imaginary, or that any difference between them is insignificant ("quantitative only"), and so on, is to reason in a typically totalitarian, primitive way. One could, of course, say the difference between the income of a

Neutrality and Academic Values

Rockefeller and that of a garbage collector is "only quantitative"; or, similarly, that since nobody is perfect, there is no significant difference between St. Francis and Hitler. And so on. There is a point of view that allows us to consider all the differences under the sun as insignificant; but nothing compels us to accept this view. No one with any experience of both kinds of universities – open and totalitarian – could honestly claim that the differences between them are insignificant or merely ostensible (while accepting both that deviations from impartiality and political abuses are to be found in many open universities, and that some honest and unprejudiced research is carried out in totalitarian ones).

The claim that universities are necessarily political tools and that there are no significant differences between them because, strictly speaking, they are all by nature equally servile, is a totalitarian attempt to justify the aspirations of one particular group to assume control over all aspects of intellectual life in its desire for power. To accept this claim is to accept the total corruption of the university, for there is indeed no reason to condemn political abuses of any kind if all of them are equally inevitable. Moreover, it contains the suggestion that there are no real ("substantial," "significant," "qualitative," etc.) differences between Nazi universities, which were transformed into instruments of indoctrination and were obliged ruthlessly to expel anyone who refused to take part in this activity, and open universities, where some ideological bias can certainly always be found and some political prejudices will always be expressed, but where discussion is always possible and the teacher is not answerable to the police and the ruling party. However imperfect the pressure which requires the teacher to accept certain universally acknowledged rules of thought and to assume responsibility before his colleagues, his students, and public opinion, the existence of this pressure is always infinitely preferable to the constraints imposed by a ruling political group which, unencumbered by any knowledge of science or by the slightest idea of what a scientific method might even look like, claims to possess the solution to important scientific problems.

Impartiality, not neutrality, is the immanent value in the life of the university we have been talking about here; neutrality is not an immanent value, although it must be observed because of its causal relation to impartiality. Probably no one would today deny that any inquiry in the humanities and social sciences is grounded in certain value judgments – present, implicitly at least, in the choice of categories used and in the hierarchy of importance given to the phenomena under study. This contention may be considered well founded in the light of the large number of studies that have been devoted to the subject. But there is not the slightest proof, nor even any demonstrated probability, that all these values are necessarily bound to particular interests of conflicting political groups. Nor does the presence of value judgments exclude impartiality within the broad perspective that they determine. There are many simple technical rules which may or may not be observed in the course of an inquiry and which determine the validity of the result, although admittedly they do not by themselves unequivocally predetermine what that result will be. Research done on the same topic by two scholars with different philosophical backgrounds and differently biased perspectives can differ widely; nevertheless, the validity of their results is determined by their observance of such modest rules as: taking into consideration all data relevant to the topic; analyzing existing conceptual distinctions that may influence the interpretation of the data; continually anticipating possible objections to one's interpretation and considering their validity; and so on. This modest code cannot eliminate disagreement that flows from fundamental differences, but it can to a considerable extent weed out purely ideological or simply dishonest work. To accept the general claim that everything in the humanities and social sciences is determined purely and simply by political preferences and interests – as do, notoriously, those who would like to subordinate the university to political ends, alleging that such subordination is in any case inevitable – is to deny, despite obvious evidence to the contrary, that human reason is capable of following rules which it has itself created. But this variant of the Protestant belief in the irreparable corruption of the human mind is self-destructive: it can only avoid the antinomy of the liar if it is supplemented by a belief in another, incorruptible source of knowledge, a source of divine origin (and advocates of the totalitarian university nowadays rarely seek this kind of assistance).

However, attacks on the possibility of neutrality follow exactly the same pattern as those aimed at impartiality and other traditional academic values. Their aim is to demonstrate that since bias is evident in many studies in the humanities and the social sciences, in these realms at least impartiality is impossible; and that, furthermore, no "qualitative" differences exist between the products of these disciplines, owing to their inevitable ideological bias or their servile nature. Thus in addition to ignoring the fact that (as I have argued above) the value judgments in which all inquiry in the humanities and social sciences is grounded exclude neither impartiality nor the spirit of tolerance nor logical consistency, totalitarian claims appear to invite the conclusion that there is no real ("qualitative") difference between the scientific value of Marx's *Das Kapital* and Hitler's *Mein Kampf*, or between the works of Weber and the program of the Black Panthers; all these apparently differ only in their politics and the interests they represent, but not in the extent of their validity, as determined by (non-existent or inapplicable, according to the totalitarian claim) rules of inquiry.

The same desire to reduce all forms of social life to this single pattern may be seen in the totalitarian denial of the possibility of impartial justice: since the law and judicial institutions are in any case tools of certain higher social entities – classes, races, or nations – there is no ("qualitative") difference between living under a system where the mediating role of the law is strongly pronounced and living under the most extreme form of despotism. The difference between the British legal system and the legal system of a state where people generally confess under torture to whatever is required, and where justice is simply an instrument of the police, is merely an insidious ploy thought up by reactionaries. Why should we think that there is any significant difference between feudal systems where the master regularly acted as judge in conflicts between himself and his serf, and modern legal systems which exclude such a possibility? It is only the "form," not the "content," that has changed, since in every case the legal system as a whole serves the particular interests of ruling groups.

Discussions with people who think in this way are not particularly fruitful, because for them, from the perspective of their thought system, anyone who defends the idea of impartiality is in fact defending the partiality which invariably lurks beneath all ostensible impartiality. Since impartiality is impossible by definition, one can only wonder why its lack is condemned with such moral indignation.

I do not, of course, maintain that all universities which are not part of a totalitarian system are in all respects to be considered models of scholarly impartiality, political neutrality, and kindred virtues. I maintain only that they have a much greater chance of safeguarding these values and that, despite all abuses, they do in fact uphold them incomparably better than openly totalitarian ones. And I maintain, above all, that efforts to safeguard them are by no means hopeless or absurd (as totalitarian doctrines would have us conclude). The whole of modern intellectual culture would be inconceivable without the medieval struggle of the *facultates artium* against their dependence on faculties of theology – a struggle, in fact, for the neutrality of secular thought with respect to theological controversies. It was the victory in this struggle that made possible the spiritual development of recent centuries. The idea that such development can continue if we reject that achievement is on a par with the idea that since we are not perfect on two legs, we should go back to crawling on all fours.

I do not pretend to have considered all aspects of the question of neutrality. We must face the fact that the immanent logic of intellectual development usually does not run parallel with the development of social needs or the requirements universities are supposed to meet; thus it will sometimes turn out that the structures which correspond to the former are no longer adapted to the latter. Universities periodically experience crises brought on by this misalignment, and these can be resolved only by various kinds of compromise. Such compromises are usually possible without abandoning fundamental academic values. Whether we are facing such a crisis at present is not a question I propose to discuss here; such a discussion cannot usefully be conducted on a general level. It is undeniable, however, that in some circumstances full political neutrality is impossible for the university. In a general crisis where the whole existence of society is threatened, it would be ridiculous to expect the university to remain uninvolved. For – I repeat – in abandoning neutrality the university does not betray its mission, as it does when it abandons impartial thought, logical rules, and tolerance in scholarly matters. In situations which patently involve the structure of society as a whole, the neutrality of the university would be no more than an empty slogan. To be sure, we cannot exactly define such conditions or the precise moment at which they may be said to obtain. In such cases definitions are necessarily imprecise – as indeed they are in all cases, except when formulated in the conventional languages of deductive systems (it seems that even the definition of a five-pence coin cannot be formulated in such a way as to eliminate all uncertainty in particular cases). But this is not a good reason to abandon attempts to improve them. The requirement of neutrality, the impossibility of always remaining neutral, and the impossibility of formulating absolutely strict definitions of the conditions of neutrality – all these are consequences of the same imperfections: imperfections which can gradually be reduced, but which can never be entirely eliminated.

Where Are Children in Liberal Philosophy?[1]

Criticism of liberal ideas – whether conservative, socialist, or Christian – is widespread. It is aimed at liberalism both as a normative doctrine (which replies to the question, *By what criteria ought social institutions to be judged?*) and as an empirical, quasi-empirical, or historical one (which seeks answers to questions such as, *What are the motivations or real aspirations of individuals? What kind of institutional frameworks will best promote wealth and general prosperity? What historical forces created the institutions that guarantee liberties in contemporary liberal societies?* etc.).

Let me stress from the start that I accept the liberal concept of negative liberty, defined as that sphere of activities which the law leaves to individual choice and toward which the state is indifferent. It goes without saying that this concept, negative in its relation to the law, is not applicable to the Hobbesian hypothetical state of nature: for where there are no laws to impose restrictions on liberty, there can be no liberty either; unrestricted liberty becomes *conceptually* impossible.

It also goes without saying that the concept of liberty presupposes an indefinite number of degrees. And here doubts have inevitably arisen: for if liberty comes in a continuous gradation, how can one establish the dividing line between liberal and totalitarian societies, given that areas of free choice, however tiny and restricted, persist even in the latter (except perhaps in the most extreme of them, like Maoist China or

1 Originally a lecture delivered in Vienna at a conference organized by the Viennese Institut für die Wissenschaften vom Menschen. Translated from the French ("Où sont les enfants dans la philosophie liberale?") by Lissa McCullough and published in *Critical Review* (Winter, 1993). Used with the kind permission of the publisher. This version was revised by Agnieszka Kolakowska.

communist Albania)? One might be tempted to conclude from this that liberal and totalitarian societies differ from one another only quantitatively. But this is not an insurmountable problem. For what distinguishes totalitarianism is not that it has "less liberty," but that it wants to destroy, to the greatest technically possible extent, civil society in all its aspects: all human bonds, all forms of communication, information, exchange, and organization that are not arbitrarily imposed by the government. This naturally implies the absence of civil liberties which are fundamental in a liberal society: freedom of speech and movement, freedom of association to defend particular interests by nonviolent means, freedom to pursue all sorts of economic activities. And it is these essential liberties, not liberty *tout court*, that enable us to make a clear "qualitative" distinction between liberal and totalitarian societies, regardless of the obvious truth that societies can be liberal to a greater or lesser extent, and totalitarianisms more or less perfect in their destruction of civil society.

Liberal rejoinders to critiques of the concept of negative liberty seem to me to be well justified. Certainly there are no grounds for saying that this concept presupposes the absence of any fundamental and legitimate human claims which might lie beyond its scope, or that it automatically abolishes the distinction between good and evil, or that a guarantee of liberty will suffice to resolve all human problems to general satisfaction, for it presupposes none of these things. We all have to eat, but there is no serious reason to claim that having enough food means being "free from hunger"; and it would be absurd to suggest that liberal theorists simply failed to notice that people need to eat. Not to suffer hunger is an elementary claim, but it need not be considered as some special kind of liberty. Similarly with "freedom from unemployment." Nor does liberty negatively conceived preclude the possibility of conflict between liberty and other desirable goods. On the contrary; we know that such conflicts appear at every turn in all liberal societies. Indeed, most major controversies – for instance, those that concern laws about abortion, monopolies, the possession of firearms, restraints on the press and television, etc. – are reducible to this basic conflict.

One might argue that definitions are arbitrary and that, provided a definition is reasonably clear, it can be constructed however one likes. But definitions are not innocent. Since the word "liberty" has always been associated with positive values, there is a tendency to impose intolerable burdens on it: it is supposed to carry all the goods we consider desirable. Defenders of communist regimes have always exploited this vague conception of liberty as encompassing all legitimate human aspirations: "Yes, it's true that under these regimes there is no freedom of speech or association, but on the other hand there is no unemployment."

The result is a draw: some liberties are enjoyed in the United States, others in Pol Pot's Cambodia.

The Augustinian doctrine whereby we are free not if we are able freely to choose between good and evil, but only if we actually choose good, can come in very useful for totalitarian ideologies. For indeed, according to this philosophy, the fewer possibilities of choice we have, the more, in other words, our lives are regulated and hemmed in by constraints – by a power that knows how to distinguish good from evil – the freer we are. And if we believe that most of our actions have moral significance, then the ideal embodiment of perfect liberty will be a regime that leaves no room for individual choice – i.e., a totalitarian state. A conflict between two political ideologies which embrace this doctrine would not be a conflict between an ideology that is totalitarian and another which is not; it would be a conflict between two kinds of totalitarianism, each of which would defend its monopoly on defining the distinction between good and evil. Communist totalitarianism was always strongly moralistic (although it did not usually employ the terms "good" and "evil" because of their Christian origins); it knew precisely what was permitted and what commanded by higher historical reasons.

Accepting the liberal definition of liberty by no means implies the acceptance of liberal philosophy, in either its normative or its quasi-empirical version, since nothing in this definition indicates what degree of liberty is possible or most desirable, or how to resolve its inevitable conflicts with other values. Nevertheless, it should be stressed, once again, that definitions are not innocent, and this applies to the liberal definition of liberty no less than to others. On this definition, the extent of liberty depends on the amount of choice that the law leaves to the individual under any given circumstances. These circumstances themselves, however, are not defined, since they are always subject to chance and will always limit the range of actions open to the individual, thus also limiting the ends he can actually accomplish. I can never accomplish everything I want; circumstances always impose limits on the ends I can accomplish. But I am free insofar as no one has the right to force me to choose one thing rather than another. Thus what matters here is choice itself, not choice between good and evil. The liberal definition has no need of the latter distinction; it can function without it. However, it does not logically exclude it. But can liberalism, as an ideology which promotes a certain kind of behavior, assimilate this distinction?

A radical liberal might reply that while the distinction between good and evil is not necessary for the proper functioning of the state, each of us is free to establish it for ourselves. The concern of the state should be with what is permitted and prohibited, not with what is morally good or evil. Otherwise the state would be arrogating to itself a doctrinal privilege to which it can lay no legitimate claim, and would become an ideological regime – which is precisely what the liberal program wants to prevent.

This is easy to say, but questions immediately arise: what is the foundation of the law, and according to what criteria are the restrictions imposed by the state to be established? The liberal definition of liberty may not state explicitly that the virtues of a political regime are to be measured by the range of freedom granted to individuals, but it certainly suggests this. Yet liberal theorists always assume that certain legal restrictions are necessary. The aim, then, is not some kind of anarchist utopia, but rather the ideal of a minimal state. But how is this minimum to be established? The traditional restriction of liberty to whatever does not harm others is not a happy solution: when I write a negative book review I am harming the author; moreover, I harm others by the sheer fact of my existence, since I take up space and use goods that others might enjoy if I were not there. On the other hand, to say that liberty is whatever does not diminish the liberty of others is either to utter an empty tautology or to imply that everyone ought to have the same degree of liberty, but without defining what that degree should be.

One could attempt another solution, and say that the degree of liberty allowed by the law should be such that only those acts are forbidden which, if they were permitted, would make social order impossible. The principle is somewhat vague, but it is a rational one; it is, to some extent, practically useful; and in itself it is scarcely contestable. It may suffice to distinguish between what is and what is not legal in certain categories of human acts (murder versus attempted suicide, rape versus homosexuality, etc.). But it is of little value if we want to establish, for instance, the desirable degree of state intervention in economic matters, since both partisans of far-reaching interventionism and advocates of extreme economic liberalism will always find arguments predicting disastrous consequences for their opponents' political programs. In any case, it is widely recognized (even by Hayek) that unrestricted *laissez-faire* is not successful, regardless of cultural conditions, and that it cannot be imposed on societies other than those shaped by the historical traditions of Europe and North America.

But I do not want to venture into an area where my competence is slight. The question I want to address is whether a radically liberal society is possible. I think it is not; and one of my main reasons for thinking this is children.

The radicalism of liberal ideologies can be gauged by listing the institutions they would like to remove from state control, beginning with those that seem least vulnerable to attack. Heading this list are the army

Where Are Children in Liberal Philosophy?

and the police, which only a few maniacal liberals, obsessed with a striving for total consistency, would want to privatize. Next comes the monopoly on printing money; then laws concerning the environment; then education and, finally, socialized medicine, the most often attacked of all these.

By education we mean here, of course, universal compulsory education. Obviously, a society without compulsory education is conceivable, since such societies have existed in the past and still exist today. But few would deny that compulsory education – and thus education which is, in practice, organized by the state – is a necessary condition of general prosperity and technical and economic progress. At this point, however, liberal doctrine is confronted with the issue of coercion: compulsory education is a constraint; it allows people no choice. Freedom of choice conflicts with what is clearly in the social interest (at least insofar as the latter notion retains any meaning, which liberals sometimes flatly deny). But whose freedom of choice are we talking about here? The choice is given or denied to the parents, not to the children; but it is the children who suffer the consequences. We should therefore consider the status of children in liberal ideology.

Let us put aside the problem of defining childhood. Since it is a continuous process of growth, such a definition can only be arbitrary, for one must establish the exact point at which adulthood begins, and with it certain legal rights, relating to marriage, sex, driving, military service, voting, civil contracts, etc. This point is defined differently and independently in different cultures, but in all cultures it is invariably marked by rites of initiation or passage. These are indispensable. Even supposing, however, that a consensus were reached on the point when adulthood begins, what is the status of those beneath this age?

We assume that children are incapable of making their own decisions. Should we say, then, that they are the property of their parents? No, because this would mean that parents could do whatever they like with their children; but children are human beings just as much as their parents. Are we then to say that children are their own masters, autonomous individuals? No, because then not only would they have the right to make decisions they are incapable of making – to engage in sexual relations, to vote, etc. – but their parents would also have no responsibility for them and no duty to take care of them. Both of these options are absurd; the question cannot be as neatly and unambiguously resolved as liberal philosophy would like. We must recognize, in accordance with common sense and age-old tradition, that parents are responsible for their children and must make decisions on behalf of them, and that while children are not objects, they depend on the decisions of others. Consequently, we must also recognize that these decisions cannot be haphazard, and that parents are responsible for leading their children into adulthood, which means giving them an education.

A human being in the proper sense of the word is defined not just in biological terms but also in cultural terms, as a being capable of participating in culture. This implies that education is just as obligatory as vaccinations against contagious diseases. (These latter are elementary proof that society as such, and not just the individual, is real. Though it may be recalled that when compulsory vaccinations were first introduced they were objected to, at least in England, in the name of liberal principles.)

The argument against compulsory education – "Why should the state know better what is good for children than their parents?" – is no more convincing than similar arguments against compulsory vaccination or certain requirements for cars that are necessary for the safety of both passengers and other road-users. To be sure, the idea of "making people happy by force" has been discredited by the experience of totalitarian regimes, which showed us what happens when the self-anointed privileged possessors of higher historiosophical wisdom (as reliable as numerology) oppress people in the name of a universal happiness to come in some undefinable future. The cases under scrutiny, however, concern very specific measures; and in a democratic order the population has instruments at its disposal to reject a compulsion it considers excessive. Moreover, there is hardly any opposition to compulsory schooling. Most of us are ill-informed in many areas of knowledge that are relevant to our lives, and must rely on some authority, even though it is not infallible. There is nothing wrong with the general principle that the state is responsible, within limits, for the welfare, both physical and mental, of its citizens; the point of contention is how those limits are to be defined. No one persecutes the members of the Flat Earth Society, but even a liberal state would not tolerate teachers who tell children that the Earth actually is flat or that two and two make seventeen. This shows that even a liberal state sees itself as, to some extent, a guardian of truth.

But this is where the problems really begin. A liberal can admit, reluctantly but without contradicting his principles, that compulsory schooling is desirable and that it is an area in which parents should not be given freedom of choice: whether to give their children at least an elementary education or to leave them in ignorance and illiteracy. But he will insist that schooling be "neutral" with respect to views about the world, since the state is neutral and cannot impose any philosophy or religion on its citizens.

Of necessity, however, school equips children not only with a certain amount of knowledge but also with an elementary introduction to culture, and thus to a variety of norms, symbols, and values accepted in the culture; it teaches them language, history, art, and literature, all of them full of strongly normative elements. A school cannot escape the obligation to teach children how to distinguish good from evil. Liberals claim that the task of school is to teach the young, not to indoctrinate them. This is easy to accept as a general principle, but the distinction is far from precise. I accept the principle of the separation of church and state; I am opposed to mandatory religious instruction. But even enemies of religion must concede that one cannot assimilate the culture of nominally Christian societies without becoming acquainted with their religious symbols and their past, of which religious history is a major component. Is it possible to teach this in a neutral way – without, on the one hand, attacking, condemning, or ridiculing religious dogmas, or, on the other, presenting them as truths on a par with the truths of arithmetic? It is; it is very difficult, and requires a great number of highly cultured, open-minded, and tolerant teachers, but it is not impossible.

But when we speak of "indoctrination," we do not mean only religious or anti-religious instruction. Teaching the moral norms and symbols specific to a culture, its customs and rituals, can also be considered "indoctrination." Moreover, language itself is not "neutral," since it abounds in elements which contain value judgments and normative distinctions. Given this, the question arises whether schools should be neutral in the sense that they should abstain from teaching the distinction between good and evil? And should the state itself also be neutral in this sense, so as not to run the risk of being condemned as an ideological – communist or theocratic – state? But do not the very foundations on which liberal law reposes already entail a certain choice of values – the values essential for the protection of civil rights?

One can imagine a reply in the spirit of liberal philosophy: "The state should be neutral with respect to morality, but of course the state involves a system of laws. The responsibility of the citizen consists in obeying these laws. Yes, laws should be constructed so that they safeguard order, ensure social stability, and prevent civil war, but none of these aims should be cause for controversy. As for instruction, it can, and indeed should, include elementary instruction about the law; children must learn to distinguish between what is allowed and what is forbidden by law. But this need not involve the distinction between good and evil; the school must remain neutral."

If this reconstruction is fair, then according to liberal philosophy citizens need not (although they may) distinguish or even be capable of distinguishing between right and wrong and good and evil; it is enough that they obey the laws. This means that, to ensure a reasonably stable and well-functioning society, it is enough that people fear the law and the punishment they risk by violating it; they need not also believe that there are norms of behavior which should be observed because they are right.

Is such a society – a society where only the law and fear of the law regulate social relations, and where people have no beliefs about good and evil – conceivable? Conceivable – yes, although we know of no such case empirically, because some vestiges of moral consciousness still persist even in the most advanced and developed societies. But if such a society is conceivable, it is inconceivable that it would last long. The stability of a society where fear was the only basis on which public life was organized would be extremely fragile. Such a society could not survive any serious trial; when faced with a crisis – if the law ceased to function well and became hard to enforce, and if social bonds, which cannot be maintained by legislative measures, disintegrated – it would collapse. In a crisis, the perfect society constructed according to the liberal recipe would descend into uncontrollable chaos.

The idea and institution of the contract is as fundamental for a liberal order as for a democracy. But why should I honor my contracts? If fear of punishment is the only reason, then there is no reason for me to honor them if the penal system functions in such a way that I can disregard its obligations. If nothing remains but penal coercion, all contracts and promises are rendered void the moment I am (for whatever reason) beyond the reach of the police and the gallows. (Hobbesian philosophy seems contradictory on this point, for it appears to assume that only the coercive force of the law can be relied on, but at the same time that *pacta sunt servanda*.)

Indeed, liberal states display an obsessive tendency to legislate, in minute detail, about every aspect and variety of human relations – between men and women, parents and children, wives and husbands, employers and subordinates. Thus liberal principles turn against themselves: for the fewer the factors, in addition to the punitive power of the law, that regulate collective life, the more laws and regulations are needed that intervene in our lives. And so the law becomes more and more repressive and leaves less and less freedom to the individual.

It is not always clear in liberal philosophy whether liberty is considered a value in itself or merely an instrument for ensuring social stability and, above all, economic growth and prosperity. If the former, the state is not neutral, because it accepts liberty as an end that requires no higher justification. If the latter, liberal philosophy accepts that circumstances will dictate the need for a greater or lesser degree of liberty, and sometimes for none at all, if this is how higher ends can best be achieved. And there is no empirical evidence that these ends – i.e., economic growth and prosperity – are in all circumstances best achieved by greater liberty, though in some conditions this is obviously true.

To this, too, liberal doctrine has an answer. It says that it is a natural aspiration, common to all, to want fewer rather than more external restraints, and more rather than less scope for personal expression and activity in one's own interest, and therefore that liberty requires no theoretical justification; the demand for it is justified by an appeal to nature. But this answer is inadequate, for two reasons.

First, even though this argument may be valid in many cases, and even if it is true that we – by which I mean we who participate in European civilization – simply desire liberty by nature, it is also true that our desire for security is equally fundamental, and that the conflict between freedom and security is a permanent element of human existence. People are often willing to forgo freedom, or suffer restrictions on it, in order to gain security (or more security); the temptations of totalitarianism are rooted in this need. This is particularly true in the case of children. A school is founded upon discipline; it is assumed that the institution and the administrative authorities, not the schoolchildren, establish the educational programs. And children do not seem to want much freedom of choice at school, though this is a need that gradually increases with age.

The second, and perhaps more important, reason to restrain our belief in the benevolent desire for freedom instilled in us by nature, is this. Assuming that we all share this natural desire (whatever its description would be in biological terms), we also share another, equally natural and very strong desire: the desire to dominate, to be obeyed, and to impose on others our own "authentic" ideas of happiness, truth, and the good. Despotism is no less natural than freedom. This is why the anarchist ideal is impracticable: its realization would require the fulfillment of an utterly implausible negative condition, namely the non-existence of any political movements that aspire to absolute power and could, in conditions of anarchy, impose their will on a disorganized society. The absence of such movements is so highly improbable that anarchism may in practice be considered an ideology in the service of tyranny.

This is not an objection that can be made against liberal ideology, which has always insisted on the need for the state as an essential instrument for safeguarding social order and security, even if it regarded the state as a necessary evil. But there is an analogous problem. In order that liberty may be maintained within the limits of the law, it is not enough that the law exist; it must be enforced and obeyed, and this depends on social conditions that law alone cannot ensure. The idea of the welfare state, the network of social services organized by the state, is often attacked in liberal thought. But the welfare state, though it can be improved, is irreversible once established, with its massive bureaucratic machinery. To replace it with voluntary private insurance would provoke upheavals which would destabilize the social order to such an extent that the state might fall victim to totalitarian forces.

Whatever one thinks of the justice of the welfare state, the idea of abolishing it is a symptom of ideological dogmatism. Freedom demands constant vigilance; it is never secured by inaction.

It would be even more absurd to return to the idea – already abandoned by many liberals by the end of the nineteenth century – that the state and the law may not intervene in contracts as long as they are free, that is to say, entered into without physical coercion. If this idea were taken seriously, all legislation concerning labor contracts – and even civil contracts, such as those concerning loans and interest rates – would be invalidated. Such legislation was implemented in many countries under pressure from various sides – socialists, conservatives, unions. It was justified by the principle that it is right for the state to protect the weakest (again, within limits; for this principle can be abused, and used to produce support for a totalitarian regime), and also by the observation that it is not true that an unemployed worker is as free – that is, has as much scope for choice – as the company that might employ him. This principle may be moralistic, but it is not clear why this should necessarily be condemned. However, practical considerations are, and always have been, no less important than their moral justifications. It might be the case (although it is difficult to distinguish the ideological from the empirical in such a claim) that the abolition of labor legislation would prove generally beneficial after a number of decades or generations. But it is highly likely that before this happened the entire fabric of society would be shattered by social unrest.

To summarize:

1. The liberal negative definition of liberty is not only acceptable; it is also unique in being protected against the abuses of tyrannical ideologies. It does not presuppose that liberty resolves all social problems or that liberty may not be restricted where it conflicts with other values.

2. The idea of the minimal state is acceptable, but only as a very general rule, since it says nothing about the content of this minimum. Acceptable, too, is the idea of the state as a necessary evil, not as the object of a cult, as in Hegel and other German metaphysicians.

3. The radically liberal state is a utopia whose principles finally turn against themselves. The liberal state cannot survive by mere inertia, mere neutrality and non-intervention; it requires (as has often been remarked) vigilant attention on the part of its citizens – those responsible for the common cause, the *res publica*. And the civic virtues on which the viability of the liberal state depends are not born spontaneously; they require a certain kind of "indoctrination." A perfectly neutral liberal state is not viable; it could last no more than a moment. We should

defend the imperfect liberal state, constructed on a system of compromises between a number of legitimate but conflicting objectives: a neutral state and neutral public education on the one hand, the absolute necessity of civic and moral education on the other; freedom to enter into contracts on the one hand, the need to safeguard the social equilibrium through a system of social services on the other.

Certain commendable principles, such as the protection of the weak, the welfare state, equality of opportunity, and the need for moral education, can easily, if taken to their extreme and applied with perfect consistency, be used to argue for the benefits of an ideological and economic dictatorship. But certain equally commendable opposing principles, such as free contract, the neutral state, the minimal state, personal responsibility, and the encouragement of individual initiative and inventiveness, can just as easily, if they are consistently applied, produce a picture of a political system that would not be viable, and would collapse under the weight of its own virtues. The expansion of moral nihilism and hedonistic indifference, the disappearance of civic-mindedness, the decline of the educational system, and the growth of inequalities to the point where envy becomes explosive can leave society prey to despotism. This, too, is a well-known truth.

Freedom will always be a fragile plant, notwithstanding the recent victories of democracy and liberal ideas in Central and Eastern Europe. And the police are never omnipotent, even in totalitarian regimes, much less in liberal societies.

Justice is not my concern here. I am concerned only with what is practicable and reliable.

From the very beginning, the liberal philosophy of the Enlightenment was attacked as a form of utopian thinking. Liberalism, according to its critics, starts from the idea of an ahistorical individual who is everywhere the same, with the same needs, aspirations, and ways of thinking, and upon this foundation builds an ideal constitution that is supposed to be fully applicable to all societies of the world, since it is philosophically deduced from universal human nature. But this model individual simply does not exist and never has, and for this reason the liberal project is doomed to failure.

This critique, in its general form, is justified, as today's postcommunist world confirms well enough. But we must also remember its dangers. Granted, if we accept that some degree of indoctrination is inevitable, we must accept, too, that the content of this indoctrination will be historically determined by the experiences of a given community, that it should be adapted to these experiences, and that it cannot be simply deduced from the list of human rights. But it is also true that this list is essential if we are not to succumb to extreme relativism, which could lead us, as it has led many, to say that while freedom may be a good thing for us, despotism and theocracy may be better for other peoples, whose aspirations are different from ours. There are communal interests that cannot be reduced to the interests of each member of society separately, and people need to identify with national or tribal communities and to preserve their inherited symbols. But we also need the idea of humanity as a moral concept, not just as a zoological category, and it would be dangerous to renounce this idea. For without it there would be no reason not to treat others who do not belong to my nation, my race, or my mythology, as a different biological species – in other words, as objects. And it would be catastrophic if the heritage of the Enlightenment, and of the great universal religions, sank into oblivion. Here, as in all human affairs, a compromise must be forged: between, on the one hand, the noble naiveté of the liberal utopia, which imagines that it can erase history, community, cultural differences, symbols, and myths, and, on the other, the unrestricted affirmation of specificity and exclusivity, which dispenses with the concept of humanity altogether.

Man Does Not Live by Reason Alone[1]

Leszek Kolakowski in an Interview with Nathan Gardels

Nathan Gardels: The title of your recent book is *Modernity on Endless Trial*.[2] But isn't the trial over, the verdict in? With the resurgence of religious fundamentalism and ethnic strife across the globe – in effect the revenge of the sacred and the soil against modernity – aren't we living out the final days of the last modern century?

Leszek Kolakowski: We are living through the realization that many rationally constructed predictions made in the nineteenth century are more wrong than the so-called illusions they were trying to dispel. Both secular liberals and socialists expected that national, or tribal, passions would gradually disappear, while improved means of communication and a better scientific understanding of the universe would take its place. But it turned out not to be so. The need to belong to a tribe, so to speak, is as strong as ever. National conflicts don't appear to be disappearing. Indeed, in the Soviet Union and some countries recently liberated from communism, the "return of the repressed" may take a particularly nasty form.

There is, of course, always a potential for conflicts to erupt into bloody wars of global consequence, or massacres, as has happened time and again in the course of European history. But, in principle, there is nothing wrong with people trying to define themselves, or identify themselves with a particular culture. For Europeans, it is almost impossible to be a cosmopolitan in good faith. Each of us belongs to a national community.

1 Originally published in *New Perspectives Quarterly* (Spring, 1991).
2 Leszek Kolakowski, *Modernity on Endless Trial* (Chicago: The University of Chicago Press, 1991).

Moreover, the rationalist predictions about religion also turned out to be wrong. I don't expect the death of religion or the death of God. Secularization hasn't eradicated religious needs. Of course, it is true that secularization spread with the process of rural uprootedness and urbanization, general education, and technological advance. But there is no strict connection between them. After all, the most mobile, technologically developed country in the world, the United States, is by no means the most secularized. Not only is the traditional Christian Church alive and very well there – more than half the American people go to church regularly – but there is also a flowering of oriental cults, sects, and so-called "new age spirituality."

To be sure, Christianity has been enfeebled. But as it adjusts to the civilization of the next millennium, it might experience a renewal. However wrenching the process might be, as we can witness today on the issue of abortion, conflict and adjustment of just this nature has occurred several times over the centuries. After confrontations such as the one with Galileo, Christianity accepted the autonomy of reason and gave up trying to control science. Hostile to the notion of human rights after the French Revolution, Christianity now accepts and promotes them. Theocratic pretensions have been given up altogether in Christianity.

So, far from secularization inexorably leading to the death of religion, it has instead given birth to the search for new forms of religious life. The imminent victory of the Kingdom of Reason has never materialized. As a whole, mankind can never get rid of the need for religious self-identification: who am I, where did I come from, where do I fit in, why am I responsible, what does my life mean, how will I face death? Religion is a paramount aspect of human culture. Religious need cannot be ex-communicated from culture by rationalist incantation. Man does not live by reason alone.

Gardels: Speaking about the collapse of communism in Europe last year, your compatriot, the Polish poet Czeslaw Milosz, said: "What is surprising in the present moment are those beautiful and deeply moving words spoken in Prague and Warsaw, words which pertain to the old repertoire of honesty or the dignity of the person. I wonder at this phenomenon because maybe underneath there is an abyss. After all, those ideas have their foundation in religion. And I am not over-optimistic about the survival of religion in a scientific-technological civilization. How long can such notions stay afloat if the bottom is taken out?"

Kolakowski: I hope Milosz is wrong, but I can't be sure. If we imagine a technologically advanced Brave New World in which mankind has forgotten its religious heritage and historical tradition – and therefore has no basis for interpreting its own life in moral terms – that would be the end of mankind. It is most unlikely that mankind, deprived of its historical consciousness and religious tradition because they are technologically useless, would be able to live peacefully, satisfied with its achievements.

In fact, I would expect the opposite, since it is in the very constitution of humanity that our wants have no definite limits. They can grow indefinitely in an endless spiral of greed. During the last few decades of rapid economic growth, we got used to the idea that all of us moderns could have everything and, indeed, that we deserved everything. But that is simply not true. Since there are natural limits on our planet – ecological and demographic limits – we will be compelled to limit our wants. Without a consciousness of limits, which can only come from history and religion, any attempt to limit our wants will result in terrible frustration and aggression that could take on catastrophic proportions. The amount of frustration and aggression doesn't depend on the absolute level of satisfaction, but on the gap between wants and their effective satisfaction.

Religious tradition has taught us to limit ourselves, to place a distance between our needs and our wants. All the great religious traditions have taught us for centuries not to become solely bound up in one dimension – the accumulation of wealth and the exclusive preoccupation with our present material life. It will be a cultural catastrophe if we lose the ability to maintain this distance between our wants and needs. The survival of our religious heritage is the condition for the survival of civilization.

Gardels: The cultural catastrophe being that without a set of rules that comes from religious tradition there are no moral brakes on man, particularly on the gluttony of *homo consumptus*?

Kolakowski: Yes, no moral brakes. When culture loses its sacred sense, it loses all sense. With the disappearance of the sacred, which imposes limits on the perfection that can be attained by secular society, one of the most dangerous illusions of our civilization arises – the illusion that there are no limits to the challenges we can undergo; that society is an endlessly flexible thing subject to the arbitrary whims of our creative capacities.

In the end, as I have written in the essay "The Revenge of the Sacred in Secular Culture," this illusion sows disastrous despair. The modern chimera, which would grant man total freedom from tradition or all preexisting sense, far from opening before him the perspective of divine self-creation, suspends him in a darkness where all things are regarded with equal indifference.

To be totally free from religious heritage or historical tradition is to situate oneself in a void and thus to disintegrate. The utopian faith in man's self-inventive capabilities, the utopian hope of unlimited perfection, may be the most efficient instrument of suicide human culture has ever invented. To reject the sacred, which means also to reject sin, imperfection, and evil, is to reject our own limits. To say that evil is contingent, as Sartre did, is to say that there is no evil, and therefore that we have no need of a sense given to us by tradition, fixed and imposed on us whether we will it or not.

As you put it, there are thus no moral brakes on the will to power. In the end, the ideal of total liberation is the sanctioning of greed, force, and violence, and thus of despotism, the destruction of culture and the degradation of the Earth. The only way to ensure the endurance of civilization is to ensure that there are always people who think of the price paid for every step of what we call "progress." The order of the sacred is also a sensitivity to evil – the only system of reference that allows us to contemplate that price and forces us to ask whether it is exorbitant. The values whose vigor is so vital to culture cannot survive without being rooted in the realm of the sacred. This is true not only of the values of which Milosz spoke – honesty and personal dignity – but others as well.

Gardels: This emphasis on pre-existing sense, or tradition, has led you to ask whether society can survive in the absence of the conservative forces that resist the upheaval of endlessly changing modernity that perpetually undermines its foundations. Without conservative structures, unbounded development explodes; yet without dynamic development, society stagnates and dies. Each alone entails destruction; the tension between the two creates balance.

Trying to maintain this appropriate tension is the perspective, you say, of a "conditional conservative." With the ecological imperative so pressing, why can't a new set of conserving values, which seek to preserve the future, instead of conservative values, which preserve the past, constitute a new realm of the sacred?

Why not look toward the greening of religious heritage instead of looking back toward orthodoxy?

Kolakowski: Religion is about the meaning of Being, about the meaning of the universe and our place in it. Such meaning can only be established by historical explanation, by paying homage to origins and foundational events. In this sense, there can be no such thing as a religion that is not conservative. Thus, no religion can survive without a certain wealth of tradition, which inevitably brings it into conflict with the trend of civilization toward constant change. With everything casting off origins and overthrowing all form and structure, the tension between past and future is bound to be with us. Life is tension and suffering. That is the human condition and mankind cannot be liberated from it.

Gardels: Can't the religious imagination not only be rooted in origins but in hope and belief in a destination; for example, in a world that survives ecologically?

Kolakowski: Certainly, religious belief can limit human ambition and conserve the future. But one should be as careful about believing in a green utopia as in a red one.

It is obvious that some elements of the German Green Party, for example, are hostile to freedom and are totalitarian in nature. As with the communist movement, there is a danger in some of the more absurd and grotesque forms of the environmental movement which would sacrifice everything now for some distant salvation. In any event, we don't need religion to worry about ecological catastrophe. Religion cannot replace what science and technology can cope with; it can only give us the belief that the world is not self-explanatory, that there is a meaning that cannot be directly perceived and established as a scientific fact. Religion is of another dimension, one that enables us to cope with an existence of frustration, failure, suffering, and death. In this sense, religion is not about survival, but about not surviving. It is man's way of accepting inevitable defeat. For mankind, there is no such thing as ultimate victory. In the end, we die.

Gardels: We've talked about the illusions of modernity. But the Reformation and the Enlightenment have also brought modern acquisitions of civilization to the West that we don't want to discard: individual conscience and freedom, human rights, the autonomy of reason, the separation of church and state, pluralism and tolerance.

Yet, as we've discussed, the West has not only weakened itself through the loss of tradition, moral indifference, and bad faith; it has engendered a reaction to the inadequacies of modernity that now threatens many of its positive contributions. As the modern West weakens, it faces two challenges in the next century: the absolutism of Islamic fundamentalism and the absolute relativism of homogeneous, polytheistic Japan, the rising economic superpower.

Kolakowski: I quite agree. The West faces these two challenges in the future and, as you say, it challenges itself. One has the feeling that Japan is really an alien civilization. Their way of seeing reality is very different from ours. We can feel this strangeness in the films of Akira Kurosawa, for example. His film *Ran* is an aesthetic masterpiece, visually beautiful and technically exquisite. So much so in fact that one greets with indifference the bloody battles where heads are being chopped off and bodies mangled.

While Japan's way of seeing the world certainly is a challenge to ours, it at the same time lacks the menacing messianic impulse of America or Russia.

When visiting Tokyo, I once asked a Japanese intellectual, "Aren't you destined to conquer the world? After all, you are the only industrial society in existence that has kept its social hierarchy and social structures intact. You are quickly able to assimilate scientific knowledge and technical skills, you are relatively healthy, and you are terribly crowded on your islands." He was not astonished at my question. "No, I don't think so," he said, "because we Japanese don't feel that we have a cultural mission, to impose our ways on the rest of the world. Our imperialist adventures, both in the Middle Ages and in this century, ended disastrously."

Gardels: The mentality of indifference that accompanies the tolerance of contradiction is a mentality that lacks absolute notions of good and evil and that does not make room for the sacred. What we call nihilism in the West has been the Japanese condition for millennia. It is perhaps rooted in the polytheism of Shinto, which has it origins in the ancient forest culture of Jomon.

Kolakowski: I have been told that if you tally the membership of the Japanese in the various religious groups in Japan, you end up with a number greater than the entire population of the country. It is not unusual for the same people to go to a Shinto shrine, a Buddhist temple, and a Christian church, depending on the need and the circumstance. Of course, this phenomenon is very different from the monotheistic cultures where exclusivity is the basis of any religion or sect.

Gardels: In the sixteenth century, the writer Fukian Fabian polemicized against what was already then a secularized Buddhism, asking where is the lord who punishes evil and thus preserves morality. That seems to be your question about modernity at the end of the twentieth century. What is the difference between the tolerance of contradiction, or religious inclusivity, in Japan and the indifference you so scorn in the West?

Kolakowski: Of course, indifference is the main form of tolerance in the West. Our tolerant attitude is often little more than lack of interest or disbelief; we are as indifferent to our own beliefs as to those of others. But the intolerance of the church is not the only alternative to such a nihilistic attitude in the West. After the religious wars of the sixteenth century a certain tolerance combined with commitment to a set of beliefs took root in Christian culture. Individuals and groups can be strongly committed to their religious values and at the same time practice tolerance toward others. The Catholic Church is preaching something like this now.

Gardels: For example, in Pope John Paul II's encyclical *Redemptoris Missio*, released during the war with Islamic Iraq, he claims the superiority of Christianity. One might say then that *Redemptoris Missio* is an attempt by Pope John Paul II to distinguish between "pluralistic tolerance" and what we might call "indifferent tolerance."

Kolakowski: Yes, I think so. Christianity cannot renounce its claims to superiority, of course. It is bound to make claims to truth, but there is no reason in principle why Christianity cannot accept a plurality of religions without renouncing its own claims to truth. One cannot say with consistency that this is my religion, and it is as good as any other. That is absurd. In what sense, then, is it mine? Despite the miserable record of repressions and persecutions, there is in Christianity a history of toleration that was preached for the sake of preserving Christian values.

Gardels: Islam, the other evangelizing monotheistic religion besides Christianity, hasn't accommodated to the European experiences of the Reformation and the Enlightenment. Islamic culture thus lacks the modern indifference characteristic of the West, leading the French social critic Jean Baudrillard to remark that Islam offers the only resistance to the radical indifference sweeping the world.

As a result, might not the renaissance of religion worldwide also mean the renaissance of religious conflict, of conflict between civilizations?

Kolakowski: Medieval Islamic culture produced great achievements in the history of civilization, in philosophy, poetry, architecture, mathematics, and medicine.

To be sure, there were pogroms against the Jews and genocide during the First World War in the Ottoman Empire. But it is wrong to think that the history of Islam, whether in the Ottoman period or earlier in Spain, to take two examples, is the history of the systematic persecution and extermination of religious minorities. One cannot say with any certainty that it is the destiny of Islam to be bellicose, aggressive, and repressive.

Nonetheless, for reasons I cannot explain, at a certain moment Islamic civilization fell into a slumber. Culturally speaking, Islam has not been very fertile in recent times.

The meaning of today's Islamic renaissance, which is a renaissance of religious fanaticism and aggression, is not clear. It may be more related to the rise of petro-power, and the resultant economic imbalances and resentments in the Islamic world, than to religious invigoration.

In any event, this occult fundamentalism has been proven an efficient device to channel the frustrations and aggressivity of nationalism.

The central point of conflict with Western civilization, the point of departure between our two cultures, is the institutional separation of the secular and the sacred. Theocratic nationalism confronts the secular states of the West in international relations. As long as there are theocratic states, there will be conflict with the West. That is inevitable.

Gardels: If these two civilizations must battle it out in one independent world, where will that lead?

Kolakowski: We cannot predict how the so-called modernization of Islamic countries will affect religious life. In Iran, modernization engendered the theocratic counter-revolution of Khomeini and led to his desperate attempt to medievalize the country. Although he once said that all traditional religions — Islam, Judaism, Zoroastrianism, and Christianity — should be tolerated, he ruthlessly persecuted and killed Bahais.

But since the rest of the world does not live in the twelfth century such religious totalitarianism must sooner or later be exhausted. Indeed, the clash with the demands of technical modernization will lead to a loosening of rigid theocracy.

Islamic theocracy ultimately can no more resist the autonomy of reason required by technological progress than could Christian theocracy. Islam cannot have both. A medieval religious regime will mean medieval material and technical conditions; economic modernization means the end of theocracy.

For now, oil resources cushion the clash. But when the wells run dry, so too, I suspect, will this kind of fanaticism.

Still, of this we cannot be sure. The only certainty in history is its utter unpredictability and incoherence.

Gardels: At the end of the last modern century, can secular man reintroduce the sacred? Can we base ethical values on reason instead of revelation? Must personal responsibility be rooted in *transcendental beliefs*?

Kolakowski: It is obviously possible for individuals to keep high moral standards and be irreligious. I strongly doubt whether it is possible for civilizations. Absent religious tradition, what reason is there for a society to respect human rights and the dignity of man? What is human dignity, scientifically speaking? A superstition?

Empirically, men are demonstrably unequal. How can we justify equality? Human rights are an unscientific idea. As Czeslaw Milosz says, these values are rooted in a transcendent dimension.

Gardels: It strikes me that totalitarianism of a different kind could emerge from the new global capitalist order – a totalitarianism of immediate gratification in which reason is conditional to self-interest.

What is to defend dignity and human rights from total commercializaton?

Kolakowski: The absence of a transcendent dimension in secular society weakens this social contract in which each supposedly limits his freedom in order to live in peace with others. Such universalism of interest is another aspect of the modern illusion. There is no such thing as scientifically based human solidarity.

To be sure, I can convince myself that it is in my interest not to rob other people, not to rape and murder, because I can convince myself that the risk is too great. This is the Hobbesian model of solidarity: greed moderated by fear. But social chaos stands in the shadows of such moral anarchy. When a society adheres to moral norms for no other reason than prudence, it is extremely weak and its fabric tears at the slightest crisis. In such a society, there is no basis for personal responsibility, charity, and compassion.

Now, with the ecological imperative, a new ethos of species self-preservation is being discussed. To some extent, it may be true that we are instinctively programmed for self-preservation of the species. But the history of this last modern century has certainly demonstrated that we can destroy members of our own species without great inhibitions. If there is species solidarity at some deep biological level, it hasn't saved us from civil destruction.

Thus we need instruments of human solidarity that are not based on our own instincts, on self-interest, or on force. The communist attempt to institutionalize solidarity ended in disaster.

Bibliography of Leszek Kolakowski's Writings[1]

I. Editions and Translations

1. *Spinoza's* Ethics, edited by L. Kolakowski, 1954; contains an introductory essay "Spinoza i tradycje humanizmu nowozytnego" ("Spinoza and the Traditions of Modern Humanism").

2. Leibniz, Gottfried Wilhelm, *Nowe rozwazania dotyczace rozumu ludzkiego* (*New Essays Concerning Human Understanding*), edited by Izydora Dambska, 1955; contains an introductory essay by L. Kolakowski, "Racjonalne i irracjonalne elementy filozofii Leibniza" ("Rational and Irrational Elements in Leibniz's Philosophy").

3. *Z Dziejow polskiej mysli filozoficznej i spolecznej* (*The History of Polish Philosophical and Social Thought*), ed. by L. Kolakowski, Warsaw, 1956, vol. I; contains an article by Kolakowski, "Problematyka historii polskiej filozofii i mysli spolecznej XV–XVII wieku" ("Problems of the History of Polish Philosophy and Social Thought in the XV–XVIIth Centuries").

4. *Filozofia XVIIgo wieku. Wybrane teksty z historii filozofii: Francja, Holandia, Niemcy* (*17th Century Philosophy: France, Holland, Germany*), selected and edited by L. Kolakowski, 1959; contains an introductory essay by L. Kolakowski, "Swiatopoglad 17go stulecia" ("The Seventeenth-century Worldview"), and his translation of fragments from the writings of Spinoza, Guelinx, Louis-Paul du Vaucel, Martin Becan, Johannes Coccejus, Martin de Barcos, Henricus Regius, Peter Balling, Henry de Boullainvilliers, Hieremias Drexelius, Puffendorf.

---

1 An extensive bibliography of his writings which also includes articles (published in, or translated into, various languages), up to 1971, was prepared by George Kline in a special edition of *TriQuarterly*, Fall 1971, entitled *A Leszek Kolakowski Reader*.

5. *Listy mezow uczonych do Benedykta de Spinozy, oraz Odpowiedzi autora, wielce pomocne dla wyjasnienia jego dziel* (*Spinoza's Letters*), 1961, translated and edited by L. Kolakowski, 1961; contains Kolakowski's introductory essay "Spinoza wsrod przyjaciol i wrogow" ("Spinoza among Friends and Foes").

6. *Filozofia Egzystencjalna. Wybrane teksty z historii filozofii* (*Existentialist Philosophy. Selected Texts*), edited and prefaced by L. Kolakowski and K. Pomian, 1965; contains an introductory essay by L. Kolakowski, "Filozofia egzystencji i porazka egzystencji" ("The Philosophy of Existence and the Failure of Existence").

7. *Spinoza. Pisma Wczesne* (*Spinoza's Early Writings*), edited by L. Kolakowski, 1968; contains Kolakowski's translation of Spinoza's *Short Treatise, On the Improvement of Human Understanding* and *The Theologico-Political Treatise*.

8. *The Socialist Idea: A Reappraisal*, edited by Leszek Kolakowski and Stuart Hampshire, 1974; also in Spanish as *El mito de la autoidentiedad humana: La unidad de la sociedad civil y la sociedad política*, 1976.

II. Books

1. *Szkice z filozofii katolickiej* (*Essays on Catholic Philosophy*; Polish only), 1955.

2. *Wyklady z filozofii sredniowiecznej* (*Lectures on Medieval Philosophy*; Polish only), 1956.

3. *Swiatopoglad i zycie codzienne* (*Worldview and Everyday Life*), 1957; also in Serbo-Croatian (1964).

4. *Jednostka i nieskonczonosc: Wolnosc i antynomie wolnosci w filozofii Spinozy* (*Freedom and the Antinomies of Freedom in the Philosophy of Spinoza*; Polish only), 1958.

5. *Der Mensch ohne Alternative. Von der Möglichkeit und Unmöglichkeit, Marxist zu sein*, 1960; also in Hebrew (1964), Swedish (1964), Finnish (1966), Norwegian (1966), Danish (1967), Japanese (1967), English (1968, 1986, 1971), Dutch (1968), Spanish (1970), and Russian (Florence, 1974).

6. *Notatki o wspolczesnej kontreformacji* (*Notes on Contemporary Counter-Reformation*; Polish only), 1962.

7. *Trzynascie bajek z krolestwa Lailonii dla duzych i malych* (*Tales from the Kingdom of Lailonia for the Big and Small*), 1963; also in German (1965), Dutch (1968), Spanish (1969), and English included in *Tales from the Kingdom of Lailonia and the Key to Heaven* (1989).

8. *Klucz niebieski albo Opowiesci budujace z historii swietej zebrane ku pouczeniu i przestrodze* (*The Key to Heaven*), 1964; also in German (1964),

Dutch (1968), Spanish (1969), Czech (1969), Italian (1968), and English included in *The Key to Heaven, and Conversations with the Devil* (1972), reprinted in *Tales from the Kingdom of Lailonia and the Key to Heaven* (Chicago: The University of Chicago Press, 1989).

9. *Rozmowy z Diablem* (*Conversations with the Devil*), 1965; also in German (1968), Dutch (1969), Czech (1969), Spanish (1977), Italian (1978), and English included in *The Key to Heaven: Edifying Tales From Holy Scripture to Serve as Teaching and Warning* and *Conversations with the Devil* (1972).

10. *Swiadomosc religijna i wiez koscielna. Studia nad chrzescijanstwem bezwyznaniowym siedemnastego wieku 1965*; also in French as *Chrétiens sans église: La conscience religieuse et le lien confesionnel au XVIIe siècle* (1969), and Spanish (1982).

11. *Filozofia pozytywistyczna. Od Huma do Kola Wiedenskiego* (*Positivist Philosophy. From Hume to the Vienna Circle*), 1966; also in German (1972), Serbo-Croatian (1972), Italian (1974), French (1976), and English published as *The Alienation of Reason: A History of Positivist Thought* (1968).

12. *Kultura i Fetysze: Zbior Rozpraw* (*Culture and Fetishes: A Collection of Essays*), 1967; also in Spanish (1971) and English as *Marxism and Beyond: On Historical Understanding and Individual Responsibility* (English edition, 1968; an American edition appeared under the title *Toward a Marxist Humanism: Essays on the Left Today*, 1968).

13. *Traktat über die Sterblichkeit der Vernunft: Philosophische Essays* (1967).

14. *A Leszek Kolakowski Reader*. A collection of essays published in a special issue of *TriQuarterly*, Fall 1971.

15. *Geist und Ungeist Christlischer Traditionen*, 1971; also in Italian as *Senso e non-senso della tradizione cristiana*, 1975.

16. *Obecnosc Mitu* (*The Presence of Myth*; published by the Polish emigré publishing house KULTURA, Paris), 1972; also in Hebrew (1971), German (1973), Spanish (1975), Portuguese (1981), English (1989), and Italian (1992).

17. *Der revolutionäre Geist*, 1972; also in French translation as *L'Esprit révolutionaire; suivi de Marxisme-utopie et anti-utopie* (1978).

18. *Husserl and the Search for Certitude*, 1975; also in German (1977), French (1985), and Polish (1989).

19. *Glowne Nurty Marksizmu* (*Main Currents of Marxism*), 1976–79; also in German (1976), English (1997), and French (1987; the third volume has never appeared in French).

20. *Leben Trotz Geschichte*, 1977.

21. *Toleranz und Absolutheitsansprüche*: Leszek Kolakowski, Bernhard Welte, und Johann Maier (1980).

22. *Religion: If There Is no God*... 1982; also in French (1985), Spanish (1985), Dutch (1987), Polish (1989), Bulgarian (1996), and Italian (1997).

23. *Gespräche mit Manès Sperber und Leszek Kolakowski* (1982).

24. *Czy Diabel moze byc zbawiony i 27 innych kazan* (*Can the Devil be Saved and 27 other Sermons*; a collection of essays) (1984).

25. *Bergson*, 1984; also in French (1985), Hebrew (1988), and Polish (1997).

26. *Le village introuvable*, 1986 (a collection of essays).

27. *Intelectuales contra el intelecto*, 1986.

28. *Metaphysical Horror*, 1988 (corrected edition, Penguin, 2001); also in French (1989), Italian (1990), and Bulgarian (1996).

29. *Pochwala niekonsekwencji: Pisma rozproszone z lat 1955–1968* (*In Praise of Inconsistency: Collected Essays Written Between 1955–1968*; in Polish only), 3 vols., 1989 (contains a complete bibliography of Kolakowski's articles written between 1955–1968).

30. *Modernity on Endless Trial* (1990); also in Polish (1989), and Bulgarian (1994).

31. *God Owes Us Nothing: A Brief Remark on Pascal's Religion and the Spirit of Jansenism* 1995; also in Polish (1994), Spanish (1996), and French (1997).

32. *Debating the State of Philosophy: Habermas, Rorty, Kolakowski, and Others*, 1996; also in Polish (1996) and Spanish (2000).

33. *Mini Wyklady o Maxi-Sprawach* (a collection of mini-lectures delivered for Polish Television; 1996, 1998, 2000); also in German (1997), in English as *Freedom, Fame, Lying and Betrayal* (1999), and French as *Petite philosophie de la vie quotidienne*, 2000.

34. *The Two Eyes of Spinoza and Other Essays on Philosophers* (South Bend, Ind.: St. Augustine's Press, 2004).

35. *O co nas pytaja wielcy filozofowie* (*What Great Philosophers Ask Us About*. A collection of short TV lectures broadcast by Polish Television, TVP2), Part I (Krakow: Znak, 2004).

36. *Wsrod Znajomych* (*Among Friends*), ed. by Zbigniew Mentzel (Krakow: Znak, 2004).

Leszek Kolakowski

Leszek Kolakowski was born in 1927 in Radom, Poland. He studied at Lodz University and at Warsaw University. He received his Ph.D. in 1953 for his dissertation *Jednostka i Nieskonczonosc. Wolnosc i Antynomie wolnosci w filozofii Spinozy* (*Freedom and the Antinomies of Freedom in the Philosophy of Spinoza*). From 1953 to 1968 he was Professor of the History of Philosophy at Warsaw University. During this period he also worked at the Institute of Philosophy of the Polish Academy of Sciences. Between 1957 and 1959 he was editor-in-chief of *Studia Filozoficzne* (*Philosophical Studies*), the main philosophical journal in Poland, until he was removed upon the request of the Soviet authorities.

In 1945 Kolakowski joined the Communist Party; however, already in 1954 he was accused of "straying from Marxist-Leninist ideology." Soon after the "October thaw" Kolakowski was attacked by Wladyslaw Gomolka, the First Secretary of the Polish Communist Party, and acclaimed as the "main ideologue of the so-called revisionist movement." In 1966, after delivering his famous speech on the 10th anniversary of the Polish October, Kolakowski was expelled from the Party. On May 25th, 1966, he became the object of malicious attacks in the press and was removed from his university chair for "forming the views of the youth in a manner contrary to the official tendency of the country." In 1968 Kolakowski left Poland. Between 1968 and 1981 he was on the Index of forbidden authors; his publications could not be cited or referred to.

Kolakowski was visiting Professor in the Department of Philosophy at McGill University, Montreal, in 1968–69; at the University of California at Berkeley in 1969–70; and at Yale University in 1975. From 1981 to 1994 he was Professor in the Committee on Social Thought and the Department of Philosophy at the University of Chicago. He is a fellow of All Souls College, Oxford, where he was Senior Research Fellow from 1970 until his retirement in 1995.

Kolakowski is a fellow of the British Academy; the Académie Universelle des Cultures; the Academia Europea and the Bayerische Academie der Künste; a Foreign Fellow of the American Academy of Arts and Sciences; a member of the International Institute of Philosophy; the Pen Club, the Polish Academy of Sciences, and philosophical associations in Britain and Poland.

He is the recipient of numerous awards: the Jurzykowski Prize (1969), the Friedenspreis des Deutschen Buchhandels (1977), the Prix Européen de l'Essai (1981), the Praemium Erasmianum (1982), the MacArthur Fellowship (1983), the Jefferson Award (1986), the Prize of the Polish Pen Club (1988); the Lang Award (1992) awarded by the University of Chicago Press for the best book of the year (*Modernity on Endless Trial*), the Prix Tocqueville (1993), and the Premio Nonino (1997).

Leszek Kolakowski is the recipient of the first John W. Kluge Prize in Human Sciences (2003), presented by the Library of Congress.